# PLANNING AND BUILDING
# FENCES
## AND
# GATES

**AAVIM**

TAB BOOKS Inc.
Blue Ridge Summit, PA 17214

## Part 1: Planning Fences and Gates

**AUTHOR**

**J. Howard Turner**, Editor, AAVIM

**GRAPHIC DESIGN**

**Tom Brown,** Art Staff, AAVIM

**CONSULTANT**

**Roland R. Harris**, Professor Emeritus, Agricultural Engineering Department, University of Georgia

## Part 2: Building Fences and Gates

**STAFF**

Executive Director:
*W. Harold Parady*

Editor:
*J. Howard Turner*

Research & Development Specialist:
*Thomas C. Colvin*

Art Director:
*George W. Smith*

Assistant Art Director:
*James E. Wren*

Staff Artist:
*Sheila Rutherford*

Revised by **J. Howard Turner**, Editor, and **George W. Smith**, Art Director, AAVIM.

**ACKNOWLEDGMENTS**

Special acknowledgment is given to **Ivan L. Winsett**, Executive Director, Georgia Electrification Council, for consultation in the revision of this publication.

Original manuscript was prepared by **G. E. Henderson**, former Executive Director, AAVIM, and Professor Emeritus, University of Georgia.

FIRST EDITION
FIRST PRINTING

Copyright © 1986, 1980, and 1974 by the American Association for Vocational Instructional Materials (AAVIM).

Printed in the United States of America

Library of Congress Cataloging in Publication Data

Main entry under title:

Planning and building fences and gates.

Includes index.
1. Fences—Design and construction. 2. Gates—Design and construction. I. American Association for Vocational Instructional Materials.

TH4965.P55   1986      624      85-30401

ISBN 0-8306-0443-X
ISBN 0-8306-2643-3 (pbk.)

# Contents

# Part 1
# Planning
# Fences and Gates

# Foreword

In these days when good management and efficiency are so important to livestock operations, it is essential that a person has the information necessary for making decisions for selecting types of fences, wire and posts. This information has been thoroughly researched and brought up to date.

We are indebted to the many people in industry, education and research who contributed to the success of this publication. Special recognition is also extended to authors, illustrators, graphics personnel, typists and editors whose efforts helped to produce this manual.

W. Harold Parady
Executive Director
AAVIM

Planning Fences and Gates is designed for the persons who wish to plan their own fences or prepare themselves for the job entry level of marketing and/or constructing fences. This part is prerequisite to the study of Part 2, Building Fences and Gates.

Upon completion of your reading, you will be able to perform the following:

—Determine **location** and **layout** of permanent and temporary fences.
—Determine what **kind** of **fence** to use.
—Determine what **quality** of **fencing materials** to use.
—Determine what type of **anchor-post assemblies** to use.
—Determine what **type, size** and **number** of **line posts** to use.
—Determine what kind of **electric** fence controllers to use.
—Estimate **costs** of **passageways**.
—Determine the **cost** of **materials.**

**NOTE:** Metric equivalents are given in approximate values whenever practicable with S.I. units listed first followed by U.S. Customary in parentheses.

# Introduction

If you are raising livestock, you are certain to have problems in building new fences and maintaining old ones. Fences are one of your most important production tools.

If you have been in the livestock business for a while, you may have pretty definite ideas about where fences should be built and how to build them. However, it is easy to get behind with your information. There have been no radical changes in fencing; still there have been constant changes and improvements in fencing methods (Figure 1), in the quality of materials and in fencing techniques.

There is ample evidence, as you drive through the countryside, that some fence builders are not familiar with the best methods of building a corner or end to provide ample strength with a simple design (Figure 2). Some have attached fence fabric—that will last 50 years—to posts that will last 10 years. Others have selected fence posts and fencing fabric that will last about the same length of time but fastened it with staples that have pulled out only a few years after construction, allowing the fence to slump. None of these situations is necessary if you have the proper information on fencing materials and contruction.

Fencing usually represents a rather large investment. When you make mistakes, such as those just mentioned, fencing becomes even more expensive and less effective. Consequently, as you develop or expand your farming operations, you need to protect your fencing investment with the latest information and the best practices.

FIGURE 1. Large-scale fencing can now be accomplished with machines. Some operators of these units do custom fencing.

FIGURE 2. It took almost as much work and material to build this poorly designed, low-strength corner as to build a well-designed, high-strength corner.

9

FIGURE 3. Good fencing is a reflection of good farm and ranch management.

It is sometimes difficult to measure the financial return on your fencing investment. Yet it is easy to recognize that the following results are very direct advantages:

—**Boundary lines** are permanently established.

—**Animal diseases** are more easily controlled.

—**Rotation of crops** is more orderly.

—**Appearance** of the farm is improved.

—**Quality livestock** can be kept separated from scrub animals; breeding is controlled.

—**Friendly relationships** with neighbors are more easily maintained.

—**Loss of livestock** on highways is **prevented.**

Until rather recently, it was generally believed that pasture fencing could be justified only on highly productive land or small ranches. More recently, a type of low-cost fencing has been found to be very suitable to ranches. According to a Rocky Mountain Regional Publication[1]*:

Fencing pastures and rangeland has several advantages (Figure 3).

They are as follows:

—**Eliminates** need for **herders.**

*Refer to References on pages 81-82.

—**Increases grazing capacity** of land as much as 25 percent.

—**Permits grazing both cattle and sheep** in the same pasture.

—**Permits rotational and deferred grazing** so pastures can be rested.

—**Results in heavier calves and lambs** in the fall.

—**Results in cleaner wool.**

—**Permits loose-lambing and calving.**

—**Permits segregation of classes** and kinds of animals.

—**Controls straying and trespassing.**

—**Permits seasonal contol** of hazardous areas such as bogs or poisonous plants.

—**Permits new seedlings** until they are established.

What has been said thus far applies almost totally to **permanent fences.** But there is also a place for **movable or temporary fences** on most farms. They, too, can be expensive if the wrong materials are used, if they are not properly built or not fitted to the type of use you have in mind.

This publication is intended to give you the latest information on planning a fencing layout and selecting the equipment and materials for your livestock. These are discussed under the following headings:

  I. Determining Location and Arrangement of Fences.

 II. Determining What Kind of Fence to Use.

III. Determining What Quality of Fencing Materials to Use.

IV. Determining What Type of Anchor-Post Assemblies to Use.

 V. Determining What Type, Size and Number of Line Posts to Use.

VI. Determining What Kind of Electric Fence Controller to Use.

VII. Determining What Types of Passageways to Use.

VIII. Determining the Cost of Fencing Materials.

# I.
# Determining Location and Arrangement of Fences

Few farmers or ranchers have taken time to do a systematic job of planning their fence arrangement. Some thinking and planning ahead will save you time and money.

You will need to consider the following factors:

—The **capability** of your **land.**

—How to **fit** your **fields** to your **cropping plan.**

—How to **fit** your **fences** to your **soil conservation** practices.

—How to **arrange** your **fields** and **passageways** for **convenience** and **labor saving.**

—Where you can **justify permanent fences** and **movable fences.**

—**In what order** you should **build** your permanent fences.

Factors that will influence your decisions are given under the following headings:

A. What Kind of Layout to Use.

B. Where to Locate Permanent and Temporary Fences.

## A. What Kind of Layout to Use

From your study of this section, you will be able to **lay out a fence** on a plat of your farm or ranch. Follow procedures under the heading:

### 1. PLANNING THE FENCE LAYOUT

Proceed as follows:

1. *Sketch layout of your farm or ranch (Figure 4).*

   This step and the next one may have already been completed if you are in the Soil and Water Conservation District program. If not, the layout of your farm can be most easily sketched from an aerial map, if one is available (Figure 4). Aerial photographs have been made of practically all of the farming

areas. Get one that includes your farm from the Soil Conservation Service, Production and Marketing Administration, or Cooperative Extension Servce.

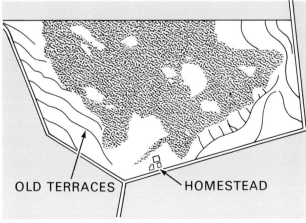

OLD TERRACES    HOMESTEAD

FIGURE 4. An aerial map is helpful in planning your fencing program.

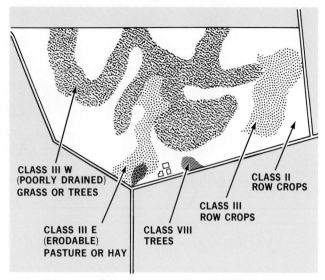

FIGURE 5. A land-capability map will look something like this if prepared by the Soil Conservation Service.

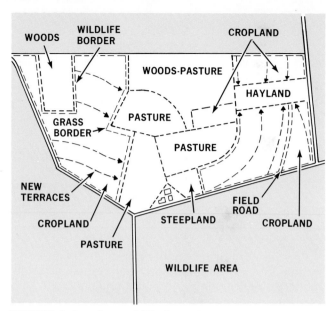

FIGURE 6. Land capability layout.

2. *Plot the capability of your land on the sketch (Figure 5).*

If your land is in a Soil and Water Conservation District, and is included in the program, you should have a land-capability map and a plan of use and management. If you have one, you can use it for planning your fence layout.

If you have no land-capability map, use the sketch you completed in step 1. Divide your land into areas that are best suited to the following uses:

—**Permanent pastures** or **hay** production.

—**Woodlands not pastured.**

—**Woodlands pastured.**

—**Cultivated areas.**

3. *Divide each area into the number and size of fields needed for your type of cropping system as related to your land capability (Figure 6).*

To do this means you will need to blend the following points into a workable field-arrangement plan:

—Fences in terraced fields should **follow the crest end of terraces** or other natural water divides (Figure 6). Don't plan to run your fences across terraces.

—If your field needs to be cross-fenced, **use a contour fence** parallel to a terrace ridge (Figure 7).

—If a cross fence is to be located at the outlet end of terraces, put it where it will **not block water** movement from terrace channels.

—Where you can use **straight fences,** you will save time and money.

FIGURE 7. Cross fence on a contour.

—Where fence is installed adjacent to a waterway, locate it **parallel to the grass waterway.**

Compare Figure 5 with Figure 6. You will note the fence lines, as established, include some woodland in cultivated fields. Also, some crop land is included in pastures. If your fields are to have straight fences on this kind of farm, there is no choice but to arrange your fencing in this manner, following your land-capability map as closely as possible.

Note in Figure 6 how natural drainageways are planned for hayland. These grassed areas provide good outlets for terraces in adjoining fields.

4. *Sketch in proposed lane to connect farm buildings with permanent pastures (Figure 8).*

If you plan to pasture all of your fields, your lane should connect all fields if possible. This may require some rearrangement of the fields as you have them planned now. An exception is when you have a permanent pasture that joins several fields; it then serves as a lane.

To keep a gully from forming on rolling land, plan the lane fence to follow either a natural ridge or a terrace ridge. If it is to follow a terrace ridge, place it immediately below the ridge. This puts the lane at the driest location and out of the way of terrace maintenance.

Keep in mind that the **lane should provide access to streams, ponds or watering tanks.** The pond in Figure 8 is used for livestock watering. This makes the lane fence less important for this farm than if all watering were done at the barn.

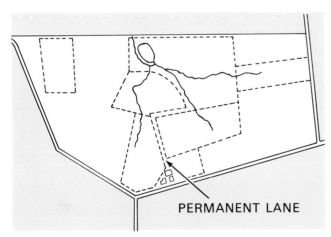

PERMANENT LANE

**FIGURE 8. Locate permanent lanes to avoid erosion, yet allow access to as many fields as possible.**

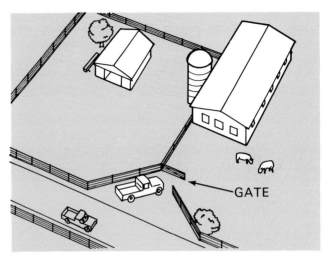

—GATE

**FIGURE 9. It is usually best to plan your gates in the corners of your fields. Gates along roads and highways should be far enough from the road to provide space for a tractor and wagon.**

If you cannot locate a lane to meet the above conditions, you will probably have to use a movable fence and change it from year to year to avoid gullying.

Recheck your plan to see if the lane can be shortened by a slight readjustment of some of the field fences.

5. *Indicate gates and other passageways (Figures 8 and 9).*

**If possible, gates and passageways for livestock and equipment should be in the corner of each field** closest to the buildings. Corner gates enable you to use the field fences as a guide in driving livestock to the passageway. The passageways should be located in well-drained areas.

**If your fields are on opposite sides of the highway,** the gates should be located directly opposite each other. For your own safety and the safety of others, locate the gates along a highway where there is good visibility from either direction.

Gates along highways should be located far enough back from the road to **provide ample clearance for a tractor and wagon** to be parked while you open or close a gate. Some highways have ample clearance — the side of the roadway may be 7.6 or 9.2 m (25 or 30 ft.) from the fence line. But many rural roads, and some highways, provide very little such space. With this situation, it is important that you provide a drive-in area at the gate (Figure 9) as a matter of safety — one with enough space so that no part of your equipment extends into the roadway.

# B. Where to Locate Permanent and Temporary Fences

The general rules for locating permanent and temporary fences are about the same. From your study of this section, you will be able to **locate** both **permanent** and **temporary fences.** Procedures are given under the following headings:

1. Locating Permanent Fences.

2. Locating Temporary Fences.

## 1. LOCATING PERMANENT FENCES

"Permanent fences" as referred to here are ones that are well built and of durable material — ones which will last from 35 to 50 years or longer.

There are no set rules for determining where permanent fences should be built. The best that can be done is to give you the generally accepted ideas resulting from experience and let you make your own decision.

**If you are not sure about some of the permanent fences, mark them as movable fences** until you get some experience with your fence arrangement. After two or three years of experience, you can decide where they should be.

Proceed as follows:

1. *Indicate a permanent fence around the farm boundary with a heavy line and dots (Figure 10).*

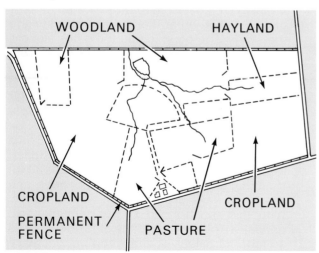

FIGURE 10. Permanent fences are often built around the farm boundary first.

The reasons for a boundary fence:

—To establish a **fixed property line** between you and your neighbor, or between you and the highway.

—To **confine your livestock.** Losses due to livestock killed on a highway and payment for damages to your neighbor's crops may be more than the cost of permanent fence. At the same time, your neighbor's livestock is fenced off of your property. This arrangement saves your crops from damage and prevents the mixing of scrub animals or diseased animals with your livestock.

—This permanent fence will **probably never be moved** unless the adjoining property becomes part of your farm.

If you think you cannot afford so much boundary fence at one time, install the part that is most helpful in your operations. In Figure 10, this would be the upper portion of the sketch from A around to B.

2. *Indicate fences around permanent pastures and ponds (Figure 11).*

Well-maintained ponds should be fenced if they are where livestock can get to them. This helps keep the pond clean and sanitary. If pond water is needed for livestock watering, provide a watering trough below the dam.

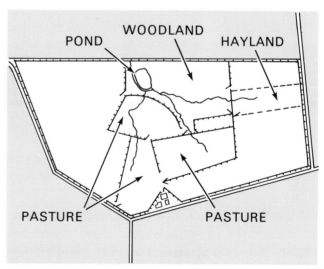

FIGURE 11. Fences around permanent pastures and ponds usually get second priority.

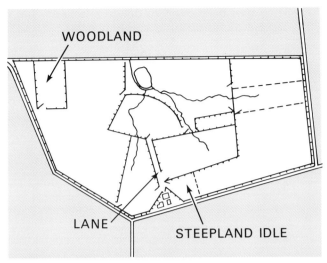

**FIGURE 12. Your lane and unpastured woodland may need fences next.**

3. *Indicate a permanent lane fence or a fence around the woodland (Figure 12).*

The lane fence will probably be most important if it is needed to provide access to water for livestock. If not, it may be best to fence your cultivated fields first.

The lane fence may have to be movable if your land is sloping and there is no natural ridge, terrace or contour line to follow.

If you have a **well-managed woodland,** it is good to fence it. This discourages campers and trespassers, keeps other farmers' livestock from damaging small trees, and keeps your livestock out.

4. *Indicate permanent fence around cultivated fields used for pasture (Figure 13).*

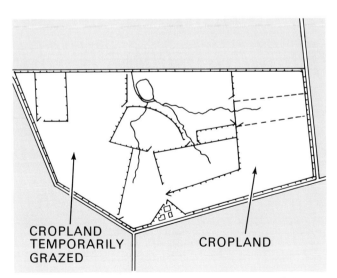

**FIGURE 13. Permanent fence around crop land that is temporarily grazed.**

If you follow the practice of hogging corn or peanuts or of turning your livestock into a field for grazing after it has been harvested, a permanent fence is desirable. Often the extra feed that is salvaged from a harvested field will go a long way towards paying for a permanent fence.

5. *Indicate any additional permanent fencing needed.*

## 2. LOCATING TEMPORARY FENCES

Movable fences and poorly built permanent fences are often called "temporary" fences. Temporary fences are intended for use over a period of a few weeks, or possibly a few months. After that, they will be removed and used in some other place or stored until needed.

Movable fences cost less to build than permanent fences. But they are not as effective and will not last more than one to three years, the way most of them are built. For these reasons, they do not take the place of permanent fences. On the range illustrated here, they would have a very important place when pasturing parts of the large cropland areas (Figure 14).

**FIGURE 14. Movable electric fence used for temporary pasture.**

15

Movable fences have a definite place in any livestock program. Their principal advantages are as follows:

—They **can be used temporarily** in place of permanent fences until you can afford to invest in permanent fencing.

—They **can be relocated** from year to year until you are certain what field layout best fits your needs.

—They **can be moved** to divide a field so that it can be pastured on a rotation basis.

—They help you **adjust the size of a temporary pasture** to the amount of livestock being grazed, thus assuring good use of the pastured area while new growth develops in the rest of the pasture.

# II

# Determining What Kind of Fence to Use

Now that you have your fencing plan laid out, your next job is to decide what kind of permanent or movable fence to select to fit your needs best.

There are several different kinds of fences from which to select, such as **barbed wire, woven wire, board, electric, combinations, cable, mesh, rail, stone** and **hedge fences.**

Fences are generally referred to by the kind of materials used in them. In this publication, you will study only those fences made of wire and lumber. Commonly used wire fences are barbed, woven, cable, mesh, electric, and a combination of any of these. Board fences are made from lumber. The kinds of posts used in these fences vary greatly and are not a part of the name of the fence.

A wire is sized by its diameter as set by a standard and designated by a gage number (Figure 15). There are many different standards for wire. Steel fencing wire is sized by the Standard Steel Gage. The American Wire Gage is used for copper and aluminum. For the same wire gage number, the standard steel wire is larger and stronger than the copper or aluminum.

From your study of this section, you will be able to **describe the different types of fences and their characteristics.**

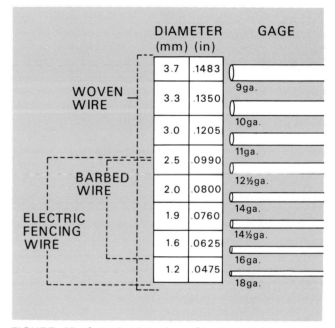

**FIGURE 15. Actual wire sizes for the various gage fences. Note that as wire size increases, smaller gage numbers are used.**

Fences are described under the following headings:

A. Understanding Kinds of Fences.

B. What Kind of Fence to Use.

# A. Understanding Kinds of Fences

From your study of this section, you will be able to **describe the different types of fences.** They are described under the following headings:

1. Barbed Wire Fences.

2. Woven Wire Fences.

3. Cable Wire Fences.

4. Mesh Wire Fences.

5. Board Fences.

6. Electric Fences.

## 1. BARBED WIRE FENCES

Barbed wire fences are made of two or more strands of smooth, galvanized steel wire twisted together with two or four sharp barbs spaced every 10.2 to 12.7 cm (4 to 5 in). They are classified as follows:

a. Standard Barbed Wire Fences.

b. Suspension Barbed Wire Fences.

## a. Standard Barbed Wire Fences

Standard barbed wire fences usually have five or six posts per 33 m (100 ft) and three to five strands of wire (Figure 16).

**FIGURE 16. Standard barbed wire fence.**

## b. Suspension Barbed Wire Fences

The suspension fence (Figure 17) consists of four to six strands of 12½-gage barbed wire. Each strand is stretched taut so there is no more than 7.6 cm (3 in) of sag between posts. The barbed wire strands are held apart by twisted wire stays or short pieces of fiberglass post spaced 4.9 m (16 ft) apart. Line posts are spaced 24.4 to 36.6 m (80 to 120 ft) apart.

The fence sways back and forth in the wind or when animals hit it. The swaying motion beats animals away from the fence and discourages them from fighting through it. For this reason, the lower ends of the stays must not touch the ground or the effectiveness of the suspension will be reduced.

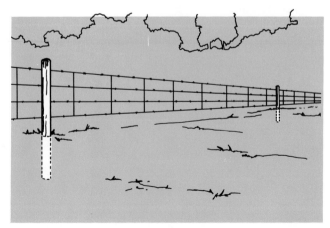

**FIGURE 17. A suspension barbed wire fence.**

In areas where windborne weeds are a problem, a suspension fence gives less trouble than the conventional type because weeds tend to work under or over the flexible wire.

## 2. WOVEN WIRE FENCES

These fences consist of a number of horizontal lines of smooth wire held apart by vertical wires, called stays (Figure 18). The spacing between the horizontal line wires may vary from close [4 cm (1½ in)] at the bottom for small animals to wide [23 cm (9 in)] at the top for large animals. The spacing of the wires generally gets wider as the fence gets higher. This variation of line spacing makes the fence more effective for restraining animals and is more economical. Stay wires are spaced 15 cm (6 in) apart for small animals and 31 cm (12 in) for large animals. The height of most woven wire fencing materials ranges from 66 to 122 cm (26 to 48 in). The height to use depends upon the size and jumping ability of the animals.

Many combinations of wire sizes and spacings as well as number of line wires and fence heights are available. These are designated by "design" or "style" of fence. Both words have the same meaning as used by different manufacturers.

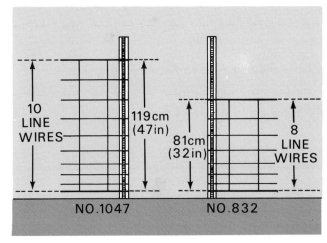

FIGURE 19. Design numbers assigned to woven wire fences indicate the number of line wires and the height.

A fence with a design number of "1047" has 10 line wires and is 1.2 m (47 in) high (Figure 19)*. If the style number is "832", the fence has 8 line wires and is 81 cm (32 in) high* (Figure 19). The last two numbers always give the height in inches. The one or two numbers ahead of the last two always give the number of line wires. Line wires are those that run lengthwise.

Some manufacturers add numbers to the design number which give more information of value to

*To reduce the number of styles and cost of production and sales, the U. S. Department of Commerce and fence manufacturers have agreed on certain style numbers as standard. The standards are given in "Simplified-Practice Recommendations R9-47" issued by the Department of Commerce, Washington, D.C. However, there are many fence designs still being made that are different from the standard style numbers.

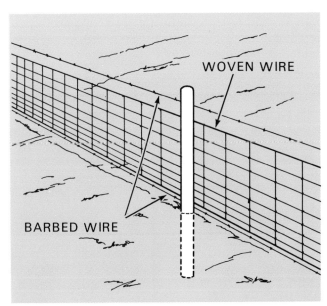

FIGURE 18. Woven wire fence protected with barbed wire.

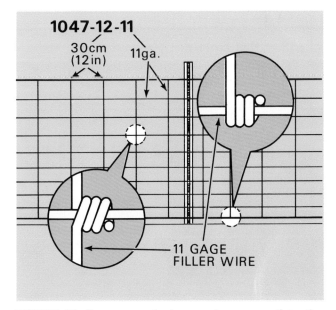

FIGURE 20. Some manufacturers show more than the design number on their fence tag. The two additional numbers indicate a 30 cm (12 in) stay-wire spacing, and 11-gage filler wires.

you. For example, suppose the style number is "1047-12-11" (Figure 20). The 1047 means the same as it did before but "12" is the inches of space between the stay wires and "11" is the size of filler wires used in the fence (11 gage).

**Filler wires** are those between the top and bottom line wires. These wires are smaller than the top and bottom line which is usually 9 gage. Extra heavy fences may have 9-gage wire throughout.

Woven wire fence materials are marketed in four weights—light, medium, heavy and extra heavy (Table I). Lightweight wires are small and have a short life, while heavyweight wires are made from large wires and have a longlife. The cost of heavyweight fencing is from 25 to 50 percent more than lightweight and will last from 2 to 3 times longer. Upkeep is greater for the lightweight materials.

## 3. CABLE WIRE FENCES

This fence consists of 1 cm (³/₈ in) smooth, steel wire cables stretched from one anchor post to another one. Each cable is normally made of seven strands of wire twisted together. Heavy springs are placed at one end of each cable to absorb the shock of any force on the wires. The other end is rigidly attached to the next anchor post (Figure 21).

The cables pass through holes in wooden posts. When other kinds of line posts are used, the cables are attached with heavy wires.

A fence may have as many cables as desired; however, a 6-cable fence is common for large animals. The spacing between wires depends upon the kind of animals to be held.

Because of high costs, cable wire fences are used mostly for confinement areas such as holding pens, feed lots, and corrals. When compared to woven and barbed wire fences, cable fences:

—Are **stronger.**

—**Do not catch snow.**

—**Permit maximum air circulation** in the enclosed area.

—**Permit the enclosed area to dry faster.**

—**Have no sharp barbs** to injure the animals.

—**Are very expensive.**

## 4. MESH WIRE FENCES

The mesh pattern wire fence is strong and provides great safety to animals. It is replacing the expensive wooden board fence in many areas, but it is more expensive, even more than good woven wire. Because of cost, it is used primarily for confinement fencing—corrals, feed lots, and small acreage areas. It makes an excellent large area fence for valuable horses (Figure 22).

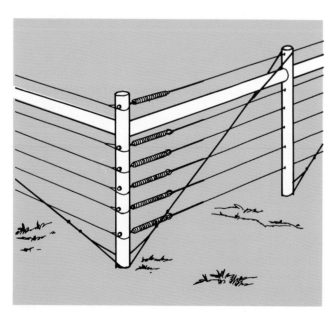

FIGURE 21. A 6-cable fence used primarily for close confinement.

FIGURE 22. A mesh wire fence for high value livestock in close confinement.

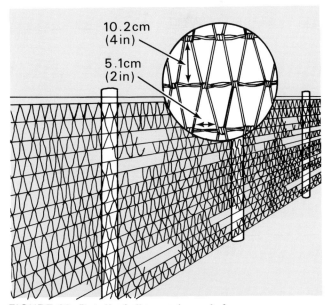

**FIGURE 23. Detail of diamond-mesh fence.**

The diamond-mesh wire design uses two smooth wires twisted together for all line wire. These wires are spaced 10.2 cm (4 in) apart which provides for strength and springiness. The vertical wires are also single smooth ones of the same size as the line wires and are wrapped around adjacent line wires to form a triangle with a 5.1-cm (2-in) base. When the bases of two triangles are fitted together, they form a diamond shape (Figure 23).

This mesh wire is made in 11, 12½, 14 and 16 gages. Fence materials vary in height from 1.27 m to 1.83 m (50 to 72 in). A treated 2.5 x 15.2 cm (1 x 6 in) wooden board or an extra strand of barbless twisted wire should be placed above the mesh wire fence as a visual barrier for animals, particularly horses.

The square knot mesh is another wire design that has single horizontal line wires spaced 10.2 cm (4

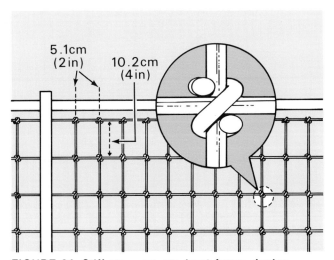

**FIGURE 24. Stiff-stay, square-knot fence design.**

in) apart. Vertical wires are 5.1 cm (2 in) apart, thus forming a rectangular pattern. The joints are stiff rather than hinged and are held by a piece of short wire formed into a knot (Figure 24). Both of these two fence designs are very hard to climb.

---

## 5. BOARD FENCES

---

Board fences normally consist of strips of lumber 10.2 or 15.2 cm (4 or 6 in) wide fastened to wooden posts which are spaced 2.4 or 3.1 m (8 or 10 ft) apart. The thickness can be either 2.5 or 5.1 cm (1 or 2 in). A piece of 5.1-cm (2-in) thick lumber is much stronger than 2.5-cm (1-in) lumber.

Many fence designs offer attractiveness, strength, and safety. Numerous heights are possible; however, 1.37 m and 1.53 m (4.5 ft and 5 ft) heights are most common for livestock (Figure 25).

Lumber fences are somewhat expensive to build and maintain. They are susceptible to splintering, breaking, and rotting. Rot can be reduced by using treated lumber, and appearance is improved by painting. The cost of lumber, nails, paint, etc. along with labor is considerably higher than most permanent wire fences. Upkeep is high for 2.5-cm (1-in) boards, especially untreated lumber.

**FIGURE 25. Board fence.**

# TABLE I. FENCE SELECTION FOR LIVESTOCK
## (Includes common fence designs)

### A. PERMANENT TYPES

| A. PERMANENT TYPES | Height (cm) (in) | Stay Spacing (cm) (in) | Comparative[1] Cost Index (Material Only)* | Approx. Life[2] Humid Climate | Dry Climate | Upkeep | Cattle | Hogs | Sheep & Goats | Horses & Mules | Combination | Remarks |
|---|---|---|---|---|---|---|---|---|---|---|---|---|
| **Barbed-Wire Fencing** | | | (One post per 5.0m rd.) | yrs. | yrs. | | | | | | | |
| **2-point, 10.2-CM (4-in.) spacing** | | | | | | | | | | | | |
| 3 strands, 12½ gage | | | 12 | 33 | 59 | High | Fair | Poor | Poor | Poor | Poor | |
| 4 strands, 12½ gage | | | 13 | 33 | 59 | High | Good | Poor | Fair | Fair | Poor | |
| 5 strands, 12½ gage | | | 14 | 33 | 59 | High | Good | Poor | Good | Good | Poor | |
| 3 strands, 14 gage | | | 11 | 19 | 33 | High | Fair | Poor | Poor | Poor | Poor | |
| **4-point, 12.7-cm (5-in.) spacing** | | | | | | | | | | | | |
| 3 strands, 12½ gage | | | 12 | 33 | 59 | High | Fair | Poor | Poor | Poor | Poor | Barbs pull |
| 4 strands, 12½ gage | | | 13 | 33 | 59 | High | Good | Poor | Fair | Fair | Poor | fleece on |
| 5 strands, 12½ gage | | | 14 | 33 | 59 | High | Good | Poor | Good | Good | Poor | Sheep. |
| **Suspension Fencing** | | | 8 | | | | | | | | | |
| **4-point, 12.7-cm (5-in.) spacing** | | | | Posts 30.5m | | | | | | | | |
| 4 strands, 12½ gage | | | 8 | (100 ft.) | | Medium | Good | Poor | Poor | Fair | Poor | |
| 6 strands, 12½ gage | | | 10 | apart 33 | 59 | Medium | Good | Poor | Poor | Fair | Poor | |
| | | | | 33 | 59 | Medium | Good | Poor | Poor | Fair | Poor | |
| **Woven Wire Fencing** | | | | | | | | | | | | |
| **Light Weight** | | | | | | | | | | | | 15.2-cm |
| Top & bottom wires: | | | | | | | | | | | | spacing |
| 11 gage | 66  26 | 15.2  6 | 14 | 19 | 33 | High for large | Fair 4B[3] | Fair | Good 1B | Poor | Poor | needed for small |
| Filler wires: 14½ gage | 81.3  32 | 15.2  6 | 15 | 19 | 33 | animals | Fair 3B | Fair | Good 1B | Poor | Poor | pigs |
| **Medium Weight** | | | | | | | | | | | | 15.2-cm |
| Top & bottom wires: | 66  26 | 30.5  12 | 15 | 33 | 59 | Medium | Fair 4B | Good 2B | Good 1B | Poor | Poor | (6-in) stay |
| 10 gage | 66  26 | 15.2  6 | 16 | 33 | 59 | Medium | Fair 4B | Good 2B | Good 1B | Poor | Poor | spacing |
| Filler wires: | 81.3  32 | 30.5  12 | 16 | 33 | 59 | Medium | Fair 3B | Good 1B | Good 1B | Poor | Poor | needed |
| 12½ gage | 81.3  32 | 15.2  6 | 17 | 33 | 59 | Medium | Fair 3B | Good 1B | Good 1B | Poor | Poor | for small |
| | 99.1  39 | 30.5  12 | 16 | 33 | 59 | Medium | Good 2B | Good | Good | Good 2B | Good 2B | pigs |
| | 99.1  39 | 15.2  6 | 18 | 33 | 59 | Medium | Good | Excl | Good | Good 2B | Good 2B | |
| | 119.4  47 | 30.5  12 | 17 | 33 | 59 | Medium | Good 1B | Good | Good | Good 1B | Good 1B | |
| | 86.4  34 | 15.2  6 | 20 | 33 | 59 | Medium | Fair 3B | Excl 1B | Good 1B | Poor | Poor | Sometimes |
| | 101.6  40 | 15.2 | 21 | ?? | ... | Medium | Good 2B | Excl | Excl | Good 2B | Good 2B | called |
| | 116.8  46 | 15.2  6 | 22 | 33 | 59 | Medium | Good 1B | Excl | Excl | Good 1B | Good 1B | "hog-tight" fence |
| **Heavy Weight** | | | | | | | | | | | | |
| Top & bottom wires: | 66  26 | 30.5  12 | 17 | 40 | 60+ | Low | Fair 4B | Good 2B | Good 1B | Poor | Poor | |
| 9 gage | 66  26 | 15.2  6 | 19 | 40 | 60+ | Low | Fair 4B | Good 2B | Good 1B | Poor | Poor | |
| Filler wires: | 81.3  32 | 30.5  12 | 17 | 40 | 60+ | Low | Good 3B | Good 1B | Good 1B | Poor | Poor | |
| 11 gage | 81.3  32 | 15.2  6 | 21 | 40 | 60+ | Low | Good 3B | Good 1B | Excl 1B | Poor | Poor | |
| | 99.1  39 | 30.5  12 | 19 | 40 | 60+ | Low | Good 2B | Good | Excl | Good 2B | Good 2B | |
| | 99.1  39 | 15.2  6 | 23 | 40 | 60+ | Low | Good 2B | Excl | Excl | Good 2B | Excl 2B | |
| | 119.4  47 | 30.5  12 | 20 | 40 | 60+ | Low | Excl 1B | Good | Excl | Excl 1B | Good 1B | |
| | 119.4  47 | 15.2  6 | 25 | 40 | 60+ | Low | Excl 1B | Excl | Excl | Excl 1B | Excl 1B | |
| **Extra Heavy Weight** | | | | | | | | | | | | |
| Top, bottom & filler wires: | 99.1  39 | 30.5  12 | 23 | 60 | 65 | Very Low | Excl 2B | Good | Excl | Good 2B | Good 2B | |
| 9 gage | 119.4  47 | 30.5  12 | 25 | 60 | 65 | Very Low | Excl 1B | Good | Excl | Excl 1B | Good 2B | |
| | 119.4  47 | 15.2  6 | 31 | 60 | 65 | Very Low | Excl 1B | Excl | Excl | Excl 1B | Excl 1B | |
| **Cable Fence** | | | | | | | | | | | | |
| 4 cable-1.5m (5') high | 121.9  48 | | 84 | 30 | 50 | Low | Good | Poor | Poor | Good | Poor | |
| 5 cable-1.5m (5') high | 152.4  60 | | 102 | 30 | 50 | Low | Excl | Poor | Poor | Excl | Poor | |
| 6 cable-1.5m (5') high | 182.9  72 | | 120 | 30 | 50 | Low | Excl | Poor | Fair | Excl | Poor | |
| 7 cable-1.8m (6') high | 213.4  84 | | 137 | 30 | 50 | Low | Excl | Poor | Fair | Excl | Poor | |
| **Mesh-Wire Fences** | | | | | | | | | | | | |
| 14 gage | 127  50 | | 30 | 20-40 | | Medium | Excl | Excl 1B | Excl | Excl | Excl 1B | |
| 12½ gage | 127  50 | | 38 | 33-60 | | Low | Excl | Excl 1B | Excl | Excl | Excl 1B | |
| 11 gage | 127  50 | | 45 | 60-65 | | Very Low | Excl | Excl 1B | Excl | Excl | Excl 1B | |
| **Board Fences** | | | Treated  Untreated One post per 2.4m | | | | | | | | | |
| 2.5x15.2cm boards, (1" x 6") rough | | | 68.6  27      63.5  25 | | | Untreated high | Good | Good | Excl | Good | Good | |
| 2.5x15.2cm boards, (1" x 6") smooth | | | 73.7  29      68.6  27 | | | | Good | Good | Excl | Good | Good | |
| 5.1x15.2cm boards, (2" x 6") rough | | | 94.0  37      81.3  32 | | | Treated low | Excl | Excl | Excl | Excl | Excl | |
| 5.1x15.2cm boards, (2" x 6") smooth | | | 99.1  39      88.9  35 | | | | Excl | Excl | Excl | Excl | Excl | |
| **Electric, Smooth Wire** | | | | | | | | | | | | |
| **For permanent installation** | | | | | | | | | | | | |
| 3 strands, 12½ gage spacing 30.5, 25.4, 40.6 cm (12", 10", 16"**) | | | 4 | 25 | 50 | Medium | Good | Poor | Poor | Good | Poor | |
| 3 strands, 12½ gage spacing 15.2, 20.3, 30.5 cm (6", 8", 12") | | | 4 | 25 | 50 | Medium | Poor | Excl | Good | Poor | Poor | |
| 4 strands, 12½ gage spacing 15.2, 15.2, 15.2, 30.5 cm or 15.2, 15.2, 15.2, 30.5 cm (6", 6", 6", 12") | | | 5 / 5 | 25 / 25 | 50 / 50 | Medium / Medium | Good / Good | Excl / Fair | Good / Good | Good / Good | Good / Fair | |
| 4 strands, 12½ gage spacing 20.3, 25.4, 25.4, 30.5 cm (8", 10", 10", 12") | | | 5 | 25 | 50 | Medium | Excl | Poor | Poor | Excl | Poor | |
| 5 strands, 12½ gage spacing 15.2, 15.2, 15.2, 20.3, 25.4 cm (6", 6", 6", 8", 10") | | | 6 | 25 | 50 | Medium | Excl | Excl | Excl | Excl | Excl | Deterrent for most predators. |
| 8 strands, 12½ gage spacing 15.2, 20.3, 20.3, 20.3, 20.3, 30.5, 30.5 cm (6", 8", 8", 8", 8", 12", 12") | | | 10 | 25 | 50 | Medium | Excl | Excl | Excl | Excl | Excl | Control for most predators. |
| 10 strands, 12½ gage spacing 15.2, 15.2, 15.2, 15.2, 20.3, 20.3, 20.3, 25.4, 25.4 cm (6", 6", 6", 6", 8", 8", 8", 10", 10") | | | 10 | 25 | 50 | Medium | Excl | Excl | Excl | Excl | | |

### B. MOVABLE ELECTRIC FENCES[4]

| B. MOVABLE ELECTRIC FENCES[4] | Comparative Cost Index One post per 7.6 m (25 ft.) | Humid Climate | Dry Climate | Upkeep | Cattle | Hogs | Sheep & Goats | Horses & Mules | Combination | Remarks |
|---|---|---|---|---|---|---|---|---|---|---|
| **Barbed Wire** | | | | | | | | | | Wires for movable |
| **4-point, 12.7 cm (5-in.) spacing** | | | | | | | | | | fences wear |
| 1 strand, 12½ gage | 4 | 33 | 59 | High | Fair | Poor | Poor | Good | Poor | more from |
| 2 strands, 12½ gage | 5 | 33 | 59 | High | Good | Good | Poor | Good | Poor | handling |
| **Steel wire (Smooth)** | | | | | | | | | | than from |
| 1 strand, 12 gage | 3 | 33 | 59 | Medium | Fair | Poor | Poor | Good | Poor | weather. |
| 2 strands, 12 gage | 3 | 33 | ... | Medium | Good | Good | Poor | Good | Poor | |
| 1 strand, 17 gage | 3 | 17 | 32 | Medium | Fair | 'Poor | Poor | Good | Poor | |
| 2 strands, 17 gage | 4 | 17 | 32 | Medium | Good | Good | Poor | Good | Poor | |
| **Copper-Covered, Steel Wire (Smooth)** | | | | | | | | | | |
| 1 strand, 18 gage | 3 | Very weather resistant | | Medium | Fair | Poor | Poor | Good | Poor | |
| 2 strands, 18 gage | 4 | Very weather resistant | | Medium | Good | Good | Poor | Good | Poor | |
| **Aluminum Wire (Smooth)** | | | | | | | | | | |
| 1 strand, 9 gage | 5 | Very weather resistant | | Medium | Fair | Poor | Poor | Good | Poor | |
| 2 strands, 9 gage | 7 | Very weather resistant | | Medium | Good | Good | Poor | Good | Poor | |
| 1 strand, 13 gage | 4 | Very weather resistant | | Medium | Fair | Poor | Poor | Good | Poor | |
| 2 strands, 13 gage | 5 | Very weather resistant | | Medium | Good | Good | Poor | Good | Poor | |

[1]Cost index figures are to show relative cost, no actual costs. For example: fence with an index figure 25, costs about twice as much per meter or rod as fence with an index figure of 12.
[2]Wire fence life based on combination of Tables III and V.
[3]B following a numeral refers to lines of barbed wire needed. Excl — abbreviation for "excellent."
[4]Costs of electric controller not included.
[5]Add two additional wires (one hot and one ground) above the top wire for wild deer control.
*Costs are based on use of galvanized wire.
**Underlined wires indicate ground returns to controller.

# 6. ELECTRIC FENCES

Electric fences may be built for temporary or permanent use. The temporary or movable fence is usually made with one or two strands of barbed or smooth wire (Figure 26). The moist earth is used for completing the electric circuit. A conventional electric fence controller is used to energize the wire(s). Corner and end posts require a minimum of bracing. Line end posts may be small with wide spacings since the fence will be used for a short period of time.

Today more permanent electric fences are built. These use from two to eight smooth wires placed on stronger and longer lasting posts. Instead of using the earth as a return for the electric flow, one or more of the wires serves as a grounded return to the charger[25] (Figure 27). Solid state electric controllers are now available, and they permit many long lines of wire to be charged for excellent control of animals.[24] (Controllers are discussed under Section VI.) The cost of the permanent electric fence is about half that of comparable barbed or woven wire fences.

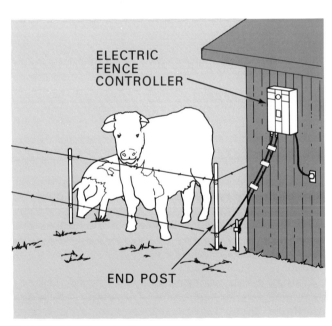

FIGURE 26. Electric fence.

A barbed or woven wire fence may be made more effective by adding one or more electrically charged wires on the inside. They are offset with brackets.

You may have already had experience with these fences and know what they are. In case you haven't, their purpose is to supply sufficient electrical shock to any animal that touches a charged fence wire so that it will respect the wire and stay away from it.

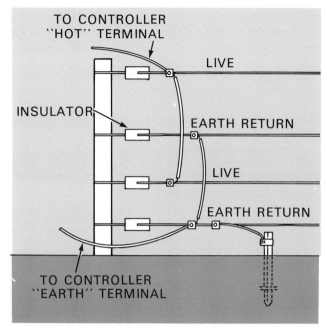

FIGURE 27. A permanent type of electric fence with two line wires and two return wires.

**Advantages** of electric fencing are:

—**Low-cost,** simple fencing materials and methods can be used.

—It is **cheap to operate.**

—Fence can be **easily built or removed.**

—It can be used to **protect any livestock or poultry from many predatory animals.**

—It can be used to **protect** and extend the usefulness of **old permanent fences.**

—It is **easy to keep** fence row clean.

Disadvantages are:

—A homebuilt or unapproved controller unit **can be** highly **dangerous.**

—**Livestock require training** when you first start using it.

—The charged wire with conventional controllers **may** short and **become less effective** when grass, weeds, or brush touch the wire. Solid state electonic controllers are designed to reduce this problem.

—It **must be kept in operation full time** to be fully effective.

—Without a return ground wire, it **may not be effective in extra-dry weather,** particularly if controller is not well grounded.

23

# B. What Kind of Fence to Use

Your decision on the kind of fence to use will be influenced by the following factors:

—The **kind of livestock** you are fencing.

—**Whether** you will keep **different kinds of livestock** in the same field.

—**How often you inspect** your animals for pests or injury.

—**Whether** you will **need** to **fence out dogs or wolves.**

—**How closely** the animals will be **confined.**

—**How much money you have** available for fencing.

—**How long** you expect your fence **to last.**

From your study of this section, you will be able to **select the proper type of fence for different livestock.**

The various points to consider in selecting the kind of fence you need are summarized in Table I. A short discussion of these data as they apply to fences is given under the following headings:

1. Fences for Cattle.

2. Fences for Hogs.

3. Fences for Sheep and Goats.

4. Fences for Horses.

5. Fences for a Combination of Animals.

6. Fences on Land Boundaries.

## 1. FENCES FOR CATTLE

A **3-strand barbed** wire fence is rated **fair** for cattle; however, a **4-or 5-strand** fence is much **better.** The upkeep for this kind of fence is high. Gage 12½ wire will last about 33 years, while 14 gage has a life of about 19 years in a humid climate. The cost of materials for the 5-strand fence is about 70 percent of that of an excellent woven wire fence (1047-11-12 design).

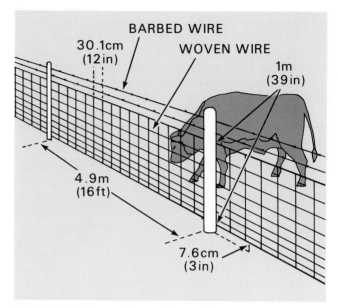

**FIGURE 28. A good fence for cattle.**

The heavy-and extra-heavyweight woven wire fence with a height of 1 m (39 in) or more and one or more strands of barbed wire above it makes an excellent fence for cattle (Table I and Figure 28). Upkeep is low. Its cost is about 130 to 175 percent of the cost of a 5-strand barbed wire fence. A fence whose height varies from 0.76 to 1.0 m (30 to 39 in) with 2 or 3 strands of barbed wire over it is good for cattle, while lower heights with barbed wire over them are rated only fair. Maintenance for these fences is low.

Light-and medium-weight woven wire fences with heights below 81 cm (32 in) are rated only fair for cattle and cost from 10 to 20 percent more than a 5-strand barbed wire. Upkeep for the lightweight wire is high while that of the medium-weight is medium.

**Cable, mesh** and **board** fences make strong, excellent fences for cattle. The **costs** are **high;** therefore, these fences are used in areas where cattle are confined. A 5-or 6-cable fence is normally adequate for cattle and horses.

Electric fences with four or more lines of smooth galvanized wire make excellent permanent fences for cattle. Three-strand fences are rated good. The cost of a 4-line electric fence is about 50 percent of that of a 4-strand barbed wire and 30 percent of a 1047-11-12 woven wire fence. A moderate amount of upkeep is necessary with electric fences.

The suspension fence is good for cross fencing or boundary fencing for cattle. It should be used only on straight slopes and on level land.

For temporary fencing for cattle, the movable electric fence is sometimes used. Its effectiveness is rated fair to good depending upon fence design. A moderate amount of upkeep is necessary with this fence.

## 2. FENCES FOR HOGS

Barbed, suspension and cable wire fences are not effective for swine confinement. **Woven wire with one or more strands of barbed wire** makes very good fences. Lightweight woven wire with low fence heights is fair. Medium-and heavyweight wire fences with close spacing of line and stay wires are excellent for restraining hogs (Table I and Figure 29).

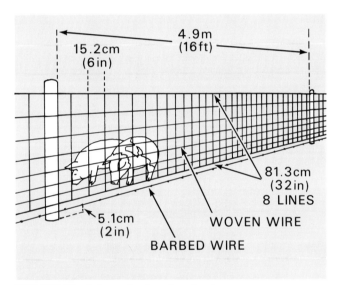

**FIGURE 29. Adequate fencing for hogs.**

Effective fences can be built from **lumber,** but initial material costs as well as annual maintenance are high.

Mesh wire makes an excellent fence for hogs but its cost is very high. Also, hog production does not require the height of commonly available mesh wire fencing materials.

## 3. FENCES FOR SHEEP AND GOATS

**Four and five strands of barbed wire** will give from fair to good control of sheep and goats. Two and three strands are poor. One disadvantage of barbed wire with sheep is that the barbs pull the fleece.

Suspension, cable and movable electric fences are poor ones for these animals. Permanent electric fences are good for sheep and goats.

**Light- and medium-weight woven wire makes good fences.** Excellent fences for sheep and goats can be built from heavy- and extra heavy-weight woven wire that is 1 m (39 in) or higher (Table 1 and Figure 30). Mesh wire fences along with 5-strand permanent electric fence also make excellent fences for these animals.

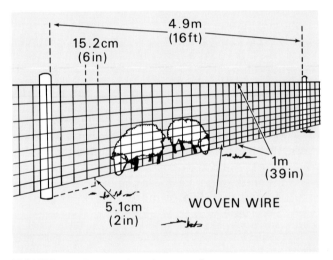

**FIGURE 30. Fences for sheep and goats.**

## 4. FENCES FOR HORSES

Fences for draft horses may be different from fences for high-value horses because of the costs. These fences are discussed under the following headings:

   a. Draft Horses.

   b. High-Value Horses.

## a. Draft Horses

Using Table I, properly chosen **5-strand barbed wire and 1 m (39 in) or higher woven wire fences are good for draft horses and mules.** Excellent fences may be built with heavy-or extra-heavy-weight woven wire, 4-to 6-strand electric fence lines, lumber, cable, and mesh wires. Cost and appearance may be the deciding factor. Keep the fence taut to prevent entanglement.

## b. High-Value Horses

For leisure and high-value horses, the mesh wire fence and the board fence are excellent (Figure 31). These are also excellent fences for other farm animals, but other types of excellent fences are much cheaper for cattle, hogs, sheep, workstock, or a combination of these. For leisure horses, the mesh wire fence with a 2.5 x 15.2 cm (1 in x 6 in) board over it provides excellent protection from injury. Also a 10 wire, high-tensile smooth wire is recommended.

Horses, particularly young ones, often run, play and kick their feet into the air. They can hang a foot, pull a shoe, strain a muscle, or cut their hide on most woven and barbed wire fences. Further-more, it is important to keep unwanted animals and trespassers out of horse pastures. An excellent permanent electric fence for leisure horses can also be built with five or more strands of smooth wire. See Table I.

**FIGURE 31. Leisure and high-value horses must be protected from injury.**

## 5. FENCES FOR A COMBINATION OF ANIMALS

When cattle, hogs, sheep, goats, mules and horses are pastured together, many of the fence designs in Table I are rated poor in effectiveness to control the animals. Fences made from 1-m (39-in) high medium-heavy and extra-heavy woven wire along with extra strands of barbed wires are good.

Excellent fences for a combination of all animals can be built from 1.2-m (47-in) high heavy-or extra-heavyweight woven wire with 1 or 2 strands of barbed wire and 15.2-cm (6-in) stays. A line of barbed wire should be placed over the top of these fence materials. All mesh wire fences are excellent for these animals. Permanent electric fences with five or more strands of wire and board fences are also rated excellent.

A relatively new idea in fencing is the high-tensile smooth wire fence. It cost less than woven wire fencing to build and a 10-strand fence, when kept tight, will contain most any animal (Figure 32).

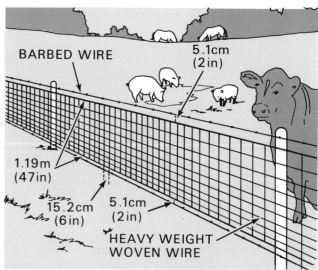

**FIGURE 32. Woven wire with barbed wire top and bottom are recommended for combinations of animals.**

## 6. FENCES ON LAND BOUNDARIES

A permanent fence around the boundary of the farm often receives first priority. This fence should resist all animals from both sides; therefore, you may want to choose one of the excellent fences under "Fences for a Combination of Livestock" as given in Table I. Figure 32 is also an example of an excellent boundary fence.

# III

# Determining What Quality of Fencing Materials to Use

After you have selected the kind of fence you need, whether permanent or temporary, your next job is to select the quality of fencing material needed for that kind of fence. This part of the discussion deals only with the materials used for the fence itself. Fence posts are discussed later.

When you buy fencing, many dealers give you a choice of fencing materials made in the United States (domestic), or of those made in other countries (imports). Immediately there is a question regarding the quality of these materials. Both can have equal quality or they may differ greatly.

As a buyer, you can easily check wire size and fence style from information on the tag and from observing the wire in the roll (Figure 33). But you can't look at wire and determine how much protective coating has been provided — the

coating that keeps fencing fabric from rusting for a period of years (Figure 34). The tag attached to the roll of fence you buy usually gives most or all of this information. Consequently, it is important that you understand what it means. It is directly related to how long your fence will stand up against rust.

These points along with others, such as the use of copper-bearing steel, the type of joint, and the effect of wire hardness on the life of a fence, are included in the following discussion.

A. Recognizing Quality in Wire.

B. Recognizing Quality in Lumber.

C. Recognizing Quality in Fasteners.

FIGURE 33. The tag on the roll of fencing you buy supplies important information.

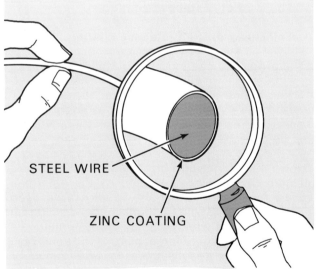

FIGURE 34. A thin coating of zinc is applied to steel wire to prevent rusting.

27

# A. Recognizing Quality in Wire

From your study of this section, you will be able to **select the wires that will last longest and require the least maintenance.**

Factors affecting the selection of materials for fences are discussed under the following headings:

1. Effect of Protective Coating.

2. Effect of Wire Size.

3. Effect of Copper-Bearing Steel.

4. Effect of Hardness of Steel.

5. Effect of Barb Spacing on Barbed Wire.

6. Effect on Types of Joints on Woven Wire.

## 1. EFFECT OF PROTECTIVE COATING

How long a **barbed wire** or a **woven wire** fence will last before it rusts out depends on the following characteristics:

—The **kind of protective coating.**

—**Thickness of the protective coating.**

The protective coating used in the past, and still in wide use, is zinc, commonly called "galvanizing." **Zinc** also acts as a "sacrificial agent." Instead of the steel wire's rusting as soon as it is exposed to the weather, the zinc on the adjoining area delays rusting.

How much galvanizing delays rusting is a question that has been studied by the American Society for Testing Materials.[2] Studies have been conducted with varying amounts of galvanizing on different sizes of wire. Samples of these materials have been placed in different parts of the country in order to secure results under a wide range of climatic conditions. A summary of the Society's findings is reported here (Table II).

### TABLE II. APPROXIMATE PROTECTION GIVEN WIRE BY CLASS 1 AND CLASS 3 GALVANIZING
#### Years till rust appears

| Wire Size | Climatic condition | | | | | |
|---|---|---|---|---|---|---|
| | Dry | | Humid | | Coastal & Industrial | |
| | Class | | Class | | Class | |
| | 1 | 3 | 1 | 3 | 1 | 3 |
| 9 | 15 | 30 | 8 | 13 | 3 | 6 |
| 11 | 11 | 30 | 6 | 13 | 2 | 6 |
| 12½ | 11 | 30 | 6 | 13 | 2 | 6 |
| 14½ | 7 | 23 | 5 | 10 | 1.5 | 4.5 |

Note — $\dfrac{1\ oz}{ft^2} = \dfrac{30.5\ mg}{cm^2}$

But first, it is important to understand that zinc is measured in $mg/cm^2$ (ounces per square foot) of wire surface. **More zinc per square meter or square foot means more years of service** before rusting starts (Table II). For your protection, fence manufacturers and the American Society for Testing Materials have established "classes" of coatings with Class 1 providing the lightest coating and Class 3 the heaviest (ASTM-A116). Each class provides for a minimum amount of galvanizing to be applied to different wire sizes. These are shown in the last three columns of Table III. Reputable domestic manufacturers work within these limits when manufacturing farm fencing materials.

When the galvanizing is listed as "regular," the wire may have less than Class 1 coating. Because of competition, most local dealers stock only wire with Class 1 coating. Fencing materials with Class 3 coating may require a special order to the manufacturer.

Imported fencing material will also meet the A. S. T. M. specifications if it is ordered that way. When the specifications have been met, it is indicated on the tag (Figure 33).

The results of tests showing how long you can expect a certain amount of zinc to keep wires from rusting under different climatic conditions are shown in Table III for coating Classes 1 and 3. Of course, when a fence wire has been damaged and the zinc peeled off, some rusting may occur. This can happen from rough handling, damage by machinery or livestock, or from grass or brush fires. The zinc coating melts at about 427°C (800°F).

You will notice from Table II that the same fencing material varies greatly in its period of service before rusting, depending on whether it is being used in a dry or humid area, or coastal or industrial area.

Note, in Table III that smaller size wires are coated with less zinc. This reduces the period of service before rusting starts on lighter weight fence.

There are several ways of applying zinc to fence wires. Some are claimed to be superior to others. Results of tests by the American Society for Testing Materials show no practical difference.

Tests with heavier gage **copper-clad steel** wire show that copper is much more effective than zinc in resisting weathering. Usually there is a thicker coating of copper than zinc. So it is to be expected that the same gage copper-coated wire will be more durable than zinc-coated wire unless the copper covering is nicked enough to expose the steel strand. Then corrosion is somewhat faster than on galvanized wire. (Copper-clad, steel wire should not be confused with ''coppered'' wire. The latter has a very thin coating and bright finish to improve appearance. It is widely used for packaging. Coppered wire has little resistance to corrosion.)

**Aluminum** wire requires no protective coating.

## 2. EFFECT OF WIRE SIZE

Once the steel wire starts to show some rust, it isn't long until your whole fence is rusty. It usually takes from one to three years from the time rust first appears until all of the wire is rusty. With the protective coating gone, the durability of your fence from then on depends on how fast rust weakens the wire. It is at this point that small wires are at a disadvantage because the surface area per unit weight of wire is so much greater than with larger wires. Table IV shows surface area with wire sizes commonly used in fencing materials.

Rusting reduces wire size; this in turn reduces its strength. Strength losses are rather rapid at first until about 25 to 30 percent of the original strength is gone. Then strength loss is rather slow. Table V shows the approximate life until the wire reaches one-half its original strength.

During the American Society for Testing Materials tests, the fences were not turning livestock, so the actual durability of fencing on farms may be somewhat less than the tables shown. On the other hand, many farmers may get this much service because they will use a fence after it has lost more than half its original strength.

**TABLE IV. SURFACE AREA PER UNIT WEIGHT OF COMMON WIRE SIZES**

| Gage of Wire | Surface Area each kg (lb) of wire | |
|---|---|---|
| 9 | 0.14 m² | .66 ft² |
| 11 | 0.17 m² | .82 ft² |
| 12½ | 0.20 m² | .98 ft² |
| 14½ | 0.26 m² | 1.29 ft² |

**TABLE III.—MINIMUM WEIGHT OR COATING ON ZINC-COATED WIRE FENCING (Furnished in 101 m (20-Rod) Rolls)**

| Size, Steel Wire Gage | Nominal Diameter of Zinc-Coated Wire | | Minimum Weight of Coating mg/cm² (oz per ft²) of Uncoated Wire Surface | | | | | |
|---|---|---|---|---|---|---|---|---|
| | Cm | (in) | Class 1 | | Class 2 | | Class 3 | |
| No. 7 | 0.450 | 0.177 | 12.2 | 0.40 | 18.3 | 0.60 | 24.4 | 0.80 |
| No. 9 | 0.376 | 0.148 | 12.2 | 0.40 | 18.3 | 0.60 | 24.4 | 0.80 |
| No. 10 | 0.343 | 0.135 | 9.2 | 0.30 | 15.3 | 0.50 | 24.4 | 0.80 |
| No. 11 | 0.305 | 0.120 | 9.2 | 0.30 | 15.3 | 0.50 | 24.4 | 0.80 |
| No. 12 | 0.267 | 0.105 | 9.2 | 0.30 | 15.3 | 0.50 | 24.4 | 0.80 |
| No. 12½ | 0.251 | 0.099 | 9.2 | 0.30 | 15.3 | 0.50 | 24.4 | 0.80 |
| No. 14½ | 0.193 | 0.076 | 6.1 | 0.20 | 12.2 | 0.40 | 18.3 | 0.60 |
| None | 0.160 | 0.063 | 4.6 | 0.15 | 10.7 | 0.35 | 15.3 | 0.50 |

**TABLE V. APPROXIMATE LIFE AFTER FENCE STARTS TO RUST UNTIL IT REACHES ONE-HALF ORIGINAL STRENGTH**

| Wire Size | Approximate Life: | | |
|---|---|---|---|
| | Dry | Humid | Coastal & Industrial |
| 9 | 50+ | 50+ | 25 |
| 11 | 50+ | 50 | 16 |
| 12½ | 50+ | 35 | 12 |
| 14½ | 50 | 20 | 7 |

For **barbed wire,** lighter weight 14-gage or 15½-gage wire is used mostly in dry country. It lasts well under dry conditions and where there is very little pressure on the fence since livestock is grazed over large areas. However, 12½-gage wire is recommended for suspension fencing in dry areas.

For **cable** fences, smooth wire is stranded into 1-cm (³/₈-in) cables. They are usually made of seven strands of smooth galvanized wire twisted together.

# 3. EFFECT OF COPPER-BEARING STEEL

Some manufacturers make fencing materials of copper-bearing steel. It is made by adding enough copper to total about 2 kg to each 1,000 kg (2 lb to each 1,000 lb) of steel.

Until the American Society for Testing Materials studies were made, it was generally believed that a fence of copper-bearing steel would last longer than steel without copper. The results of their studies show that more than .22 kg (½ lb) of copper 450 kg (1000 lb) of steel (already present without being added in most steel) appears to have no additional value.

# 4. EFFECT OF HARDNESS OF STEEL

Most manufacturers, including foreign companies, use a medium-hard steel in their fencing. This is important because of the spring action that can be built into the fence. The spring effect is

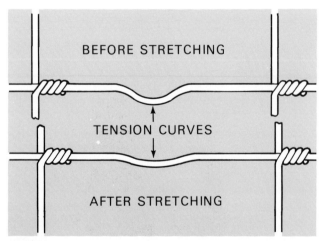

**FIGURE 35. A tension curve consists of a "U" shaped crimp in the fence wires. It has the same effect as a spring.**

secured through tension curves (Figure 35). Tension curves, which help keep the fence tight, are partly straightened when the fence is stretched. They also take up slack in the fence on hot summer days when the fence lengthens, and allow the fence to shorten in cold weather. Without tension curves, a well-stretched fence erected in summer may break in winter, or it may pull an anchor-and-brace assembly out of position.

**Barbed wire** is a problem in this respect. If it is stretched as tightly as woven wire, it will put a greater strain on the anchor-and-brace assembly than woven wire because it has no tension curves. The two wires, twisted together to make barbed wire, allow a little spring effect but not enough to equal the tension curves in woven wire. Small wire (12 to 15 gage) is used for barbed wire. The small sizes must be harder in order to have adequate pulling strength.

A fence of soft steel lacks sufficient spring action to meet these conditions. It soon sags even though the fence may have been well erected.

# 5. EFFECT OF BARB SPACING ON BARBED WIRE

Figure 36 shows different kinds of barbed wire available. Note that besides two different wire sizes, they vary in two other important respects:

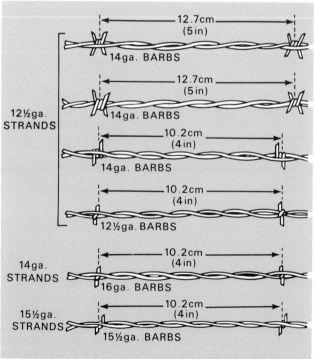

**FIGURE 36. Kinds of barbed wire available to farmers.**

30

—**Spacing between barbs** is either 10.2 cm or 12.7 cm (4 or 5 in) (approximately).

—There are **either two or four points** to each barb.

On some barbed wire, the barbs wrap around both strand wires. On other kinds. the barbs are wrapped around only one strand wire. Barbs will stay in position better if wrapped around both strand wires.

There are other differences, such as: whether the barbs are half-round or flat, and the size of wire used to make up the barbs. **Your decision** on these points is largely a matter of **personal preference.**

The first three kinds of barbed wire shown in Figure 36 are popular in humid areas where livestock is kept in smaller fields. Under these conditions, livestock may put considerable pressure on a fence. If so, a 4-point barb is more effective than 2-point ones even though the barbs are 2.5-cm (1-in) farther apart.

## 6. EFFECT ON TYPES OF JOINTS ON WOVEN WIRE

Joints in woven wire fences are where line wires and stay wires join. There are two types of joints generally recognized in woven wire fences. They are **hinge joints, stiff-stay joints** and **welded joints.**

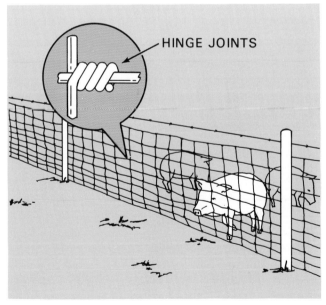

**FIGURE 37. A hinge joint allows woven wire fence to fold.**

A **hinge joint** will allow the fence to fold (Figure 37), when it is being mashed down by livestock, without the stay wires bending much. It can be straightened easily with very little wire bending. This type of joint depends on a tight wrap of the stay wire on the line wire to hold it in position. Under unusual pressure, the joint will slip sideways on the line wire.

A **stiff-stay joint** won't move sideways, but the stay wires bend when livestock mash the fence (Figure 38). To straighten the wires, you must bend them back into place. If this is done several times, there is a chance that the stay wires or the welded joint may break.

Most fences being manufactured at the present time are the hinge-joint type.

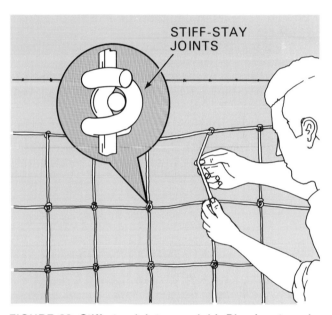

**FIGURE 38. Stiff-stay joints are rigid. Disadvantage is that stay wires bend.**

# B. Recognizing Quality in Lumber

From your study of this section, you will be able to **select the best lumber for your board fence.**

Factors are given as follows:
The following statement is taken from USDA Bulletin 1756, *Selection of Lumber for Farm and Home Building.*[5]

**Usual requirements:**
Moderate bending strength, medium decay and weather resistance, high nail-holding power, freedom from warp.

**Woods combining usual requirements in a high degree:**
Cypress, Douglas fir, western larch, southern yellow pine, redwood, white oak.

**Woods combining usual requirements in a good degree:**
Cedar, northern white pine, ponderosa pine, sugar pine, western white pine, chestnut, yellow poplar (Small tendency to warp, weathers well but low in strength and nail-holding power).

Beech, birch, red gum, mapel, red oak, tupelo (Strong, hard, high in nail-holding power, but have greater tendency to warp and do not weather so well as preceding group).

Eastern hemlock, western hemlock, white fir, spruce (Intermediate between preceding groups).

The grade of lumber to use for fences and gates will vary with different sections of the country. Select grades of hardwood are recommended. For softwoods, common No. 1 southern pine or construction grade of western woods makes very satisfactory fences and gates.

Grades lower than the above ones may be used but some waste results, strength is reduced, and good appearance is decreased.

Before using lumber not treated with a preservative, be sure it is dry. Green lumber will check, shrink and warp, causing cracks to appear. Moisture enters the cracks and speeds rate of decay.

If you plan to paint your fence, it will take less paint if you use dressed lumber.

If you plan to leave it unpainted or to whitewash or stain it, a rough finish is preferred. A do-it-yourself natural finish stain can be made following the directions outlined in a publication of the U. S. Forest Service.[6]

Consider the following factors:

—**Size and Thickness of Lumber to Use.** For most farm fences, rough lumber [2.54 cm (1 in) or 1.9 cm (¾ in)] dressed is adequate. Width is usually 15.2 cm (6 in) rough or 14 cm (5½ in) dressed. Since post spacing is usually 2.4 m (8 ft), you save labor and add to the strength of your fence by using 4.9-m (16-ft) lengths.

If you are building a fence around a corral or barn lot where livestock is to be closely confined for feeding or loading, use boards 5.1 cm (2 in) rough or 3.8 cm (1½ in) dressed. Shorten the board length to 3.7 m (12 ft) so that post spacing will be 1.8 m (6 ft).

—**Use of Wood Preservatives.** Lumber used for fences and gates should be treated with an acceptable wood preservative. The life of fences built with treated lumber will be greatly increased and annual cost lowered. If not treated, decay will soon start at joints or any place where moisture is held (Figure 39).

**FIGURE 39. Untreated lumber will rot at gate and fence joints first.**

If your fence is not to be painted, you may use a preservative such as creosote, penta (pentachlorophenol) or copper napthenate in heavy (fuel) oils.

If your fence or gate is to be painted, you will need to use a clear preservative such as penta or copper napthenate in light oils (mineral spirits is best, naptha is fairly satisfactory) or one of the many salt treatments provided by wood preserving companies before painting.

You may be able to buy commercially treated lumber in your area. If so, it will probably be either pressure-treated or soaked. Pressure treatment gives the best protection—around 20 to 30 years for board fences.

Creosote-treated wood should contain 2.7 kg (6 lb) of creosote per .03m³3 (ft³) of wood to resist decay over a long period of time.

Lumber that is treated by dipping or soaking in a 5% pentachlorophenol, water-repellent solution or a .5% copper napthenate, water-repellent solution can be expected to last 5 to 15 years, depending on how well the preservative is distributed through the sapwood. This is greatly influenced by the period of soak.

If you wish to treat your own lumber, there are several points to keep in mind. They are as follows:

—Boards should be thoroughly **air seasoned.** Green lumber will not take up enough preservative.

—It is best to first cut your lumber to the desired lengths, then **soak in the preservative** at least 15 minutes. Better yet, allow one hour of soaking time for each 2.5 cm (1 in) of thickness.

—In general, each **.3 m³ (1 cu ft) of lumber** will soak up about **.7 kg (1.5 lb) of preservative** in 15 minutes by the cold-soak method. If you can let your lumber soak longer, it will absorb more preservative and last considerably longer.

—If you cannot purchase commercially treated lumber, or are not in a position to dip-treat it yourself, it will add several years of life to your board fence or gates if you **flood-on preservative with a brush** (5% penta, water-repellent solution or copper napthenate, water-repellent solution containing 2% copper metal). Small quantities of ready-to-use wood preservatives are available from your local farm supply store for this purpose. For best results, repeat the treatment every few years.

—When treated wood is trimmed, bored or otherwise cut, some untreated wood may be exposed. You should **brush**-treat the **exposed area** with a preservative to avoid decay at that point.

—**Paint by itself will not prevent decay.** But if used over treated lumber, it helps retain the preservative and adds color to the fence.

# C. Recognizing Quality in Fasteners

From your study of this section, you will be able to select the proper fasteners for your fence.

## 1. EFFECT ON TYPES OF FASTENERS

Fasteners for wire fencing attached to wood posts may consist of **standard U-shaped staples** or **L-shaped staples** (Figure 40).

If you are using steel, concrete, or fiberglass posts, the fastener will usually be some type of **wire clip** (Figure 40).

If you are building a board fence, you will be using some type of nails — plain shank, fluted, helically threaded or annularly threaded (Figure 41).

Two qualities to consider are as follows:

a. Coating.

b. Holding Capacity.

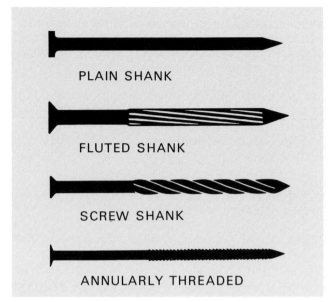

FIGURE 41. Board fasteners.

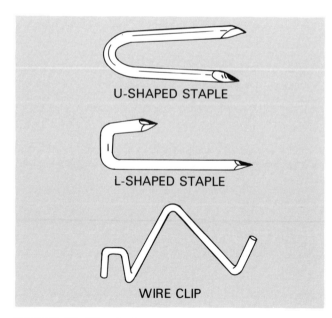

FIGURE 40. Wire fasteners.

## a. Coating

No studies are available to determine accurately how much longer galvanized staples last than ungalvanized, or bright staples. From experience and observation, it is known that galvanizing greatly increases durability (ASTM A153) — probably as much as it does for fencing fabric. Also, galvanized staples will not start rusting the attached fence wire as soon as ungalvanized ones.

Either the U-shaped or L-shaped staple is manufactured in bright or galvanized form. For some reason, dealers have been slow to stock galvanized staples of either type and frequently they are not available. This may be partly due to the fact that galvanizing softens the staple somewhat, and for hardwood posts, extra stiffness is important.

Galvanized-wire fasteners for steel, fiberglass and concrete posts (Figure 40) are expected to last about as long as the same size galvanized fencing wire except that some of the zinc may crack off where the wire makes a short bend. This will somewhat shorten the period until the first rust appears.

For board fences, the greatest durability is secured by using deformed-shank aluminum nails (Figure 41). This will completely eliminate the rust problem that develops when you use steel nails and will resist loosening in the wood.

## b. Holding Capacity

For fastening woven and barbed wire fences, you have a choice of using either U-shaped fence staples (Figure 40), made of 9-gage wire in lengths of 2.2 to 4.4 cm (⁷/₈ to 1³/₄ in), or L-shaped staples (Figure 40) made in lengths of 3.2 to 5.1 cm (1¹/₄ to 2 in).

The length of staple you select will depend on whether you are using treated or untreated posts and, if untreated, whether the posts are hard or soft wood.

If you are using untreated hardwood, shorter staples—3.2 cm (1¼ in)—may be used because they cannot be pulled out of hardwood easily. Longer staples should be used for untreated softwood posts because of low withdrawal resistance of softwood. But untreated softwood posts will last only three to five years so the holding ability of a staple is not as important as with treated posts.

With the rapid increase in the use of preservative-treated, softwood posts, the staple length becomes really important for two reasons: (1) the holding ability of a staple is reduced by the lubricating action of a preservative, and (2) the staple should be able to hold as long as the post lasts. This may be 30 years or longer with some kinds of preservatives. In that time, a short staple is almost certain to loosen and fall out.

To avoid the pulling-out action, 3.8 to 5.1 cm (1½ to 2 in) staples of either type are recommended for treated posts. The L-shaped staple was developed with this problem in mind.

According to tests[9], when treated L-shaped staples are used in pine posts, their withdrawal resistance generally increases after being in a post for a year compared to when they were first driven. The range was from .7 percent less to as high as 55 percent greater withdrawal resistance.

In general, the U-shaped staples—in the same tests—showed a substantial decrease in withdrawal resistance after a year compared to when they were first driven. The range was from 16 percent greater resistance to 51 percent less resistance. These tests included pressure-treated creosote posts.

The withdrawal resistance of nails is increasd by threading or deforming the shank, the same as with the L-shaped staple. Figure 41 shows the plain shank nail and the way other nails have been changed to make them more resistant to withdrawal. This advantage was summed up by Stern[10] as follows:

Depending on the nature of the wood the fluted nails are supposed to provide from 50 to 200 percent greater axial holding power than plain-shank nails. Properly threaded nails, however, are known to provide as much as ten times greater withdrawal resistance than the same size plain-shank nails. Furthermore, under certain conditions, fluted as well as ineffectively grooved nails achieve their ultimate holding power only after a large withdrawal which is often larger than permissible.

From this statement, you can see the importance of using something besides plain-shank nails for a board fence if you want to keep the maintenance cost down.

If you are building a high-tensile strength fence, do not drive the staples all the way. The wire must be allowed to slide through the staples for adjusting tension.

# NOTES

# IV

# Determining What Type of Anchor-Post Assemblies to Use

Now that you have selected the type and kind of fence you plan to use, you need to decide what type of anchor post construction to use. **End** construction refers to an anchor-and-brace assembly where fence pull is from only one direction (Figure 42). **Corner** construction is used when pull on an anchor-and-brace assembly is from two or more different angles. **Gate** posts and **line-braced** posts have a pull on them that is similar to the corner and end posts.

Building a movable fence does not present much of a problem. But if you are building a permanent fence, it is important for you to understand what it takes to make a strong, well-built, anchor-and-brace assembly at corners and ends of fences.

As you drive down almost any country road, it is evident that farmers are wasting lots of money and material. Many do not know how to build an anchor-and-brace assembly that will last. Others don't regard an anchor-and-brace assembly as important. They think each line post should hold its share of the pull. The discussion that follows is to help you to understand the problem and to select the kind of anchor-and-brace assembly that will best fit your needs.

Anchor-post assemblies are discussed under the following headings:
A. What Type of Anchor-Post Assembly to Use for Permanent Fences.
B. What Type of Anchor-Post Assembly to Use for Temporary Fences.

**FIGURE 42. A-well-constructed anchor-and-brace assembly will prevent failures.**

# A. What Type of Anchor-Post Assembly to Use for Permanent Fences

A well-constructed permanent fence, whether of woven or barbed wire, puts a tremendous pull on the anchor-and-brace assembly. Under normal conditions, when a fence is first stretched, the pull may be around 13.3 kN (3,000 lb). In cold weather, when the fence shortens, the pull may be as much as 20 kN (4,500 lb).

How to build an anchor-and-brace assembly that will stand this much pull is not well understood by many farmers. One result is the condition shown in Figure 43.

When constructing a permanent wire fence, attach the wires securely to **only** the four types of anchor posts. These are called the **corner, end, gate** and **center** of a line-braced unit. The fence wires should never pass these posts without being cut and tied around them. These four types of anchor posts must be braced if they are to withstand the 13.3-to 17.8-kN (3,000-to 4,000-lb) pull on them. The anchor-brace-assembly has been found to withstand these forces and to keep the fence wire tight during all seasons of the year.

From your study of this section, you will be able to **select the proper anchor-post assembly for permanent fences.**

Factors are given under the following headings:

1. Importance of Anchor-Post Assemblies.

2. Types of Anchor-Post Assemblies.

3. Types and Sizes of Posts.

4. Depth to Set Posts.

5. Types and Sizes of Compression Braces.

6. Sizes of Brace Wire.

## 1. IMPORTANCE OF ANCHOR-POST ASSEMBLIES

An anchor-and-brace assembly may fail for one or several of the following reasons:

—**Improper design;** will not stand fence pull.

—**Brace span too short.**

—**Brace member too light;** buckles under pressure.

—**Toe nailing on brace gives away.**

—**Brace set too low in end and brace posts.**

—**Posts set too shallow in ground.**

—**Poor quality post and brace material.**

—**Wires not properly attached to the anchor posts.**

—**Braces are nailed instead of dowelled.**

Some people use extra-heavy posts—20.3 to 30.5 cm (8 to 12 in) in diameter—in an effort to strengthen the anchor-and-brace assembly. These are expensive and hard to handle. They take lots of time to install. They are not necessary or desirable for good construction.

Others have tried various ideas of bracing and guying the end post. But if certain principles are not used in the construction of the assemblies, the anchor posts are almost certain to fail.

The number of spans of horizontal-brace, anchor-post assemblies are as follows:

For all permanent fences set in a straight line,

| Length of Fence | Number of Spans |
| --- | --- |
| 50.3 m (10 rods or less) | 1 |
| 50.3 to 201.3 m (10 to 40 rods) | 2 |
| Over 201.3 m (40 rods) | 3 |

If you are building a **high-tensile strength** fence, you will need brace assemblies on each side of the corners with angles of less than 120 degrees.

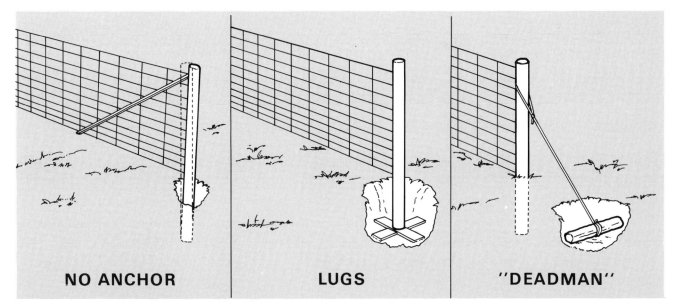

NO ANCHOR  LUGS  "DEADMAN"

FIGURE 43. Improper methods of end bracing.

## 2. TYPES OF ANCHOR-POST ASSEMBLIES

There is a wide range of methods for building fence anchor-post assemblies that are unsatisfactory. Three are shown in Figure 43. Wood posts installed without anchors are sure to pull out of the ground long before 13.3 kN (3,000 lb) of pull is applied to them. As the fence pulls, the top of the post presses forward. If the brace isn't well installed, the end post simply pulls over farther as the tension gets greater. If the brace holds solidly, more tension against the end post causes the post to move up and out of the ground.

To overcome this problem, some farmers put lugs on the bottom of the anchor post to keep it from rising out of the ground (Figure 43). The lugs help keep the post from rising but the top of the post will still move forward.

Another practice is to bury a stone or log "deadman" in the ground and run a guy wire from it to the anchor post (Figure 43). This takes lots of time and work to install. If the stone or log is large enough, it will hold satisfactorily until the log rots or the guy wire slips. The guy wire extending past the end of the fence line is unsatisfactory for fences along property lines, lanes, ditches and road rights-of-way.

There are several methods of building anchor-post assemblies that are satisfactory. One of these is the wood horizontal-brace design shown in Figure 44. As a result of both research and

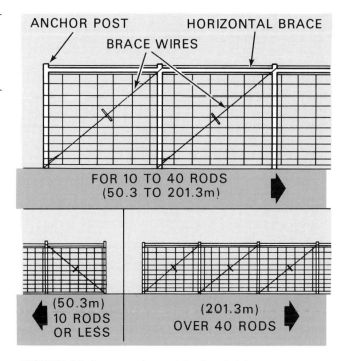

FIGURE 44. Approved wood horizontal-brace assemblies.

experience, it has been found that this type of anchor-and-brace assembly:

—Will easily **withstand 13.3 to 20 kN (3,000 to 4,500 lb) tension** exerted by the fence.

—**Requires relatively little labor** to construct.

—Can use relatively small, inexpensive posts 8.9 to 15.2 cm (3½ to 6 in) top diameters.

—Distributes the pulling pressure among three posts.

39

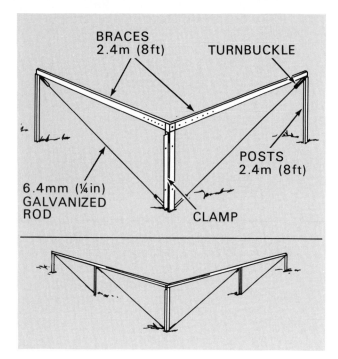

**FIGURE 45. Approved steel brace assembly.**

—Offsets tendency for anchor post to lift out of the ground.

—Eliminates the need for cutting an angle on the brace member and notching of posts.

—Can be installed with a post driver.

It has one disadvantage: if the posts are not well aligned, the assembly will buckle under pressure.

A similar type of construction is now available in steel design (Figure 45). Tests conducted with this design [12, 13] show that it has ample strength for either end or corner use and has essentially the same advantages as the wood design (Figure 44).

If you need extra strength in your end or corner, there are two other horizontal-brace designs that have proven to be very effective. They require a little more labor and material to build.

One is the **Rosemount design** (Figure 46). It is essentially the same as the horizontal-brace design in Figure 44 except with 2- or 3-span construction, the brace wires extend their pulling action over two spans at a time instead of one. This further decreases the tendency of the end post to lift out of the ground when the fence is pulling on it—more of the bracing effect is directed against the fence pull.

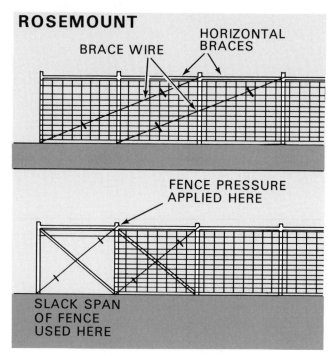

**FIGURE 46. Designs for extra heavy end pull. Rosemount anchor-and-brace assemblies designed for extra-heavy fence pull caused by wind or snow.**

This type of construction is particularly valuable in areas where snow banks against the fence or where wind loads the fences with leaves and grass.

The **cross-brace, double-span assembly** is another heavy duty design (Figure 46). But to get the extra strength, the fence is attached to the center post. This is an unusual place of attachment but tests show it is up to 60 percent stronger than the horizontal-brace assembly. With this design, the fence will be slack between the middle and the end post.

It is important with this type of assembly to attach to the center post. If you should attach to the end post, the assembly is about 20 to 35 percent less effective than the horizontal-braced assembly shown in Figure 44. (A single-span assembly of this design has a strong tendency to lift out of the ground and is not satisfactory.)

For many years, **steel diagonal-brace ends** and corners have been used satisfactorily by setting the end or corner post in concrete and placing the diagonal brace(s) in concrete (Figure 47). These are still satisfactory, but considerable work is involved in mixing and placing the concrete, and there is some delay while waiting for the concrete to cure.

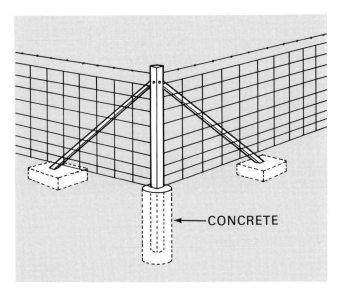

FIGURE 47. A steel anchor post and steel diagonal brace are entirely satisfactory if set in concrete and mounted as shown.

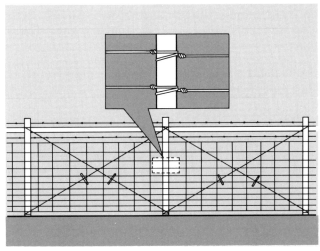

FIGURE 49. With extra-long runs of fencing [(more than 200 m (40 rd)] braced-line posts are used. The assembly has a brace wire in each direction since there may be an unbalanced pull from either direction. Each section of fence must be cut and wrapped around the center post (inset) for the assembly to be effective.

There is now available a so-called steel "dirt-set" diagonal-brace end and corner (Figure 48). It has been tested and found fully satisfactory to withstand normal fence tension. It is simple, relatively easy to install, about half the cost of the steel horizontal-brace assembly and it can be installed with a post driver.

Another type of anchor-and-brace assembly used in the fence line is known as a **braced-line-post assembly,** or as a pull-post assembly (Figure 49). These are placed about every 200 m (40 rd) in extra long lines of fence. They provide pull points for stretching a new fence. They are also used where there is a sudden change in elevation, such

as when extending from a level area down a steel slope or vice versa.

These units are built to take fence pull from either direction. The crossed brace wires along with the horizontal compression braces hold one section of the fence tightly in case the other becomes loose for some reason, such as a tree falling across one section of the fence. They are built like double-span wood or steel assemblies except that: (a) two brace wires per span are used, and (b) the fence is ended and the line wires are wrapped around the center post of each assembly to take fence tension from either direction.

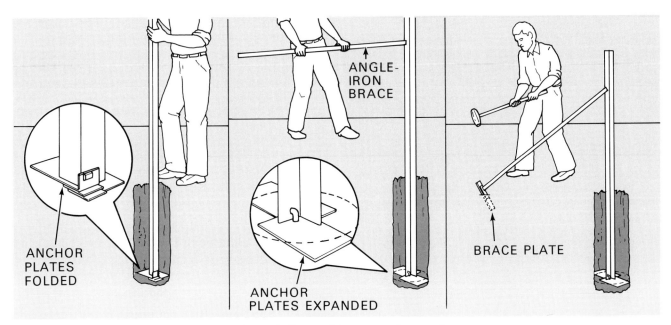

FIGURE 48. A commercially available "dirt-set" diagonal-brace anchor post.

**Steel diagonal-brace assemblies** can be used in the same manner by using a brace on each side of the anchor post to offset fence tension from either or both directions. Of course, the end wires from both fence sections must end and be attached to the anchor post.

Many farmers install braced-line-post assemblies but neglect to cut and wrap the line wires around the center (anchor) post — or the steel post of a diagonal-brace assembly. They depend on the staples that hold the fence to the posts to provide the attachment needed. Braced-line-post assemblies are useless when the fence is attached in this manner. The line wires move back and forth through the staples and the assembly does little more than regular line posts would do.

---

## 3. TYPES AND SIZES OF POSTS

---

With wood anchor-and-brace assemblies of the types just described, you can use small posts. They are easy to install and cost less than larger posts. But they will not last as long as larger posts unless they are of a durable hardwood variety or properly treated with a good preservative.

If you plan to use hardwood or preservative-treated posts, the following table can be used to determine the minimum size posts you should use:

**TABLE VI. MINIMUM SIZE WOOD POSTS FOR END OR CORNER ASSEMBLIES**

| Post Position | Top Diameter (or square) | | Length | |
|---|---|---|---|---|
| | cm | (in) | m | (ft.) |
| Corner post | 15.2 | 6 | 2.4 | 8 |
| End post | 12.7 | 5 | 2.4 | 8 |
| Gate post | 12.7 or 15.2 | 5 or 6 | 2.4 | 8 |
| Center post (LBA) | 12.7 | 5 | 2.4 | 8 |
| First corner brace post | 10.2 | 5 | 2.4 | 8 |
| Other brace posts | 10.2 | 4 | 2.4 | 8 |

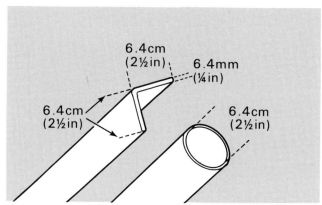

FIGURE 50. Minimum size steel posts, recommended for ends and corners.

If you are using steel anchor posts (Figure 50), the following is recommended:

| Angle iron | 6.4 cm x 6.4 cm x 0.64 cm | 2.4 m |
|---|---|---|
| | (2½ in x 2½ in x ¼ in) | (8 ft) |
| Tubing | 6.4 cm | 2.4 m |
| | (2½ in) | (8 ft) |

---

## 4. DEPTH TO SET POSTS

---

Wood or steel posts for all anchor posts and their assemblies should be set 1.1 m (3½ ft) deep. This is important if you want a strong assembly that will stand the fence pull.

If the corner post is set only 0.8 m (2½ ft) deep, the strength of the assembly is about half as much as for the 1.1 m (3½ ft) setting (Figure 51).

The 2.4-m (8-ft) posts indicated earlier as minimum length can be set 1.1 m (3½ ft) deep and still be high enough for most fences except 1.4 m (55 in) or higher woven wire fence. A 2.4 m (8-ft) length can be used with it if no barbed wire is used. With a line of barbed wire, the posts should be 31 cm (1 ft) longer so that the post can be set about 15 cm (6 in) deeper to take care of the extra height and to allow extra length for attaching the barbed wire.

Many farmers are mechanizing their post setting with power-operated post-hole diggers and power-operated post drivers (Figure 52). Posts larger than

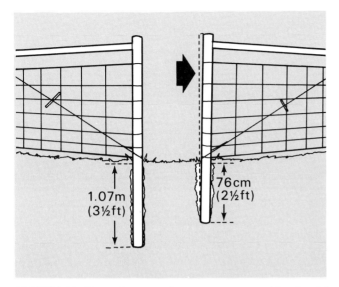

FIGURE 51. Posts in an end or corner assembly should be set 1.1 m (3½ ft) deep. An 0.8-m (2½-ft) setting is only about half as strong.

10 cm (4 in) may need to be sharpened to a dull point if you use a post driver. Only the anchor post would need sharpening with the type of construction recommended here. Large unsharpened posts will not set as firmly as sharpened posts. With a sharpened post, the soil compacts tightly around each post. This further strengthens the structure.

No comparative studies have been made on the time saved by using these machines for anchor-post assemblies as compared to hand methods. Table IX (page 54) gives comparative times for setting line posts by different methods. Power driven is faster and cheaper than hand dug or power auger.

For concreted steel end or corner construction, a hole 31 cm (12 in) in diameter is needed. This is

filled with concrete and the post is positioned in the center. The end of the steel brace is also set in concrete (Figure 47).

# 5. TYPES AND SIZES OF COMPRESSION BRACES

The compression brace is very important to a successful end or corner assembly (Figure 53). It takes the tremendous compression action that results from the fence's pulling on the whole assembly.

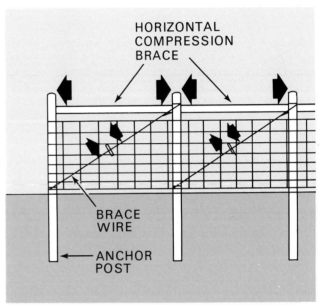

FIGURE 53. Brace wires tie anchor-and-brace assembly rigidly together. They work with the horizontal brace in holding the anchor post from overturning when fence pull is applied.

FIGURE 52. Power operated equipment for setting posts.

If you are using wood construction, the compression brace is usually a standard post which has the following characteristics:

—**Treated** with wood preservative or else is of durable wood.

—**Straight,** or almost so. In no case should it be out of line more than the amount of its own diameter.

—**Free of splits** or imperfections that may cause it to break under pressure.

Studies show that the longer the brace member(s), the less tendency there is for the anchor post to pull out of the ground. This is especially important with a single-span assembly. There are practical limits, though, which must be considered in selecting the length and diameter of wood brace members in order to keep from having to purchase special material. There is also risk of buckling. This has been kept in mind in recommending the following minimum brace sizes:

Between anchor post and first brace post.
    Length 2.4 m (8 ft), Diameter 10.2 cm (4 in).

Between first and second brace posts.
    Length 2.4 m (8 ft), Diameter 8.9 cm (3½ in).

Between second and third brace posts.
    Length 2.4 m (8 ft), Diameter 8.9 cm (3½ in).

If you are using steel pipe or tubing for a brace, it should be 5.1 cm (2 in) in diameter or larger. If the tubing is new or in first class condition, you may want to lengthen the span to take advantage of the extra length. If you are using old tubing, check it thoroughly. If it is scaling badly and shows considerable rust, it won't last. Don't risk using it. Many farmers have made this mistake.

If you are using angle iron, it should be 6.4 x 6.4 x 0.64 cm (2½ x 2½ x ¼ in) minimum size and 2.4 m (8 ft) long.

## 6. SIZES OF BRACE WIRE

With any type of wood construction, you will have to use brace wire to give the whole assembly the rigidity it needs to stand the pull of the fence. The brace wires are wrapped around the lower end of the anchor post and around the upper end of the first brace post—above the horizontal brace (Figure 53). They are then twisted to take up slack in the wires and to put pressure on the horizontal brace.

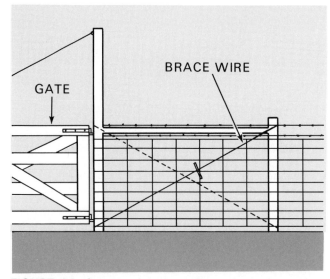

FIGURE 54. A second brace wire—shown in broken line—is not needed on a fence end except for extra-heavy gates. The tension on this brace wire should be only enough to offset the extra pull of the gate. If more than that amount, it adds to the tension the fence has already put on the anchor-and-brace assembly.

The horizontal brace pushes against the top of the anchor post so that it will not pull over when the fence is stretched. By using two or three spans, braced in this manner, the anchor-and-brace assembly is greatly strengthened since the pull is shared by each span.

Some farmers run a second brace wire from the top of the anchor post to the bottom of the first brace post (Figure 54). This should not be done for end or gate construction unless an extra heavy gate is to be mounted on the end-gate post. In that case, the second brace wire can be used in the first span and tightened just enough to have a little tension. If, at any time, the fence pull slackens enough for the gate to pull the end post away from the horizontal brace, the second brace wire will function by holding the post and horizontal brace in place. If you tighten a brace wire of this type very much, it will partly offset the fence-bracing effect of the whole assembly.

The kind of wire commonly used for a brace assembly is 9-gage, smooth, galvanized brace wire. Barbed wire should not be used. The two 12½-gage wires that make up a strand of barbed wire have about the same strength as one 9-gage brace wire but it has three disadvantages:

—Barbed wire is **more difficult to work** than smooth wire.

—It **lasts only about half as long** when exposed to weather.

—Unless the wires are evenly loaded, **barbed wire will break much quicker** than regular brace wire.

# B. What Kind of Anchor-Post Assembly
## to Use for Temporary Fences

Since movable fences are intended to stay in one location for only a few weeks, or maybe a few months, there is usually not much of an attempt to stretch the fence. This greatly simplifies the type of anchor post that is used. Figure 55 shows some of the end and corner assemblies that are commonly used, along with one commercial end assembly designed for movable fences.

If you wish to build a more permanent end or corner assembly—one that will take more fence pull—use one of the designs shown in Figures 44 through 49.

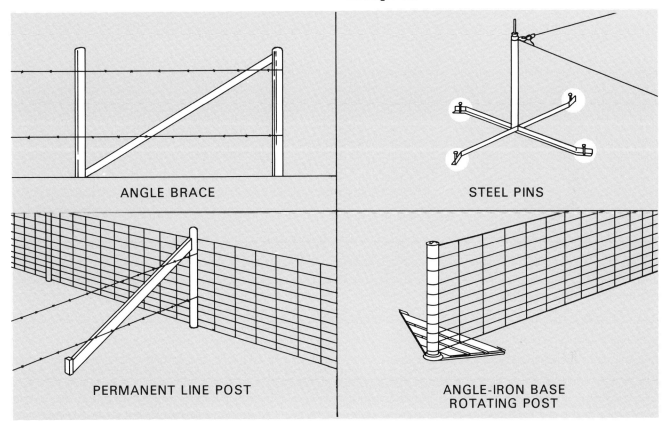

ANGLE BRACE

STEEL PINS

PERMANENT LINE POST

ANGLE-IRON BASE
ROTATING POST

FIGURE 55. Movable end corners.

# NOTES

# V.
# Determining What Type, Size and Number of Line Posts to Use

The number and kind of line posts you use will depend largely on your local conditions. Your decision will be influenced by the following situations:

—How **closely** your livestock **is confined.**

—What **kind of fence** you plan to use.

—**How long** you wish it **to last.**

—**How much it costs** to set posts.

—The **kinds of posts** available.

—**Lightning protection** needed.

—**Height of fence.**

You will need to select different posts for permanent and temporary fences. They are discussed as follows:

A. What Type, Size and Number of Line Posts to Use for Permanent Fences

B. What Type, Size and Number of Line Posts to Use for Temporary Fences

## A. What Type, Size and Number of Line Posts to Use for Permanent Fences

From your study of this section, you will be able to **select the proper line posts** for your fence.

Factors are given under the following headings:

1. Types and Sizes of Posts.

2. Spacing of Posts.

3. Lengths of Posts.

4. Durability of Posts.

5. Protecting Fences from Fires.

6. Protecting Fences from Lightning.

7. Comparing Efforts Required to Set Posts.

## 1. TYPES AND SIZES OF POSTS

**Wood** posts are available in lengths of 1.7 to 2.4 m (5½ to 8 ft) and 6.4 cm (2½ in) and larger in diameter. Reinforced concrete posts can be formed to any desired length. **Steel** posts are available in 1.5-, 1.7-, 1.8-, 2.0-, 2.1-, 2.3-, and 2.4- m (5- 5½-, 6-, 6½-, 7-, 7½-, and 8-ft) lengths. The 2.0- and 2.1-m (6½- and 7-ft) lengths are easiest to get from most dealers.

**Fiberglass** posts are available in 1.2-, 1.5-, 1.7-, 1.8-, 2.0-, 2.1-, and 2.4-m (4-, 5-, 5½-, 6-, 6½-, 7-, and 8-ft) lengths.

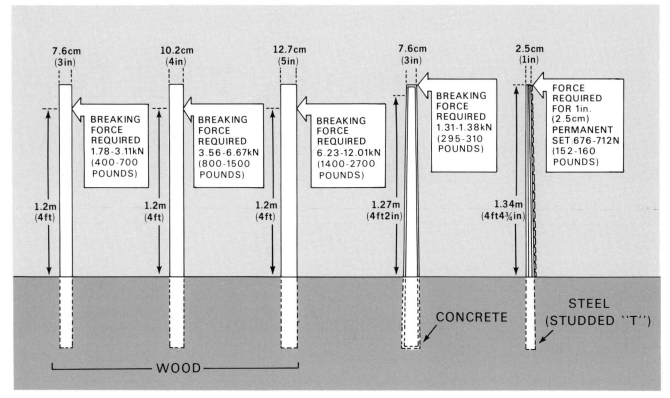

**FIGURE 56. Approximate strengths of wood posts**

Comparative strength of posts is given in Figure 56. Small values for each size of **wood posts** are for northern white cedar while larger values are for white oak, Jack pine and tamarack. Most other species fall between these extremes. Strength is computed for force exerted 1.2 m (4 ft) above ground line on green posts.

Approximate breaking strength of **square concrete posts** with 12.7-cm (5-in) base and 7.6-cm (3-in) top reinforced with four 3-gage wire is 1.3-1.4 kN (295-310 lb). Force is exerted at top of post.

The same post with 6-gage wire reinforcement has a breaking strength of approximately 721 N (162 lb). A post 9.2 x 9.2 cm ($3^5/_8$ in x $3^5/_8$ in) top and bottom with 6-gage reinforcing wire has a breaking strength of approximately 587 N (132 lb) (data from Portland Cement Association).

If you have **straight, open-field fencing,** any of the standard steel fence posts, standard 10.2-cm (4-in) concrete posts or 6.4-cm (2½-in) or larger wood posts will work very satisfactorily. In that case, your decision can be based on availability of the different posts, their cost and the cost of setting them.

If you are **fencing on the contour** and follow post-spacing recommendations, you can use the same size posts as for straight fencing. If it is necessary to lengthen the spans more than the recommended distances, use 10.2- or 12.7-cm (5- or 5 in) wood or concrete posts to get greater resistance to overturning.

You will also need to use 10.2- or 12.7-cm (4- or 5-inch) posts in **sandy** soils, or wet soils, such as in a swamp or around a lake, to resist overturning.

**At least a 10.2-cm (4-in) post** should be used around **barnlots** or **corrals.** For very **close confinement,** such as loading chutes or sorting pens, **12.7-cm (5-in) posts** are needed.

**Fiberglass** posts are excellent as line posts for **electric fences.**

In building a **board fence,** use **wood posts** with a **10.2-cm (4-in) flat face.** Besides strength, this provides a surface wide enough for you to nail on boards without splitting. Splitting decreases the strength of your fence. Posts that are sawed so that they are half-round or quarter-round are often available for this use.

A **studded "T" steel post** will withstand 676-712 kN (152-160 lb) but will result in a 2.5-cm (1-in) permanent deflection. Common types of steel posts are shown in Figure 57.

48

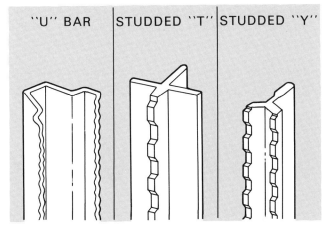

| "U" BAR | STUDDED "T" | STUDDED "Y" |

**FIGURE 57. Common types of steel posts.**

## 2. SPACING OF POSTS

In reaching your decision as to the number of posts to use, there are two major points to consider. They are the **kind of fence** you plan to use, and **how closely confined your livestock** will be.

If you are building a straight woven wire field fence, on level ground, it is common practice to space the posts about 4.3 to 4.9 m (14 to 16 ft) apart. If the ground isn't level, you may have to space your posts closer together in order to have one at each high and low point in the fence. (These and other spacing recommendations, except for contour fencing, are the result of experience rather than particular studies that have been made.)

If you are building a barbed-wire fence, posts are usually spaced about 3.7 to 4.3 m (12 to 14 ft) apart since there are no stay wires on a barbed wire fence to hold the strands apart.

There are two exceptions to this. They are as follows:

—In **dry country where barbed wire is used to fence in range areas,** post spacing may be as much as 15.3 m (50 ft) because there is very little livestock pressure.

—If **suspension fences** are used, spacing is about 31 m (100 ft) apart. Twisted wire stays are inserted every 4.9 to 7.6 m (16 to 25 ft) to hold the barbed-wire strands apart. Middle "T" fiberglass posts that are 1.2 m (4 ft) long may be used as stays.

For permanent electric fences using three or more 12½-gage smooth wires, post spacing may vary from 31 to 46 m (100 to 150 ft), depending upon the smoothness and uniformity of the land slope. Insulated stays or battens should be installed every 9.2-15.3 m (30-50 ft) between posts. With wood or steel posts, insulators must be used, while none are required with fiberglass posts because they are insulators themselves.

For high-tensile, smooth-wire fences, space posts 12 to 18 m (40 to 60 ft) apart with stays spaced from 3 to 6 m (10 to 20 ft) apart.

If wire is smaller than 12½ gage, the length of the post interval should be shortened—9.2 m (30 ft) or less.

If you are building your fence on the contour, post spacings will have to be adjusted to the amount of curvature. Complete instructions are given in Part 2, Building Fences and Gates.

For board fences around an open field, posts are spaced 2.4 m (8 ft) apart. This spacing allows for use of 4.9-m (16-ft) lengths of lumber. Around a barnlot or corral, post spacing is 1.5 or 1.8 m (5 or 6 ft). This allows for the use of 3.1- or 3.7-m (10- or 12-ft) lengths of lumber. Closer spacings greatly strengthen a fence where livestock is closely confined, and may push or pile up against it.

## 3. LENGTHS OF POSTS

Iowa studies show that 2.1-m (7-ft) posts for permanent field fences should be set 76 cm (2½ ft) in the ground. This is true whether you are planning a woven wire, barbed wire, or board fence. About the only exception is when you are building a board fence around a barnlot or corral where livestock will put considerable pressure on it. In this case, a 92-cm (3-ft) setting is used.

If you are using a low, woven wire fence without barbed wire, your posts can be shortened until you have about 7.6 cm (3 in) of height left after the post is set and the fence attached. Under most conditions, this is not a very good practice. If you change your livestock practices so that a higher fence is needed, either the posts will have to be replaced, or a wood strip nailed to the posts, to increase their height. The former is expensive, and the latter unsightly and not very strong.

# 4. DURABILITY OF POSTS

The durability of steel, concrete and fiberglass posts is one of their outstanding advantages. Under normal conditions, each type of post should last 20 to 30 years. For **concrete posts** to last, they must be well made.* Research on the durability of fiberglass posts is in progress at this writing, but preliminary indications suggest they will last as long as wood or steel.

Fiberglass posts have the following advantages:

—**Light** — about ¼ the weight of steel.

—**Easy to install** in ground with standard driving tools.

—**Economical** in cost.

—**Require no anchor plates** if driven 15.2 cm (6 in) deeper than steel posts.

—**Smooth** — thus reducing injury to animals.

—**Will bend (flex)** above ground without loosening in ground.

—**Do not rot** in ground.

—**Made in various colors and lengths.**

—**Immune to acids and other corrosive** soil conditions.

—**Good electrical insulators.**

—Excellent for **suspension** and **electric fences.**

**Wood posts** have been widely used because they are comparatively low in cost and readily available. The more durable woods such as osage-orange, black locust, and red cedar have given excellent service when they are selected with a high heartwood content. In many areas, these durable woods are almost gone and attempts to substitute non-durable, untreated woods have resulted in a short post life.

---

*If you are interested in how to make your own concrete posts, write the Portland Cement Association, 33 West Grand Av., Chicago, Illinois for their leaflet, "How to Make Concrete Posts."

**FIGURE 58. Untreated softwood posts last only one to three years in warm, humid climates.**

Untreated softwood posts, such as southern pine, rot quickly. Their average life is about 3 years. In fact, the untreated sapwood of any species will rot in 1 to 3 years (Figure 58). The heartwood of many species will not last much longer.

Southern pine and many other species of softwoods and hardwoods take preservative treatment readily and will then give 15 to 30 years or more of top service if they have 2.7-3.4 kg (6-8 lb) of a suitable preservative per .028m³ (ft³) of wood well distributed through the post. Some pressure-treated creosote posts are reported to have lasted 50 years or longer.

In view of these tests and experiences, the use of wood preservatives of various kinds has gained rapid acceptance. In recent years there has been a large increase in the number of wood-preserving plants offering well-treated fence posts for sale at a moderate price. Tests on the life of treated and untreated fence posts are being conducted by the U. S. Forest Service, the Tennessee Valley Authority, wood-preserving industries, and a number of state experiment stations. Although some preservatives and some methods of treatment are too new to provide information as to expected life, much is known about the performance of posts treated by tested preservatives and methods.

# TABLE VII. LIFE EXPECTANCY OF TREATED AND UNTREATED FENCE POSTS

Prepared by the Coordinated Wood Preservation Council, an organization of southern agricultural colleges and experiment stations; the Forest Utilization Services of the Southern and Southeastern Forest Experiment Stations; and the Division of Forestry Relations, T.V.A. Supplemented with references as numbered. Data for Rocky Mountain area posts were obtained from Forest Products Laboratory USDA, Report 068).

| Kinds of Wood | (Heartwood)* | Pressure (Creosote, pentachlorophenol or copper napthenate)† | Treated Round Posts Hot & Cold Bath (Creosote, pentachlorophenol or copper napthenate)† | Cold Soak | End Diffusion (Zinc chloride or chromated zinc chloride)§ | Double Diffusion (Copper sulfate and sodium fluoride) | Salt Treatments (Osmose, tanalith and celcure) |
|---|---|---|---|---|---|---|---|
| | (years) | (years) | (years) | (years) | (years) | (years) | (years) |
| Osage Orange | 25-30 | | | | | | |
| Red Cedar | 15-25 | 20-25[1] | 20-25[1] | 10-20[1] | | | |
| Black Locust | 15-25 | | | | | | |
| Sassafras | 10-15 | 20-25 | 15-20 | | | | |
| White Oak | 5-10 | 20-30 | 15-30 | 10-20 | 8-9 | | |
| Blackjack Oak | 5-10 | 15-25 | 10-20 | 10-20 | 8-9 | | |
| Cypress | 5-10 | 20-30 | 15-30 | | | | |
| So. Pine | 3-7 | 25-30 | 15-20 | 10-20 | 10 | 20-30[19] | 25[19] |
| Sweetgum | 3-6 | 20-30 | 20-30 | 10-20 | | | |
| Hickory | 2-6 | 15-20 | 10-15 | 10-15 | | | |
| Red Oak | 2-6 | 20-30 | 20-30 | 10-20 | 6 | | 17[19] |
| Sycamore | 2-6 | 20-25 | 15-25 | 10-20 | 8-9 | | |
| Yellow Poplar | 2-6 | 20-25 | 15-25 | 10-20 | 8-9 | | |
| Cottonwood | 2-6 | 15-20[1] | 10-15[1] | 5-10[1] | 5 | | |
| Willow | 2-6 | 30 | 28-37 | 7-20 | 5 | | |
| Ponderosa Pine | 4-14 | 35 | 30 | 18 | | | |
| Lodgepole Pine | 4-12 | 35 | 35 | 20 | | | |
| Rocky Mt. Juniper | 29 | | | | | | |
| Douglas Fir | 7-12 | 20 | 25 | 2 | | | |
| Aspen | 7-12 | 20 | 25 | 20 | | | |

*Sapwood of all species rots readily in one to three years depending on local soil and weather conditions.
†Data based on an absorption of 6 pounds or more per cubic foot of wood with complete penetration of sapwood. All preservatives applied in an oil solution. Posts barked and seasoned before treatment.
§Water solution: ¾ - 1 pound of dry salt per cubic foot of wood. Posts must be green when treated.

Table VII has been prepared to guide you in selecting posts treated by various methods with various preservatives. The table lists six different methods of post treatment. They are as follows:

—**Pressure.**

—**Hot and cold bath.**

—**Cold soak.**

—**End diffusion.**

—**Double diffusion.**

**FIGURE 59. Pressure-treated posts are sealed in a large cylinder and preservatives applied under pressure.**

The first one, **pressure treatment** (Figure 59), is done on a commercial basis because it takes considerable equipment and skill. It also gives the best results.

The other treating methods can be done on the farm. Figure 60 shows the equipment used for different farm methods of treatment. This may help you to understand Table VII.

Methods of treating your own posts are as follows:

## a. Hot and Cold Bath

Peeled, seasoned posts are first heated in preservative (water can be used) about 2 hours to drive out air, then dipped in cold preservative about 2 hours.

## b. Cold Soak

Seasoned, peeled posts are submerged in preservative 1 to 3 days.

## c. End Diffusion

Freshly cut, unpeeled posts are set in a wooden trough, or tub, containing preservative and allowed to stand from 1 to 10 days. Opposite ends of posts are then placed in trough until all preservative is absorbed.

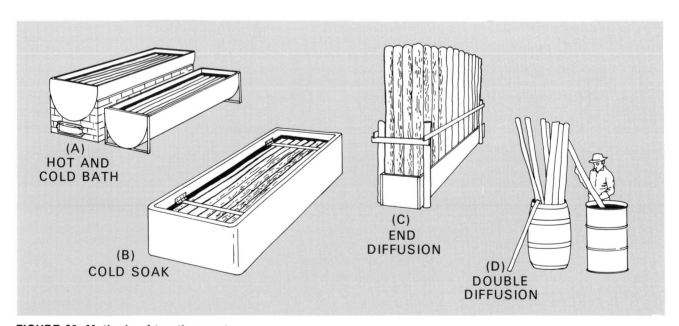

**FIGURE 60. Methods of treating posts.**

## d. Double Diffusion

Freshly cut and peeled posts are soaked, butt down, in one barrel of preservative for about 3 days. Then they are placed in the second barrel of preservative for another 3 days.

## 5. PROTECTING FENCES FROM FIRES

Damage to all fence materials by fire can be expected. A hot fire can cause wooden posts to burn or char, steel posts to lose their protective coating, and fiberglass posts to weaken or melt. Steel wire can lose its temper and zinc coating by high heat.

The fence row should be kept as free as possible of grasses and brush. Some may be cut with mowers, while others may be killed with selected herbicides.

## 6. PROTECTING FENCES FROM LIGHTNING

In areas where lightning is a hazard, it is recognized more and more that something should be done about grounding barbed wire and woven wire fences. It is rather common for lightning to hit a wire fence directly, or indirectly through a tree or building near a fence, and then travel as far as 3.2 km (2 mi) on the fence before it is grounded. Each year there is a sizable loss of livestock; occasionally a human life is lost.

It is true that lightning will strike a grounded fence quicker than one that isn't grounded, or is poorly grounded. Although no research studies have been made on the effectiveness of different fence-grounding methods, there have been extensive studies made with power and telephone lines. These studies show that it is best and least destructive to provide a quick path to ground for the lightning charge.

With wood, fiberglass, or concrete posts, there is very little grounding effect unless the posts are wet and in moist or wet soil. According to the National Associaton of Mutual Insurance Companies, fair protection can be secured with a metal post every

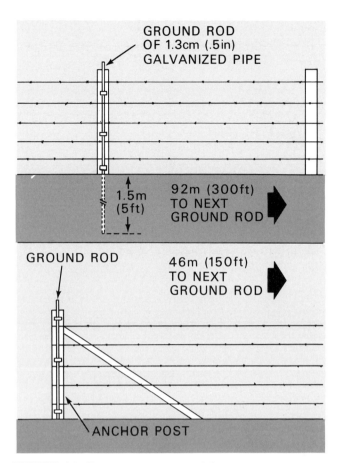

**FIGURE 61. Proper grounding of fence helps protect from lightning.**

46 m (150 ft) in a line of wood or concrete posts. An extra-long steel post is desirable for this purpose.

In moist areas, a 1.3-cm (½-in) galvanized steel pipe, 2 to 3 m (8 to 10 ft) long, may be driven at least 1.4 m (5 ft) into the ground beside the fence post. The grounding rod and wire must be firmly bonded together in the post (Figure 61). A grounding rod should be placed within 46 m (150 ft) of each anchor post and within 92m (300 ft) of each other along the fence line. Under extremely dry conditions, even this arrangement may not be adequate but under most farm conditions, it should be satisfactory.

If you plan to erect a wire fence under a power line, the ground rods will serve a second safety function. In case a high voltage wire breaks and falls on the fence, the driven ground rods will probably carry sufficient current to cause the power supplier's automatic breaker to open and turn off the current.

Steel posts will ground a fence as long as the soil is wet or moist. If you are using all steel posts, or every other post of steel, you probably have a fairly well grounded fence except under very dry conditions. In some areas, the soil will dry out below the

53

level of the post until there is practically no grounding effect. In that case, follow the same recommendations as for wood posts.

## 7. COMPARING EFFORTS REQUIRED TO SET POSTS

Another factor you need to consider is the ease with which the different kinds of posts can be handled and how quickly they can be set by different methods. Table VIII gives the approximate weight of different kinds of posts.

### TABLE VIII. COMPARATIVE WEIGHT OF DIFFERENT KINDS OF 2.1-M (7-FT) POSTS

| Size Post | | Material | Approximate Weight | | |
|-----------|---|----------|--------------------|---|---|
| cm | in. | | kg | lbs. | |
| 7.6 | 3 diam. | Untreated wood | 4.1-9.1 | 9-20 | Treated wood posts will weigh 1.8 to 3.6 kg (2 to 8 lb) more due to weight of preservative. |
| 10.2 | 4 diam. | Untreated wood | 7.3-16.3 | 16-36 | |
| 12.7 | 5 diam. | Untreated wood | 10.9-23.2 | | |
| 10.2 x 10.2 | 4 x 4 | Concrete Steel | 50.-57 3.9-5.0 | 110-125 8.5-11 | |

## B. What Type, Size and Number of Line Posts to Use for Temporary Fences

Most of what has been said about posts for permanent fences applies to posts for movable fences. The principal differences are in the size of the posts used, spacing of posts and depth of set.

Standard-size wood or concrete posts can be used for movable fences, but most farmers don't want to take the time necessary to dig holes and tamp dirt around posts that large. Since steel and fiberglass posts can be driven in the ground quickly and easily, they are widely used.

Small, pointed wood posts or stakes, pipe and small 1-cm (³/₈-in) steel rods, used for electric fencing, make up the selection for movable fences (Figure 62). The size of post you select is not very important since a movable fence is not expected to take much, if any, pressure from livestock. The most important point is that the post be of a size that can be driven into the ground easily.

Indiana studies[20] show that in building electric fences the average setting time per post is as follows: wood line posts—22.5 minutes; special steel line posts for electric fencing—7.5 minutes. (Table IX).

Spacing of posts is mostly a matter of judgment based on how closely you think the posts should be to hold the fence as long as you will need it. Spacing usually varies from 4.6 to 7.6 m (15 to 25 ft). However, some farmers will space posts for electric fencing as far as 12.2 to 13.7 m (40 to 45 ft).

### TABLE IX. APPROXIMATE TIME FOR SETTING ONE LINE POST

| Kind of Post | Method | Setting Time |
|--------------|--------|-------------|
| Wood or Concrete | Hand | 22.5 min. |
| Wood or Concrete | Power Digger | 12.5 min. |
| Wood | Power Driver | 4.0 min. |
| Steel | Hand Driven | 7.5 min. |

Depth of set is just enough to make the post reasonably firm in wet weather. In heavy soils, this is 25.4 to 35.6 cm (10 to 14 in). In lighter and sandy soils, the setting depth may have to be around 61 cm (2 ft) or more.

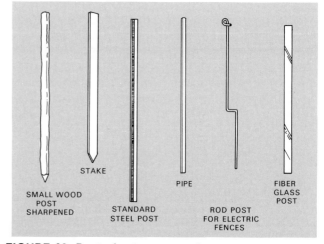

FIGURE 62. Posts for temporary fences.

# VI.
# Determining What Kind of Electric Fence Controller to Use

Electric fences are widely and successfully used throughout farming areas where livestock is raised. They can be an effective, safe and inexpensive means of providing both temporary (movable) or permanent fencing if the fences are properly constructed and if they are energized with a safe controller. (A "controller" is also commonly called a "charger" or "fence charger" or "energizer.")

On the other hand, some controllers—especially home-made ones—can be a hazard. Each year they cause serious injury and some deaths to both humans and livestock. Fires are known to have started in fields and around buildings as a result of their use.

Electric fence controllers are discussed under the following headings:

A. What Kind of Controller to Use for Permanent Fences

B. What Kind of Controller to Use for Temporary Fences

## A. What Kind of Controller to Use for Permanent Fences

Permanent electric fence installations are planned for longtime usage. They generally consist of two or more strands of smooth wire. Fences designed for the control of small predators along with coyotes may have as many as 10 or 12 strands.[3] Alternate wires are "hot" ones. Some are "ground-return" wires to the controller. Figure 63 shows an excellent general purpose fence with five line wires—three hot and two ground-return. The ground wire return design is particularly recommended where the soil may be dry some of the time.

Special controllers have recently been developed to supply an adequate electrical charge for long lengths of wires. These solid state electronics have low impedance, high power and high voltage. They are normally adequate for a multi-strand fence totaling 8 to 16 km (5 to 10 mi) of wire. They cost 3 to 4 times as much as the conventional controller but may be used for either temporary or permanent fences. Even so, the permanent electric fence will cost only 30 to 50 percent of a comparable woven barbed wire fence.

The solid state energizer produces 45 to 65 electrical pulses per minute; however, the duration

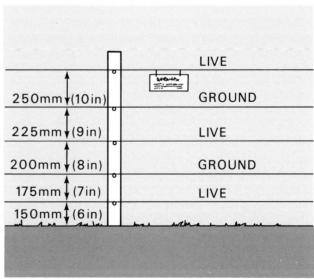

FIGURE 63. A 5-wire electric fence with three live and two ground wires.

of each electrical charge is 3/10,000 of a second, while that of the conventional controller is about 3/10 of a second (Figure 64). This short duration of shock permits the use of higher amperage on the lines, thus giving better animal control and safety over long fence lines with less maintenance.

This controller provides adequate voltage for animal control even under adverse conditions. Snell reports that at least 1000 volts are necessary for daily cattle, 2000 volts for sheep and goats and 2000 to 3000 volts for coyotes.[25]

Other features of the solid state energizer are similar to the approved conventional ones.

Table I gives the specifications for several permanent types of electric fence design. See Part 2, Building Fences and Gates, for construction details.

**FIGURE 64. This solid state electronic controller is effective for many strands of wire over long distances.**

# B. What Kind of Controllers to Use for Temporary Fences

A temporary electric fence is often built for a given group of animals. It consists of one, two or three strands of wire fastened to insulators mounted to posts. Small posts and wires are normally used. A low-cost conventional controller may be used to supply the shock that gets the respect of the animals. Depending upon its type and power strength, this controller will charge up to 8.1 km (5 mi) of wire under extremely favorable conditions.

From your study of this section, you will be able to **select the proper controller for your electric fence.** Factors are given under the following headings:

1. Power Sources for Electric Fences.

2. Effectiveness of Electric Fence Controllers.

3. Safety of Electric Fence Controllers.

4. Durability of Electric Fence Controllers.

5. Convenience of Electric Fence Controllers.

## 1. POWER SOURCES FOR ELECTRIC FENCES

From the user's viewpoint, there are three sources of electric power for fence controllers (Figure 65). They are as follows:

—6-volt batteries (DC).

—12-volt batteries (DC).

—120-volt power supply (AC).

Some controllers are designed to operate on either. Solar powered units are being developed.

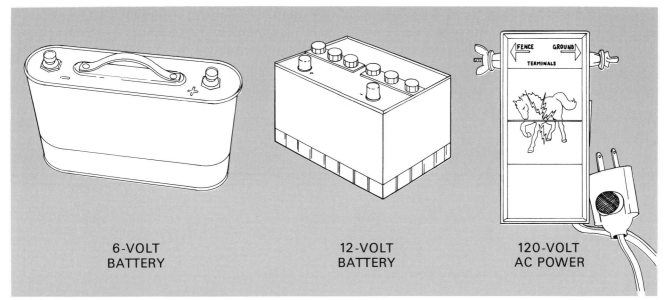

FIGURE 65. Sources of electric power for fences.

## 2. EFFECTIVENESS OF ELECTRIC FENCE CONTROLLERS

Most conventional controllers are designed for relative short lengths of fence lines while solid state electric ones can energize fence line totaling 24.2 km (15 mi) of wire. Long mileage controllers are more expensive but may be used for short lines if desired.

If all of the fields you plan to fence are not near a 120-volt power source, you have no choice but to use a battery-operated controller. It has been a very popular type of controller because it can be used at any location without connection to an outside power source. Batteries will usually last from 1½ to 3 months, so maintenance is no big problem.

A 12-volt wet battery can be used to operate a fence controller. Normally this battery will need to be recharged every 6 to 10 weeks. With a solar cell energy collector, this battery can be recharged daily for the life of the battery. This power source with an appropriate controller is especially convenient for a multi-line permanent, as well as remote, installation. The initial cost of this controller is more than that of the conventional ones, but effective permanent fences for any animal can be built with it.

If some of your fields are distant from a 120-volt power source and some are close, you may wish to select the combination unit that will operate on either voltage. The only disadvantage of the combination unit is that it costs more than a battery-operated one.

If all of your fields are where they can be served from a 120-volt controller, it is probably your best selection. There is no problem of changing or recharging batteries. Cost of operation is reasonable, averaging around 7 kilowatt-hours per month.

Farm animals must be trained to respect an electric fence if it is to be effective. This is particularly true if you are planning to use only one or two strands of barbed or smooth wire. Most animals can go either over or under fences of this type unless they have learned to respect them.

**FIGURE 66. Methods of training animals to respect an electric fence.**

Training for hogs, cattle, horses and mules consists of putting feed on the opposite side of the fence just out of their reach (Figure 66). It is best to allow them to discover the feed on their own rather than try to drive them to it. They usually learn their lesson within 1 or 2 hours.

With sheep and goats, the problem is different. It is difficult to give them a shock through their wool or hair but they are very sensitive if they touch the charged wire with a nose or ear. They can be trained in two ways. One method is to attach an ear of corn or some hay to the charged fence. The other is to attach tin cans or other bright objects to the fence wire. In either case, when they investigate, they will probably receive an effective shock. In this way, they learn to respect the fence the same as other animals. The disadvantage is that they gradually forget their training and the next time they contact the fence, they may not get a shock unless they happen to touch an ear or nose to the wire. For this reason, an electric fence is not considered as effective for sheep and goats as for other animals unless solid state energizers are used. Cattle and sheep dogs can be trained to go over or through most electric fences without being shocked.

Most manufacturers do not indicate what voltage is supplied to the fence by their controller. The battery-operated units, or the combination battery and 120-volt units may supply from around 3,000 volts to as high as 10,000 volts. (The latter is close to the voltage used to fire some spark plugs.) Modern solid state electronic energizers have an output voltage between 4,000 and 5,000 volts.

The 120-volt type may supply less than 1,000 volts to as high as 6,000 volts to the fence line.

The higher voltage is better for the short runs where the fence is checked frequently to replace cracked insulators, to clean dirty insulators and to remove grass, weeds or brush that may short the line wire. It works better than lower voltage under dry weather conditions. It is also better when used with smooth wire; the extra voltage helps overcome lack of a barb for penetrating to the skin of an animal.

Its main disadvantge is that it will short more readily unless the fence line is well maintained. Once the fence line is shorted, it may deliver little or no shock to animals touching it.

Lower voltage conventional fencing units work better on long runs of fence because they do not short as readily. Their lower voltages are effective under most farm conditions.

For any controller to be effective, it is very important that it be well grounded. The ground rod must be in contact with moist soil at all times. If your **ground rod** is driven to a **depth of 2.4 m (8 ft)**, you can be reasonably sure you have a good ground connection.

The use of one or more neutral return (grounded) wires to the controller is recommended for dry areas.

58

## 3. SAFETY OF ELECTRIC FENCE CONTROLLERS

Safety is your most important point to consider when obtaining a controller (Figure 67).

Extensive studies have been made on how much electricity it takes to kill a person or animal. These studies have been interpreted into two well recognized codes: "Standard for Electric Fence Controllers" established by the Underwriters' Laboratories, Inc., and "Safety Rules for Electric Fences" established by the National Bureau of Standards. Only the first one is concerned with actually checking and approving units for manufacturers. Many foreign countries have tested and approved their own.

You can tell whether a controller has been approved. Check the label(s) on the controller (Figure 68). They should be approved by either Underwriters' Laboratories, Inc. (UL) or by some approved testing commission or foreign country. Some controllers meet several of these codes.

If a fence controller is approved by either of these organizations, it is your best assurance of safety.

A few states have laws prohibiting the sale of controllers unless they have been approved by one of the codes.

**FIGURE 67. This homemade "controller"—a transformer from an appliance—resulted in the death of a 5-year-old youngster.**

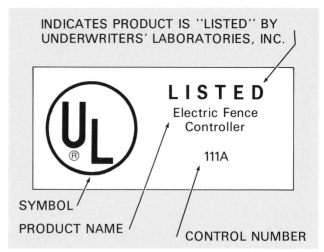

**FIGURE 68. Your controller should be approved by Underwriters' Laboratories, Inc. (UL).**

Some controllers are approved for safety by other countries of the world such as New Zealand, Australia, Great Britain, Holland, Germany, Denmark, Sweden and Norway (Figure 69). These controllers may or may not have completed the tests for UL approval, but they are considered to be safe.

There are a number of controllers on the market that have not been approved under any code. One type is called a weed burner or weed chopper When weeds or grass grow up and touch the charged wire, there is sufficient spark from the wire to burn it clear of vegetation. To do this means the controller must be "on" 5 to 15 times longer than the .1 to .2 seconds established by the codes. Consequently, it is not approved. There may also be some hazard from fire if there is material close at hand that will burn easily.

**FIGURE 69. Labels of safety approved by other countries.**

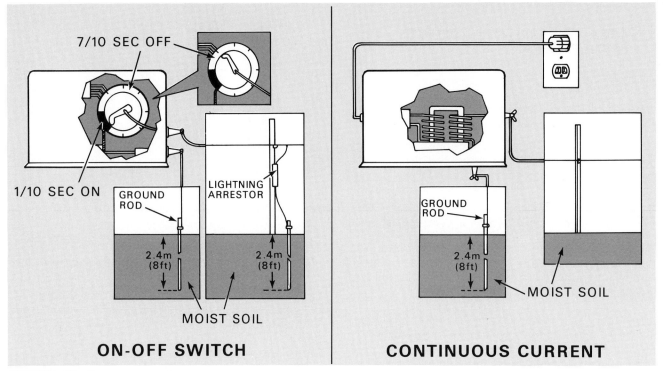

FIGURE 70. Some controllers operate intermittently while others remain "on" at all times.

Another type of controller is known as the continuous type. It keeps the fence charged continuously. The two codes shown in Figure 68 do not approve this type of controller. However, it is approved by the National Bureau of Standards. The question regarding this unit is the degree to which an animal or person tends to "freeze," or lose muscle control, resulting in an inability to break contact. There is no period when the current is off so that contact can be broken. This means that the current from these units must be held to very low values of about .003 to .005 amperes. Other approved units provide for a time-off interval so that a person or animal can get away. On-and-off units with an on time of 1/10 second may supply .025 and .040 amperes through the controller (Figure 70).

## 4. DURABILITY OF ELECTRIC FENCE CONTROLLERS

It is somewhat difficult for a manufacturer to assure the durability of a controller. The best controllers are occasionally damaged by lightning. If you install your unit so that it is well grounded and protected with lightning arrestors, this damage is reduced but not completely eliminated.

Approved units have to meet certain requirements such as corrosion resistance and protection against dust and weather (if used outdoors) which helps assure durability. The durability feature of approved units is partly offset by the delicate mechanism needed to time the on-and-off periods and to make and break the electrical circuit. Farmer experience indicates that approved controllers will last an average of 1 to 3 years if operated continuously. Few farmers operate a unit continuously so it may last much longer with normal service.

The durability of your controller will probably be influenced by the following factors:

—**Use an approved controller.**

—**Provide a good ground rod** at the controller.

—**Provide good insulators** and keep them in good condition.

—**Maintain a clean fence** with respect to weeds.

—**Provide lightning protection.**

## 5. CONVENIENCE OF ELECTRIC FENCE CONTROLLERS

There are many features that various manufacturers publicize (Figure 71). Probably the most important ones to you as a user are as follows:

—A **warning signal** to indicate if the fence is shorted. (With some controllers, this is not feasible)

—A **high-low switch** which provides for more voltage when the ground gets dry.

—**Provision for easy mounting**—important if you use a portable unit, either of the battery type or the combination battery and 120-volt type. This feature is of no particular importance for those using the straight, 120-volt, alternating-current type since there is usually very little occasion to move it about.

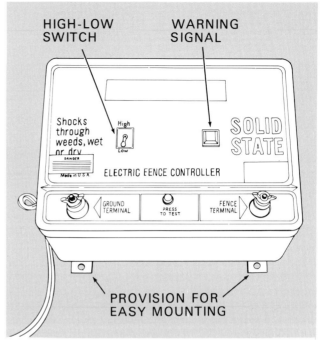

FIGURE 71. Desirable features of a controller.

# NOTES

# VII.
# Determining What Types of Passageways to Use

Many people who build good fences do not finish the job with well-built, convenient passageways. Very little research information is available on this subject, so most of the information presented here is the result of farmer experience.

In reaching your decisions as to the passageways you will need, you can select from five different types. They are discussed under the following headings:

A. What Types of Passageways to Use for Machinery and Livestock.

B. What Types of Passageways to Use for Equipment Only.

C. What Types of Passageways to Use for Livestock Only.

D. What Types of Passageways to Use for Persons Only.

E. What Types of Passageways to Use for Water Only.

## A. What Types of Passageways to Use for Machinery and Livestock

Farm gates are most used where farm machinery and livestock use the same passageway. However, some cattle guards can be used in the manner as will be discussed later. Figure 72 shows several common types of gates.

From your study of this section, you will be able to **select the proper type of passageway for your fences.**

Factors are given under the following headings:

1. Widths of Gates.

2. Durability and Cost of Gates.

3. Ease of Handling.

### 1. WIDTHS OF GATES

In determining the width of the gate, it is impossible to consider what farm machine will be passing through it. Normally a 3.1- or 3.7-m (10- or 12-ft) gate is wide enough for livestock.

Four and .3-m and 4.9-m (14 and 16 ft) gates are becoming much more popular as farmers increase their use of combine harvesters, hay balers, cotton pickers and other large farm machines that require a wide gateway. Most farm machines will pass through a 3.7-m (12-ft) opening. However, a few machines are being built that require a 4.3-m (14-ft) width and the probabilities are that more will be built in the future. A 4.9-m (16-ft) gate is needed if a turn must be made while moving large machinery through a gate such as when passing from a field into a lane.

Most gates are 1.3 to 1.4 m (52 to 54 in) high.

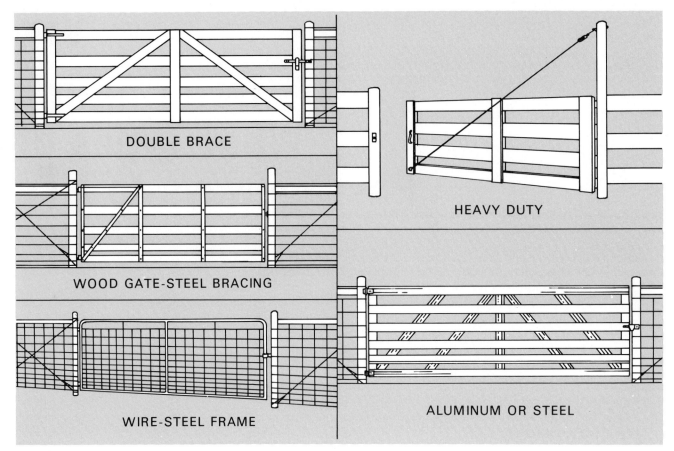

**FIGURE 72. Common types of gates.**

## 2. DURABILITY AND COST OF GATES

Studies conducted in Indiana[20] in 1949 indicate that ". . . wood-braced and wood-panel gates were estimated to have an average total life of 14 years, wood gates with steel frames 22 years, and all-steel gates 25 years. The average use cost per gate (per year) was 51 cents for wood braced, 53 cents for wood panel, $1.45 for wood, steel-frame and $1.48 for all-steel gates." Since this study was made, costs have increased greatly.

The life of wood gates can be greatly increased by treating the wood members with a preservative.

Aluminum gates have been popular with farmers. From the standpoint of weathering, they should last indefinitely since aluminum doesn't rust. However, when exposed to livestock pressure and damage from farm machinery, their durability is not as good as that of wood and steel gates.

Aluminum gates cost about 50 to 100 percent more than steel gates.

## 3. EASE OF HANDLING

Ease of handling depends on whether or not your gate is mounted so that it supports its own weight. If it is to be self supporting, it must be **well built** to avoid sagging and warping, and **mounted on a post anchor-and-brace assembly** built to carry the load over a period of years.

Most farmers do not take time to mount a gate so that it will swing. Too often it is held in place with wire. If a gate is to be used only a few times a year, it may not be worth the time and expense to mount it so that it will swing. In that case, a low-cost gate can be used and mounted as shown in Figure 73. This helps to hold the gate up straight so that it will not warp out of position. It also helps hold a wood gate off of the ground and delays rotting.

If you are planning to mount your gate so that it will swing, it is very important to use one that will not sag or warp easily. This problem is greatest with homebuilt, wood gates.

**FIGURE 73. An inexpensive way of mounting gates that are not used much.**

Lighter weight gates will also help prevent sagging due to post movement. Table X gives the approximate weight of different kinds of gates.

Practically every state college has plans for building wood gates that are well braced. If you are planning to build your own gates, get their plans.

All-steel gates will hold their shape over a period of years better than wood gates, unless you use a special method of bracing as shown in Figure 74.

### TABLE X. APPROXIMATE WEIGHTS OF DIFFERENT KINDS OF GATES
[Height 1.32 to 1.37 m (52 to 54 in)]

| | | Kind of Material | | | | |
|---|---|---|---|---|---|---|
| | | All Wood | | Wood With Steel | | |
| | | Board Size | | Bracing | Fence Filler | Aluminum |
| Length | | 4.4x15.2 cm (1¾x6 in) | 1.9x15.2 cm (¾x6 in) | 1.9x15.2 cm (¾x6 in) | | |
| m | (ft) | | | | | |
| 3.1 | (10) | 68 - 80 kg (150 - 175 lb) | 27 - 36 kg (60 - 80 lb) | 32 - 36 kg (70 - 80 lb) | 34 - 36 kg (75 - 80 lb) | 18 - 21 kg (39 - 46 lb) |
| 3.7 | (12) | 80 - 91 kg (175 - 200 lb) | 32 - 41 kg (70 - 90 lb) | 39 - 43 kg (85 - 95 lb) | 30 - 43 kg (65 - 95 lb) | 19 - 22 kg (42 - 49 lb) |
| 4.3 | (14) | 91 - 102 kg (200 - 225 lb) | 36 - 45 kg (80 - 100 lb) | 45 - 52 kg (100 - 115 lb) | 32 - 48 kg (70 - 105 lb) | 24 - 27 kg (52 - 59 lb) |
| 4.9 | (16) | 102 - 114 kg (225 - 250 lb) | 41 - 50 kg (90 - 100 lb) | 50 - 57 kg (110 - 125 lb) | 45 - 52 kg (100 - 115 lb) | 27 - 31 kg (60 - 68 lb) |

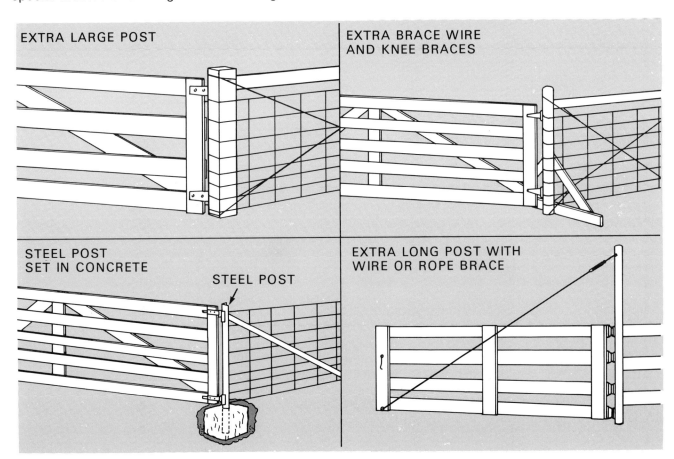

EXTRA LARGE POST

EXTRA BRACE WIRE AND KNEE BRACES

STEEL POST SET IN CONCRETE

STEEL POST

EXTRA LONG POST WITH WIRE OR ROPE BRACE

**FIGURE 74. Special bracing for free-swinging gates.**

When a gate is built in an electric fence, the electric wires may be placed above the gate or in the ground under the fence. If the wires are placed over the gate, they should be 3.1 m (10 ft) or more above the ground so that trucks and machines can pass through. Such an arrangement can be unsightly.

The best way to cross a gate is to place an insulated electric wire cable in a 1.3 cm (½-inch) polyvinyl chloride pipe placed in the ground under the gate (Figure 75). In this way, the gate is not electrified.

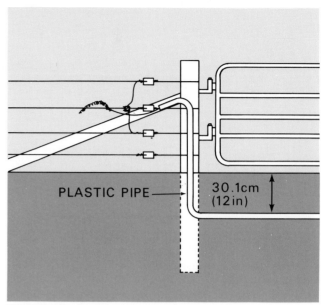

PLASTIC PIPE — 30.1cm (12 in)

**FIGURE 75. Plastic pipe conduit for electric fence.**

# B. What Types of Passageways to Use for Equipment Only

If you have occasion to drive a truck or tractor through a passageway several times a day, a cattle guard may be the answer. It can save you lots of time by your not having to open gates. Although it is called a "cattle guard," it can be used to turn most kinds of livestock. A cattle guard is **not** recommended for horses because they can injure a leg.

A permanent-type cattle guard is shown in Figure 76. It can be made of either heavy preservative-treated planks set on edge or of 3.8- to 6.4-cm (1½- to 2½-in) pipe. With either, the spacing between members is about 7.6 cm (3 in). If spaced much farther apart, there is severe jolting of the equipment as it is driven across the cattle guard. This is hard on both the equipment and the cattle guard.

A well-built cattle guard consists of a pit about 61 cm (2 ft) deep, 1.8 to 2.4 m (6 to 8 ft) wide and 3.1 to 4.9 m (10 to 16 ft) long. Concrete or heavy planking is used to supply a rigid support for the pipe or plank grating.

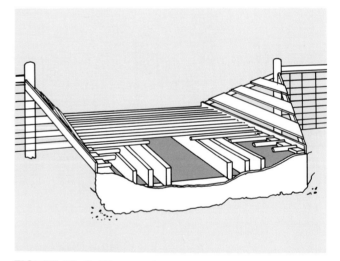

**FIGURE 76. Cattle guard.**

If a cattle guard is used to turn sheep or goats, you have to avoid any smooth strips on top of the guard. They will walk across a strip as narrow as 5.1 cm (2 in).

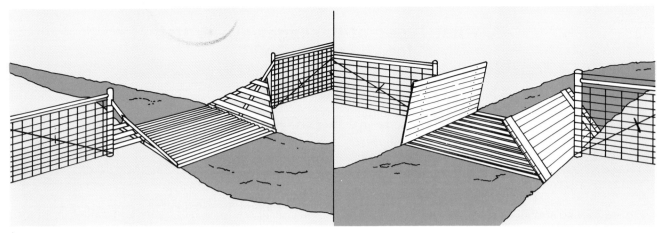

**FIGURE 77. Cattle guards with shields.**

If you don't want to build a cattle guard the full width of your passageway, you can put panels on each side as shown in Figure 77. This method works well unless you have equipment with extra-wide wheel spacing. It provides ample room for wide wagon and truck beds to pass.

If you wish to use the cattle guard for passage of livestock, you can equip it with end panels of heavy, treated planks (Figure 77). The end panels can be let down over the guard while livestock are driven through. This arrangement is not nearly as convenient as a gate for this purpose. Some farmers mount a gate next to the cattle guard as a matter of convenience.

Some farmers use temporary cattle guards (Figure 78). These can be mounted in a gate opening and towed to another location when desired. This type of guard is mounted above the ground level so it is somewhat less convenient to cross than the permanent type, and is somewhat harder on farm machinery that passes over it.

Permanent guards will cost 2 or 3 times more than temporary guards. But the permanent type is more ruggedly constructed and will last much longer.

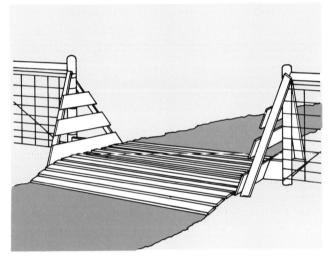

**FIGURE 78. A temporary type of cattle guard.**

You can get plans for building permanent cattle guards from most state agricultural colleges.

You may prefer to purchase a ready-made cattle guard; both types are available commercially.

## C. What Types of Passageways to Use for Livestock Only

Passageways for livestock only are usually temporary. Figure 79 shows an arrangement that will permit cattle and horses to pass but will retain hogs. Cattle and horses can step over the panels, but hogs fall between them and have no choice but to move to one end or the other.

Figure 79 also shows a creep used as a barrier for cattle, horses and mules that will let hogs pass readily. Gates that are not rigidly mounted are often raised at one end to provide sufficient room for a creep. Some rigidly mounted, commercially built gates are designed for use in a similar manner.

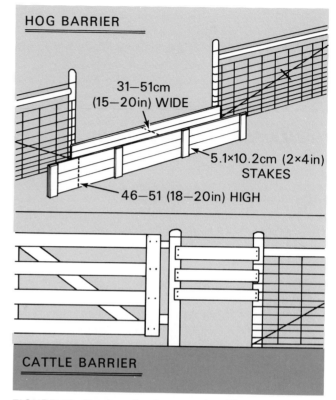

FIGURE 79. Barriers for hogs and cattle.

## D. What Passageways To Use for Persons Only

Figure 80 shows types of stiles and walk-through passageways that are in common use. Stiles provide passage for people but stop all kinds and sizes of livestock. Walk-through passageways limit

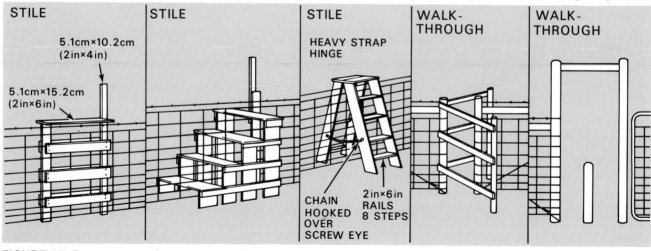

FIGURE 80. Passageways for persons only.

the turning of large animals. Except for keeping that point in mind, the type you select is largely a matter of personal preference.

A 1.2 m (4 ft) wide swinging wood or metal gate similar to the large gates in Figure 72 is often desirable in a fence for use by people and small equipment.

Durability of any of these designs will depend upon how well they are assembled and anchored and whether or not you use lumber treated with a preservative.

Walk-throughs have this disadvantage: frequently a straight line of fence must be cut to provide for a walk-through unless it is placed at the end of a line of fence. This means that standard anchor-and-brace assemblies must be installed on each side, or the posts must be extra long and fastened at the top to take the pull of the fence. This latter arrangement is also desirable for transferring the strain of a gate mounting to the end.

## E. What Types of Passageways to Use for Water Only

A structure across a stream, or a draw, that will permit water and debris to pass and still fence livestock is called a floodgate. There have been many designs of floodgates, but it is very difficult to build one that is successful under all conditions.

If you build a floodgate that has no provision for letting driftwood and rubbish get by, it will gradually clog until it starts backing water on the upstream side. During a wet period, there is often enough water backed up to finally break the floodgate.

The kind you select can be based on whether or not your fence crosses the stream (Figure 81), or ends on each side of the stream (Figure 82). You

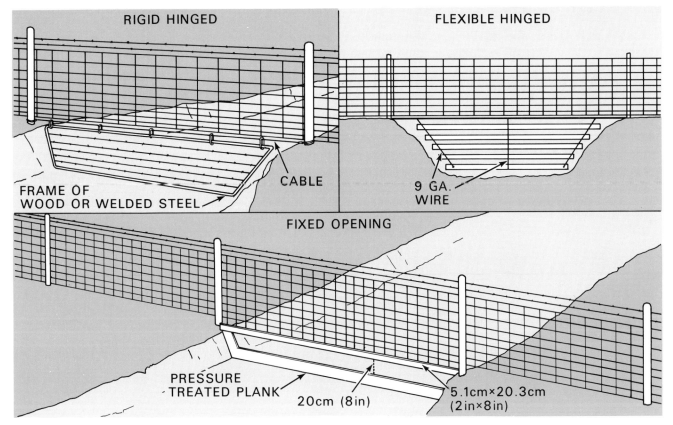

FIGURE 81. Stream passageway where fence wire crosses the stream.

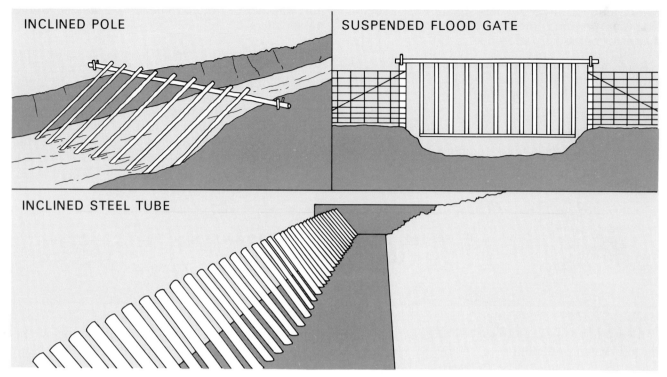

INCLINED POLE

SUSPENDED FLOOD GATE

INCLINED STEEL TUBE

**FIGURE 82. Stream passageway where fence ends on each side of the stream.**

will want to consider the experience in your area with different types of floodgates. It is highly important that all wood members be treated with a preservative if you expect them to last.

Several floodgates have been developed that are intended to be self cleaning. Those that are hinged are supposed to swing open enough when water pressure builds up, to let the floodgate clear itself of debris. Sometimes the cleaning action is not complete, and the floodgate is left partly open so that livestock can get through.

# VIII.

# Determining the Cost of Fencing Materials

When planning a fence, one of the first questions is how much will it cost. So far you have already studied fence materials and labor. In this unit, *only* the material cost will be determined since labor cost may vary greatly, because labor may be furnished by owner and family, by hired labor, or by a contractor.

Determining the cost of materials for a given fence is not difficult; however, you must follow the proper procedure. To help you understand this procedure, **an example is worked out here** and the steps are given. The procedure and forms used here make the cost calculations easy.

The procedure is given under the following headings:

A. What Kind of Fence to Build.

B. Preparing the Bill of Materials.

C. Calculating Fence Material Cost.

## A. What Kind of Fence to Build

From this section, you will be able to describe the type of fence to use for a specific need and to list the specifications for that particular fence. Procedures are given under the following headings:

1. Determining the Type of Fence Needed.

2. Determining the Specifications for Materials.

### 1. DETERMINING THE TYPE OF FENCE NEEDED

For this example, assume you want an **excellent** non-electric, permanent-type fence where **cattle,** **hogs, sheep,** and **horses** are confined. You need **two wide gates** for the passage of animals and machinery, **two small gates** for people, and **animal access to a stream.** Wood posts are used in this example. Proceed as follows:

1. *Using Table I, look under "Combination" of livestock heading, and you will find ten possible excellent fences.*

   Since two of these fences are electric (which you do not want), only eight designs will be considered for this problem.

2. *Now use the "Comparative Cost Index" column in Table I to find the relative cost for each of the fence designs.*

   Reading from top to bottom in table, you will find the comparative cost index figures to be: 23, 25, 31, 30, 38, 45, 37 and 39.

71

3. *Since the comparative cost index figure of 23 is lowest (most economical), you will find that fence's name and specifications in the first column. It is a heavyweight woven wire fence, 1 m (39 in) high with 15.2 cm (6 in) stay spacings, and with two strands of barbed wire.*

## 2. DETERMINING THE SPECIFICATIONS FOR MATERIALS

Proceed as follows:

1. *Find the design number of the fence.*

   The design number of the fence is 939-6-11-2B (Figure 19).

2. *Determine the post sizes.*

   Referring to Sections V and VI of this publication, you will find the recommendations for wood post sizes as follows:

   —**Corner posts:** 15.2 cm x 2.4 m (6 in x 8 ft).

   —**First corner brace post:** 12.7 cm x 2.4 m (5 in x 8 ft).

   —**Second corner brace post:** 10.2 cm x 2.4 m (4 in x 8 ft).

   —**End Post:** 12.7 cm x 2.4 m (5 in x 8 ft).

   —**All end brace posts:** 10.2 cm x 2.4 m (4 in x 8 ft).

   —**All horizontal compression members:** 10.2 cm x 2.4 m (4 in x 8 ft).

   —**Line-brace assembly center post:** 12.7 cm x 2.4 m (5 in x 8 ft).

   —**All line-braces assembly brace posts:** 10.2 cm x 2.4 m (4 in x 8 ft).

   —**Line post:** 7.6 to 10.2 cm x 2 m (3 in to 4 in x 6 ft 6 in).

   —**Gate post:** 12.7 to 15.2 cm x 2.4 to 3.1 m (5 to 6 in x 8 to 10 ft).

   —**Post between two gates:** 15.2 cm x 2.4 (6 in x 8 ft).

3. *Find spacing needed for line posts (V, 2).*

   Spacing of line post is 4.9 (16 ft) under normal conditions.

4. *Determine size and kind of tension wire (IV, A, 6).*

   The size and kind of tension wire is found to be No. 9 smooth medium hard galvanized steel wire.

5. *Determine specifications for barbed wire (III, A, 5).*

   Specifications for each of the strands of barbed wire is 12½ gage galvanized steel with 4 point barbs spaced 10.2 to 12.7 cm (4 to 5 in) apart.

6. *Determine specifications for gates.*

   Each of the large gates will be 4.9m (16 ft) wide, 1.2 to 1.3 m (48 to 52 in) high with 6 panels, and 4 or more braces. It will be made from galvanized steel. Each small gate will have the same specifications as the large one except it will be 1.2 m (4 ft) wide (Figure 72).

7. *Determine types of staples to use (III, C, 1, b).*

   Since treated softwood posts are used, 3.8 cm (1½ in) L-shaped staples should be used.

8. *Determine types and sizes of dowels to use (Figure 44).*

   The round steel dowels will be 1.3 to 10.2 cm (½ to 4 in).

9. *Determine type and size lightning rod to use (Figure 61).*

   Each lightning ground rod for fence should consist of one 1.3 cm x 3 m (½ in x 10 ft) galvanized steel pipe, 3 straps and 6d common nails.

10. *Determine type of water passageways to use (Figure 81).*

    Choose an appropriate design from Figure 81.

# B. Preparing the Bill of Materials

From this section, you will be able to prepare a bill of materials for a specific fence. The procedure is given under the following headings:

1. Preparing a Map of Area to be Fenced.

2. Determining the Location of Anchor-Post Assemblies Needed.

3. Determing Number and Size of Brace Posts Needed at Each Assembly.

4. Determining the Number of Posts and Compression Members by Sizes.

5. Determining Amount of Wire Needed.

6. Determining Amount of Staples, Dowels and Grounding Rods Needed.

7. Estimating Costs for Passageways.

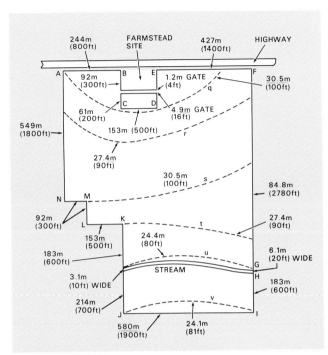

FIGURE 83. Sketch of area to be fenced showing corners, gates, stream and distance.

## 1. PREPARING A MAP OF AREA TO BE FENCED

Proceed as follows:

1. Go to area to be fenced and determine the location of fence lines, corners and passageways (gates, streams, etc.).

2. Drive a small stake at each corner and on each side of the gates and stream.

3. Measure distance between corners as well as between corners and passageways.

   Record measurements for later use.

4. Sketch an outline of the fence line on paper (Figure 83).

5. Designate all major points (corners, ends, passageways, etc.) on the fence line with capital letters—such as A, B, C, etc.

6. Place the measured distances between consecutive points on the plan.

   On the example, the distance from E to F is 427 m (1400 ft) and the stream is 6.1 m (20 ft) wide at G-H.

7. Locate the high and low contours of the land's different elevations on the map with dotted lines.

   Estimate these differences in elevation with figures such as 30.5, 27.4, 30.5, 27.4, 24.4, 24.7 m (100, 90, 100, 90, 80, 81 ft) etc. High numbers mean high land contours with lower case letters q, r, s, t, u and v. Record numbers and letters on map.

8. Draw in the location and size of streams, ditches, etc. where the fence must cross.

## 2. DETERMINING THE LOCATION OF ANCHOR-POST ASSEMBLIES NEEDED

Proceed as follows:

1. *Locate an anchor-post assembly at each corner of the fence line (Figure 84).*

   In our example, these are at points A, B, C, D, E, F, I, J, K, L, M, and N.

2. *Locate an end anchor-post assembly at every place where the fence line ends (stops).*

   These are at W, X, Y, Z, G and H.

3. *Locate a line-braced anchor-post assembly on each high and each low elevation of land on the fence line between corner and end-post assemblies.*

These are on one end of contour lines q, s, t, and u and on both ends of line n.

4. *Locate one or more additional line-braced anchor post assemblies between each of the consecutive anchor-post assemblies (corner, end, or line-braced) if the distance is more than 201 m (40 rd) (660 ft) or where you feel additional fence strength may be needed.*

5. *Now label all line-braced anchor-post assemblies as LB-1 (between A and B), LB-2, etc. in a clockwise manner around the fence line (Figure 84).*

   In this example, 14 line-braced anchor-post assemblies are needed. LB-1 and LB-14 are near corner A.

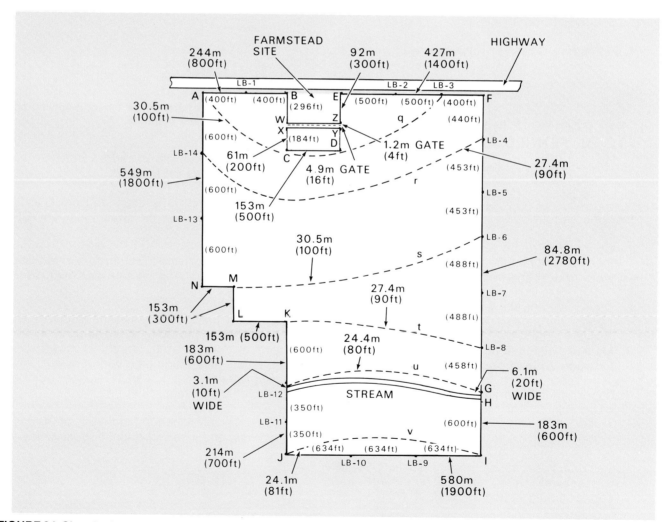

**FIGURE 84.** Sketch of area to be fenced showing corners, gates, stream and location of anchor-post assemblies.

74

# 3. DETERMINING NUMBER AND SIZE OF BRACE POSTS NEEDED AT EACH POST ASSEMBLY

Some anchor-post assemblies will have more pull on them than others; therefore, these must have more built-in strength (figure 44). Proceed as follows:

1. *Calculate the distance between consecutive anchor posts of the assemblies on your map (Figure 84).*

2. *Record each measurement in parentheses on the map.*

3. *Determine the number of brace posts needed at each post assembly.*

If the distance between any two consecutive anchor posts is less than 50 m (10 rd), place one brace post at each corner and end assembly along a straight line between the two anchor posts. Each brace post will be 2.4 m (8 ft) from an anchor post. (Figure 85).

If the distance between any two anchor posts is from 50 m to 201 m (10 rd to 40 rd), place a second brace post at each **corner** and **end** assembly but not at the line-braced assemblies. The brace posts will also be placed 2.4 m (8 ft) from the first brace post of the assembly.

For corner post assemblies the corner post should be 15.2 cm (6 in) in diameter; the first brace post, 12.7 cm (5 in); and the second brace post, 10.2 cm (4 in). All other brace posts should be 10.2 cm (4 in) in diameter and 2.4 m (8 ft) long.

Only one brace post is placed on each side of the anchor post in a line-braced assembly.

4. *Indicate each brace post on your map with dots (Figure 85).*

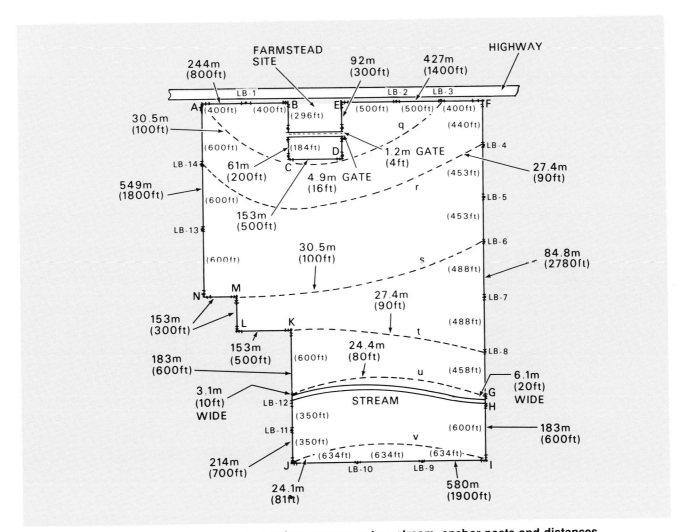

FIGURE 85. Sketch of area to be fenced showing corners, gates, stream, anchor posts and distances.

## 4. DETERMINING THE NUMBER OF POST AND COMPRESSION MEMBERS BY SIZES

Proceed as follows:

1. *Prepare a form on which to record the posts needed (Table XI).*

2. *Beginning with corner A on Figure 84, count the number of posts by sizes in each assembly along fence line AB.*

   *Record in Table XI under appropriate headings.*

   *Refer to Section VIII, A, 2, step 2 to identify various post sizes.*

**NOTE: Do not include those brace posts in these assemblies that are in fence lines AN and BC.**

3. *Count the number of horizontal compression members in the assemblies along fence line AB and record in appropriate column of this table.*

4. *Count and record the number of assembly posts and compression members by sizes for each of the other fence line intervals in entire area to be fenced.*

**NOTE: Do not count the corner and line-brace assembly anchor post twice because line wires from two separate intervals are tied to the same post.**

5. *Find the number of line posts needed.*

   *The number of line posts can be determined by (a) the short-line-post-interval method for an exact number of posts or (b) the total-fence-length method for a close estimation of the number needed. To find the total number of line posts needed by the* **Total-Fence-Length Method** *(b), use the following procedure.*

   (1) *Determine the total length of fence line by adding the length of all sides of fenced area (Figure 82).*

   *In this example, the length is 4,026 m (13, 200 ft or 800 rd).*

   (2) *Subtract from the fence's total length those short fence spaces where no line posts are used—such as under the compression members and gates and over wide streams.*

In our example (Figure 84), space under compression members is 215 m (704 ft) (88 members x 2.4 m (8 ft) each); under the large gates, it is 9.8 m (32 ft) (2 gates x 4.9 m (16 ft) each); over the stream, it is 6.1 m (20 ft).

**(NOTE:** When crossing a stream or ditch less than 14.9 m (16 ft) wide, the fence line is usually not broken.) Therefore, the fence line not occupied by line posts in this example is 3,762 m (4,026 m less 264 m) or (12,336 ft) (13,200 ft. less 864 ft).

   (3) *Divide the length of fence needing line posts 3,762 m (12,336 ft) by post spacing 4.8 m (16 ft) to find the total number of line posts needed.*

   *That number is 771 and is nine more for this example than the total number needed if calculated by the short-internal, line-post method.*

   (4) *Record this number on the TOTALS line and under the Line Posts column in Table XI.*

6. *Total each column in Table XI.*

## 5. DETERMINING AMOUNT OF WIRE NEEDED

Proceed as follows:

1. *Determine the amount of smooth wire needed.*

   *Count the number of tension brace wire units in each fence line interval. Each line-brace post assembly has two tension wire units per compression member (Figure 58). Each corner and end assembly has one unit per compression member (Figure 53). The first section of an end anchor assembly where a large gate is hinged requires two tension wire units (Figure 63).*

2. *Record in last column of Table XI by fence intervals. Add this column. There are 120 units for this illustrated example.*

3. *Find the number of 45.4-kg (100-lb) rolls of No. 9 smooth wire to get.*

76

## TABLE XI

## DATA COMPILING FORM

| Fence Line Intervals | Corner and End Anchor Post Assemblies*** | | | Line-Braced Post Assemblies | | Compression Members | Line Posts* | No. of Assembly Tension Wire Units** |
| | 15.2 cm x 2.4 m (6 in x 8 ft) | 12.2 cm x 2.4 m (5 in x 8 ft) | 10.2 cm x 2.4 m (4 in x 8 ft) | 12.7 cm x 2.4 m (5 in x 8 ft) | 10.2 cm x 2.4 m (4 in x 8 ft) | 10.2 cm x 2.4 m (4 in x 6.5 ft) | 7.6 to 10.2 cm x 2 m (4 in x 8 ft) | |
|---|---|---|---|---|---|---|---|---|
| A-B | 2 | 2 | 2 | 1 | 2 | 6 | 23+23 | 6 |
| B-C | 3 | 4 | 4 | | | 8 | 25 | 20 |
| C-D | 1 | 2 | 2 | | | 4 | 29 | 4 |
| D-E | 3 | 4 | 4 | | | 8 | 25 | 20 |
| E-F | 1 | 2 | 2 | 2 | 4 | 8 | 29+30+23 | 8 |
| F-G | | 1 | 2 | 5 | 10 | 13 | 27+27+27+ 30+30+28 | 18 |
| G-H | 2 | 0 | 1 | | | 2 | 0 | 0 |
| H-I | 1 | 1 | 1 | | | 3 | 35 | 8 |
| I-J | 1 | 3 | 3 | 2 | 4 | 8 | 38+38+38 | 8 |
| J-K | 1 | 3 | 3 | 2 | 4 | 8 | 20+20+30 | 8 |
| K-L | 1 | 2 | 2 | | | 4 | 29 | 4 |
| L-M | 1 | 2 | 2 | | | 4 | 16 | 4 |
| M-N | 1 | 2 | 2 | | | 4 | 16 | 4 |
| N-A | | 2 | 2 | 2 | 4 | 8 | 35+36+35 | 8 |
| TOTALS | 18 | 30 | 32 | 14 | 28 | 88 | 762 | 120 |

*Use this column for exact count by the fence line interval method. When a close estimation is adequate (Operation, Step 5), record only in the TOTALS line under line posts.
**See Figure 49—cross tension wire unit.
***Gate posts at W, X, Y, and Z are 15.2 cm × 2.4 m (8 in × 8 ft)

(1) *Measure or calculate the length of smooth wire needed to go from the bottom of one brace post to the top of the next one.*

This length is about 3.1 m (10 ft).

(2) *Calculate the amount of smooth wire needed per single tension wire unit.*

Since 4 strands of smooth wire are used per unit, 12.2 m (40 ft) [4 strands x 3.1 m (10 ft) each] of wire will be needed per brace wire unit (Figure 44).

The total length of wire needed for the fence will be 1464 m (4800 ft) or 12.2 m (40 ft) per unit times 120 units. Since 5.2 m (17 ft) of wire weighs about .45 kg (1 lb), 128.5 kg (283 lb), 1464 m ÷ 5.2 m/kg (4800 ft ÷ 17 ft/lb) of wire will be needed. This amounts to three 45-kg (100-lb) rolls.

4. *Find the number of 100-m (20-rd) rolls of woven wire needed.*

Divide the total length of fence, 4,024 m (800 rods) by 100 m (20 rd) per roll.

$$\frac{4,024}{100} = \textbf{40 rolls}$$

$$\frac{800}{20} = \textbf{40 rolls}$$

5. *Find the number of 402-m (80 rd) rolls of barbed wire needed.*

Divide the total length of fence, 4,024 m (800 rd) by 406 m (80 rd) per roll.

$$\frac{4,024}{406} = \textbf{10 rolls.}$$

$$\frac{800}{80} = \textbf{10 rolls.}$$

Since two strands of barbed wire are to be used, multiply the 10 rolls by 2.
10 x 2 = **20 rolls.**

## 6. DETERMINING AMOUNT OF STAPLES, DOWELS, AND GROUNDING RODS NEEDED

1. *Determine number of staples needed.*

   Usually .68 kg (1½ lb) of wire staples will be needed for each 100-m (20-rod) roll of woven wire and .68 kg (1½ lb) for each 402-m (80-rod) roll of barbed wire.

   In this example, 41 kg (90 lb) of staples should be adequate.

2. *Determine number of dowels needed.*

   Figure two round steel dowels 1.27 x 10.2 cm (½ x ¼ in) for each compression member.

   Since there are 88 compression members, 176 dowels will be needed.

3. *Find the number of lightning grounding rods needed.*

   Applying the principle for grounding wire fences (Figure 61), 52 lightning ground rods will be needed.

   You must remember that good electrical connections are not generally made between wires on two opposite sides of anchor posts. This is because all wires are cut and tied separately around these posts and not around opposite wires. Consider no electrical con-nections are made between wires on anchor posts.

## 7. ESTIMATING COSTS FOR PASSAGEWAYS

Many designs for gate, cattle and water passage-ways are available (Unit VII). You may even want to plan and build your own. Since so many of these passageways can be purchased as a complete unit, costs are estimated here rather than including a complete bill of materials for each item.

1. *Estimate the cost of gates.*

   At this writing, assume the costs for 4.9 m (16-ft) wooden gates (Figure 72) to vary from $30 to $50, depending upon design. A 1.2-m (4-ft) gate will cost from $12 to $20.

   For an assembled 4.9-m (16-ft) galvanized steel gate (Figure 72), figure the cost to be about $50, while that of a 1.2-m (4-ft) gate is about $16.

2. *Estimate the cost of passageways.*

   The fixed-opening water passageway at LB-12 (Figure 83) only requires a small amount of materials, estimated at $15. The other designs shown in Figure 81 cost more.

   To cross the wide stream at G-H, a suspended floodgate may be used (Figure 81). An estimation for this passageway is $50.

# C. Calculating Fence Material Cost

Proceed as follows:

## 1. DETERMINING THE TOTAL COST FOR FENCE MATERIALS

To determine the total cost for the farm or ranch fence, you must figure the different materials separately and then combine them. To do this, proceed as follows:

1. *Prepare a form such as Table XII for recording and summarizing the data.*

2. *List the quantity of materials in the first column and the name and size of them in the next column.*

3. *Secure the cost of materials locally. Record in Unit Cost column.*

## TABLE XII. SUMMARY OF FENCE MATERIALS COST

| Quantity | Materials and Size | Unit Cost[1] | Item Cost |
|---|---|---|---|
| 18 | 15.2 cm x 2.4 m (6 in x 8 ft) corner posts[2] | $ 6.00 | $ 108.00 |
| 44 | 12.7 cm x 2.4 m (5 in x 8 ft) end and brace posts[2] | 4.75 | 209.00 |
| 88 | 10.2 cm x 2.4 m (4 in x 8 ft) compression members[2] | 2.95 | 259.60 |
| 60 | 10.2 cm x 2.4 m (4 in x 8 ft) assembly brace posts[2] | 2.95 | 177.00 |
| 771 | 7.6 to 10.2 cm x 2 m (3 to 4 m x 6.5 ft) line posts[2] | 1.85 | 1426.35 |
| | (Less 10% on posts for volume purchases) | | (– 142.64) |
| 40 rolls | Woven wire | 45.50 | 1820.00 |
| 20 rolls | Barbed wire | 30.00 | 600.00 |
| 3 rolls | #9 smooth wire | 40.00 | 120.00 |
| 2 | 4.9-m (16-ft) steel gates | 50.00 | 100.00 |
| 2 | 1.2-m (4-ft) steel gates | 16.00 | 32.00 |
| 176 | Steel dowels | 0.20 | 35.20 |
| 90 lb. | Wire staples | 0.65 | 58.50 |
| 52 | Grounding rod units | 3.00 | 156.00 |
| 1 | Passageway at G-H | Est. | 50.00 |
| 1 | Passageway at LB-12 | Est. | 15.00 |
| | TOTAL COST | | $5024.01 |

Total length of fence: 4,026 m (13,200 ft or 800 rods or 2.5 miles). Cost of fencing materials: $0.38 per foot; $2009.60 per mile. Area in the fenced area: 72.5 hectare (179 acres). Fencing cost $69.29/hectare $28.06/acre)

[1]Local cost at time of publication.
[2]Treated pine posts.

4. *Find the total cost for each item by multiplying quantity of materials needed by unit cost. Record in Item Cost column.*

5. *Add all Item Cost figures for a TOTAL COST of all fencing materials.*

## 2. DETERMINING SUPPLEMENTAL FENCE COST FACTS

Sometimes you may want other figures about your fencing problem. Some of these are listed at the bottom of Table XII.

# NOTES

# References

1. *Pasture and Range Fences,* McNamee, Michael A. and Kinee, Edwin, Rocky Mountain Regional Publication No. 2; November 1965.

2. *Twenty-Year Atmospheric Corrosion Investigation of Zinc-Coated and Uncoated Wire and Wire Products,* Dale, Alvin C.; Agricultural Engineering Dept., Purdue University, ASAE Paper No. 63-409.

3. *Constructing an Effective Anticoyte Electric Fence,* USDA, Leaflet No. 565, 1978.

4. *New Developments in Wire Coatings;* Rigo, Jane H., U. S. Steel Corporation, ASAE Paper No. 63-410.

5. *Selection of Lumber for Farm and Home Building;* Sweet, C. V. and Johnson, P. A., USDA Farmer's Bulletin No. 1756.

6. *Forest Products Laboratory Natural Finish,* Bul. No. FPL-046, USDA, Forest Products Lab., Madison, Wis., 1964.

7. *Decay Protection for Exterior Woodwork;* Ferrall, A. F., Pathologist, USDA, Southern Forestry Experiment Station, New Orleans, Louisiana.

8. *Better Utilization of Wood Through Assembly With Improved Fasteners,* Stern, E. George, Va. Poly. Inst. and State Univ., Blacksburg, Virginia, Bul. No. 38.

9. *Effectiveness of the L-Shaped Fence Staple,* Stern, E. George; Va. Eng. Exp. Station; Bul. No. 17.

10. *Plain Shank vs. Fluted vs. Threaded Nails;* Stern, E. George, Va. Poly. Inst. and State Univ., Wood Research Laboratory, Bul. 27; Blacksburg, Virginia, 1956.

11. *Farm Fence End and Corner Design,* Giese, Henry and Henderson, S. M., Iowa State University, Research Bul. 364.

12. *An Investigation of the Factors Affecting the Design of Fence End and Corner Assemblies,* Throop, James W. and Boyd, James S., Michigan State University, East Lansing, Michigan, ASAE Paper No. 63-412; 1963.

13. *New Techniques for Efficient Fencing;* Bigalow, Ivan W., U. S. Steel Corporation, Pittsburgh, Pennsylvania.

14. *Concrete Fence Posts,* Davidson, J. B., Iowa State University, Ames, Iowa.

15. *Building Better Farm Fences,* Neetzel, J. R.; Ext. Bul. 272; Univ. of Minnesota.

16. Unpublished data, Tennessee Coal, Iron and Railroad Company, Birmingham, Alabama.

17. *Concrete Posts Still Good After 48 years,* Herman, J. Clayton, Iowa State Univ., Special Report.

18. *How to Treat Fence Posts by Double Diffusion,* Baechler, R. H., USDA Forest Products Laboratory, Bul. FPL-013, Madison, Wisconsin, 1963.

19. Unpublished data, Southeastern Forest Experiment Station, Asheville, N.C.

20. *Woven Wire Fencing Methods and Costs,* Burroff, E. L., Moor, E. H., Robertson, L. S. and Mayer, I. D., Purdue Agricultural Exp. Station, Bul. 570.

21. *Use Colorado Fence Posts,* State Forest Service, Dept. of Forest and Wood Science, and Colorado State University. 1970.

22. *Fences for the Farm and Rural Home,* USDA, F. B. No. 2247, 1976.

23. *Fence Posts for Farm and Home,* North Carolina Ext. Folder 320, 1974.

24. *Electric Fencing Do's and Don'ts,* Gallagher Electronics, Hamilton, New Zealand.

25. *New Fencing Concepts,* AFC Snell Fence Systems, San Antonio, Texas.

## GENERAL REFERENCES

*Specifications for Farm Fence Construction,* Designation R250.2, American Society of Agricultural Engineers, St. Joseph, Michigan.

*Effect of Temperature on Tightness of Fences,* Boyd, James S. and Wilson, Jack D., Transactions of the American Society of Agricultural Engineers, 1960.

*Relations of Heavy Chemical Treatment to Durability of Wood in Ground Contact,* Neubauer, L. W. and Sullivan, J. J., ASAE Paper No. 63-910, 1963.

*Zinc-Coated (Galvanized) Iron or Steel Farm-Field and Railroad Right-of-Way Wire Fencing,* ASTM Designation, A 116-57, American Society for Testing and Materials, 1957.

*Steel Fence Posts—Field and Line Type;* Commercial Standard 184-51, U. S. Dept. of Commerce.

*Serviceability of Farm-Treated Fence Posts,* Kring, J. S.; Bulletin 356, Univ. of Tenn., January 1963.

*Treated Fence Posts,* Clymer, C. L., Extension Service, Oklahoma A & M College, Circular 541.

*Farm Fencing,* Kite, G. D.; Ext. Ag. Eng., Va. Poly. Inst. (mimeo); Blacksburg, Virginia.

*Laboratory and Service Evaluation of Aluminized Steel Wire;* Rigo, Jane H., U. S. Steel Corporation, *Corrosion,* Vol. 17, No. 5, May 1961.

*Wood Preservative Treatments,* American Wood Preserver's Association Standards, Washington, D.C., 1977.

*Wood Preservation and Wood Products Treatments,* Baxter, H. O., Coleman, V. R., and Motsinger, R. E., Cooperative Extension Service, Univ. of Georgia, Athens.

*Cost Per Mile of Fence by Types,* Northwest Georgia Experiment Station, Calhoun, Georgia, 1978.

*Depth of Post-Fiberglass vs. Steel,* Quarterly Bul., Vol. 44, No. 4, Michigan State Agricultural Experiment Station.

*How to Build Fences with USS Max-Ten 200 High Tensile Fence Wire,* John W. Knapp, U. S. Steel Corporation, Pittsburgh, PA, 1980.

# ACKNOWLEDGMENTS

Recognition is given to the following individuals and industries for photographs, information or reviews:

1. **Allison, J. M.,** Agricultural Engineering Division, University of Georgia.

2. **Atlantic Steel Company,** Atlanta, Georgia.

3. **Bekaert Steel and Wire Corporation,** Atlanta, Georgia.

4. **Farmer, D. G.,** Area Teacher of Agriculture, Athens, Georgia.

5. **Gallagher, J. A.,** Director, Gallagher Electronics, Ltd., Frankton, Hamilton, New Zealand.

6. **Hutton, Charles,** Extension Livestock Specialist, University of Georgia.

7. **Knapp, John,** United States Steel Corporation, Pittsburgh, Pennsylvania.

8. **Keystone Steel and Wire Company,** Peoria, Illinois.

9. **The Langdale Company,** Valdosta, Georgia.

10. **McLendon, B. Derrell,** Agricultural Engineering Division, University of Georgia.

11. **Mueller, James G.,** Project Engineer, Electrical Department, Underwriters Laboratories Inc., Northbrook, Illinois 60062.

12. **Owen Kris,** Manager, Agricultural Wood Products, Koppers Co., Pittsburgh, Pennsylvania 15219.

13. **Powell, Roy E.,** Assistant State Supervisor of Agricultural Education, District III., Athens, Georgia.

14. **Prickard, Bud, and Larson, Mark,** Snell Systems, Inc., San Antonio, Texas.

15. **Wiley, Thomas E.,** United States Steel Corporation, Pittsburgh, Pennsylvania.

16. **Wayne A. Maley,** Taylor Associates, 1910 Cochran Road, Pittsburgh, PA.

# Part 2
# Building
# Fences and Gates

# Preface

Anyone who expects to build a fence or to oversee the building of a fence must be proficient in the skills described in this book. The procedural steps are illustrated and the book is developed into a self-study unit.

The general objectives of this manual are to help the reader become proficient in the following jobs:

1. Laying out and clearing fence lines.

2. Building barbed wire and woven wire fences.

3. Building electric fences.

4. Building cable fences.

5. Building welded panel fences.

6. Building board fences.

7. Building wood rail fences.

8. Building chain link fences.

9. Building gates.

Upon completion of your study of this part, you will be able to perform the following.

1. Layout and clear fence lines.

2. Install posts and braces properly.

3. Stretch wire and attach it to the posts.

4. Ground wire fences for lightening protection.

5. Attach board fencing to posts.

6. Attach rail fencing to posts.

7. Stack rail fencing without posts.

8. Build a gate.

# Introduction

Have you noticed, as you drive through the country, how different people build fences? If so, you have discovered there is no standard procedure. You also noticed that many fences are not standing up well enough though good materials were used. What you did not see was how much unnecessary work and expense went into building some fences.

This publication has been prepared to meet that situation. The information is based on research and experience gathered from all parts of the country. It is presented in step-by-step procedures so you can follow it easily. The tools and equipment required are those normally available on a farm or in a shop. The procedures are those considered best for hand construction from the standpoint of time savings, durability, and cost.

If you have not reached such decisions as: where to locate your fences, what kinds of fence to use, what material is most durable for your needs and the merits of different kinds of corners and ends for woven-wire and barbed-wire fence, you will find the information in Part 1, Planning Fences and Gates.

Building fences is discussed under the following headings:

   I. Laying Out and Clearing Fence Lines.

  II. Building Barbed-Wire and Woven-Wire Fences.

 III. Building Electric Fences.

 IV. Building Cable Fences.

  V. Building Welded Wire Panel Fences.

 VI. Building Board Fences.

VII. Building Wood Rail Fences.

VIII. Building Chain Link Fences.

 IX. Building Gates.

# IX. Laying Out & Clearing Fence Lines.

Before you can start to build a satisfactory fence, you must have a clear place to work. The next job is to lay out the line where you want the fence to be located.

For clearing and laying out fence lines, follow procedures under the headings:

A. Laying Out Fence Lines.

B. Clearing Fence Lines.

# A. Laying Out Fence Lines

If you want to have a straight, or uniformly curved fence, you will have to stake it out first.

From your study of this section, you will be able to **lay out fences** on (1) areas with heavy undergrowth, (2) open level areas, (3) rolling areas, and (4) contour.

Laying out fences is discussed under the following headings:

1. Tools and Materials Needed.

2. Laying Out Fence Lines On Areas Which Have Heavy Undergrowth.

3. Laying Out Fence Lines On Open Level Areas.

4. Laying Out Fence Lines On Open Rolling Areas.

5. Laying Out Fence Lines On Contour.

## TOOLS AND MATERIALS NEEDED

Axe(s)
Bank blade(s)
100′ Tape
5′ Stakes
Rags or Flags
12′ to 15′ Flag Pole(s)
Level
String

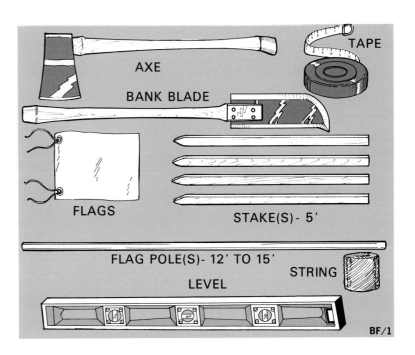

# LAYING OUT FENCE LINES ON AREAS WHICH HAVE HEAVY UNDERGROWTH

Procedures for laying out fences on areas which have heavy undergrowth are as follows:

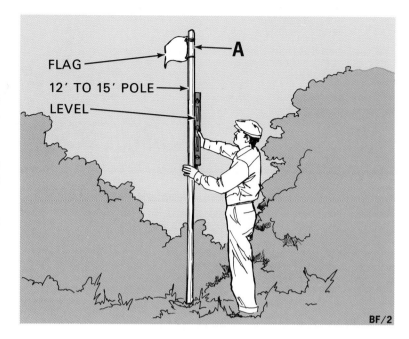

1. *Hold a twelve to fifteen-foot flag pole A at end of fence line with heaviest growth.*

   Check pole with level to make sure it is vertical.

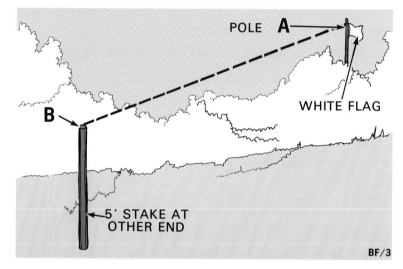

2. *Place 5' stake at other end of fence line.*

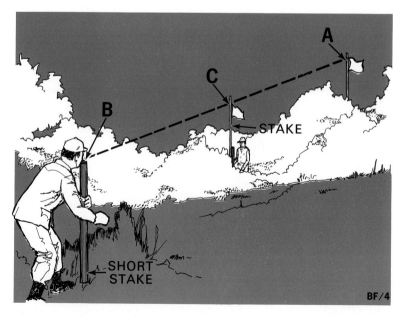

3. *While sighting from short end stake B to pole A at other end, align second stake C as far inside thicket as it can be seen.*

4. *Clear area between stakes B and C and for a distance beyond stake C.*

   See section "B. Clearing Fence Lines" for procedures.

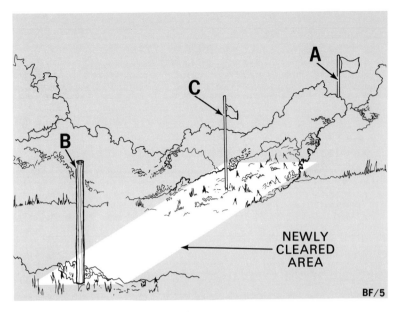

5. *Establish another stake in the same manner, and so on until line is completely established.*

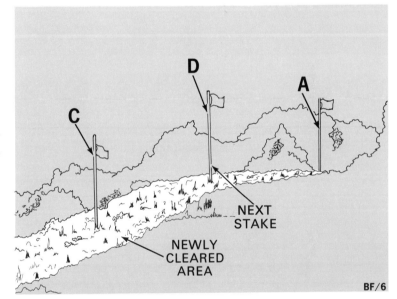

## LAYING OUT FENCE LINES ON OPEN LEVEL AREAS

To lay out fences on open level areas, proceed as follows:

1. *Set stake at each end of proposed fence line.*

   Station someone at one of the end stakes to help with alignment of remaining stakes.

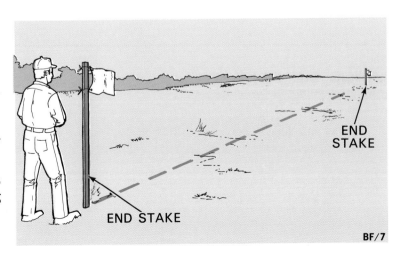

89

2. *Proceed about 100 feet towards other end, align and set stake.*

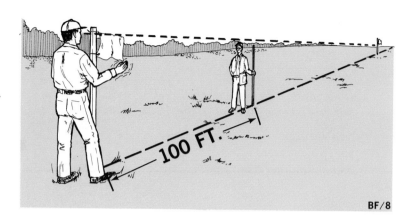

BF/8

3. *Proceed about 100 feet further and set another stake in line with all three stakes.*

This is easily done with help of person at end stake sighting through to other end stake.

Continue setting additional stakes about every 100 feet until complete fence line is staked.

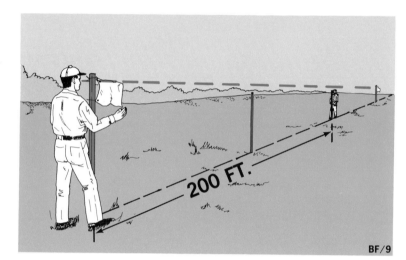

BF/9

## LAYING OUT FENCE LINES ON OPEN ROLLING AREAS

To lay out fences on open rolling areas, proceed as follows:

1. *Set stake at each end of proposed fence line, stakes A and B.*

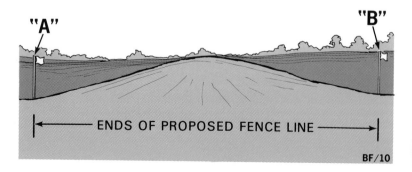

"A"

"B"

← ENDS OF PROPOSED FENCE LINE →

BF/10

2. *Place two stakes about ten feet apart on top of hill so both are visible from either end stake.*

In case of a valley, place stakes at lowest position in valley.

3. *Align two center stakes (C and D) from one of the end stakes.*

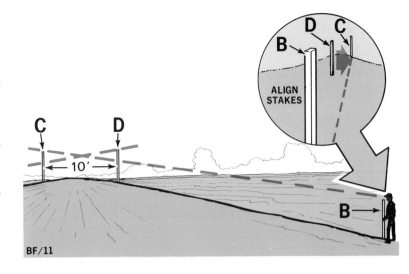

4. *Check alignment of center stakes from other end stake.*

Center stakes may have to be moved several times before satisfactory alignment can be secured from both end stakes.

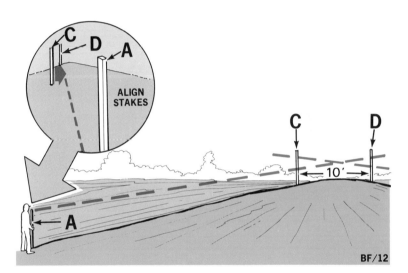

## LAYING OUT FENCE LINES ON CONTOUR

To lay out fence line on contour, proceed as follows:

1. *Stake out smooth curve along contour strip or terrace.*

Space stakes about 16 feet apart. If following terrace ridge, place stakes below ridge so terrace can be maintained.

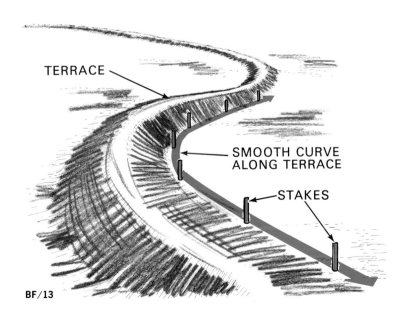

2. *If there is much curve at any one point, select three stakes at point of greatest curvature.*

3. *Stretch string between first stake (A) and third stake (C).*

4. *Measure distance from center stake (B) to string.*

5. *Decrease post spacing as shown in Table I if measurement is more than 4 inches.*

### TABLE I. POST SPACING FOR CONTOUR FENCES

| Distance from center stake to string | Recommended post spacing |
|---|---|
| inches | feet |
| 4 or less | 16 |
| 4 - 5 | 15 |
| 5 - 6 | 14 |
| 6 - 8 | 12 |
| 8 -14 | 10 |
| 14 - 20 | 8 |

6. *Set stakes to get proper spacing.*

7. *Repeat steps 3 to 6 any place there appears to be much curvature.*

8. *Check by sight to see that no single post is out of line of smooth curve.*

By keeping curve smooth, fence wire will pull equally against each post.

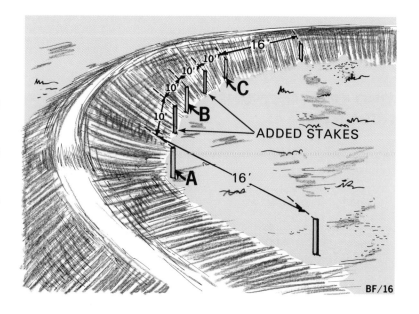

92

# B. Clearing Fence Lines

For a good job of construction and maintenance of your fence you must have a fence line free of brush, loose rocks, trees, and tall grass. This not only improves the appearance of the completed fence but saves considerable time in constructing the fence.

Do not leave trees to use in place of posts. They increase danger from lightning, the fence damages the tree and vice versa.

From your study of this section, you will be able to **give the procedures for clearing a fence line** with (1) a bulldozer and (2) a tractor and harrow.

They are discussed under the following headings:
1. Tools and Materials Needed.
2. Clearing Fence Line with Bulldozer.
3. Clearing Fence Line with Tractor and Harrow.

## TOOLS AND MATERIALS NEEDED

Leather gloves
Axe
Swing blade
Mattock
Shovel
Bank blade
Bulldozer, or tractor and harrow
Wrecking bar
Hammer

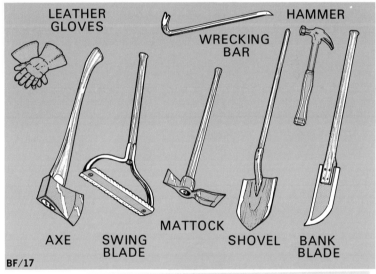

## CLEARING FENCE LINE WITH BULLDOZER

If you plan to use a bulldozer, proceed as follows:

1. *Detach fence from posts that are still in good condition.*

   Be sure to pick up nails, staples and bits of wire to keep livestock from getting them.

   Most old fence is not worth the time and effort it takes to detach it from the posts and roll it up. However, if there are any good posts, you will want to save them.

2. *Drive bulldozer ahead until blade is loaded.*

Old posts are broken off or pulled from the ground without detaching from fence.

A cleared strip about ten feet wide through a thicket or woods makes it possible for you to distribute posts and unroll fence. It will later serve as a roadway and fire lane.

Remove mounds, to fill in low places, and to remove old fence.

BF/19

3. *Empty load to side of fence line for rotting, or use material to fill gully.*

GULLY

RUBBLE

BF/20

4. *Return over cleared area "floating" blade.*

This operation does a very neat job of smoothing the fence row for easy fence construction.

CLEARED AREA

BF/21

## CLEARING FENCE LINE WITH TRACTOR AND HARROW

If you plan to use a tractor and harrow, proceed as follows:

1. *Remove old fence posts, small trees, and brush with tractor.*

   (1) *Use the hydraulic lift on your tractor, or,*

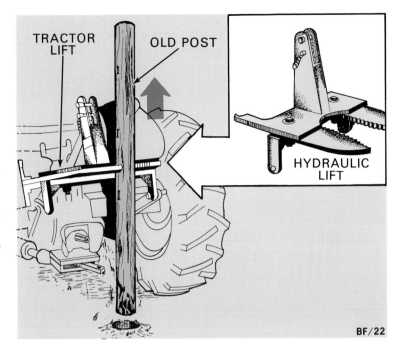

   (2) *Use an A-frame.*

   An A-frame is made from three 2″ x 4″ boards, each 3 feet long and bolted together about 6 inches from the end with ½-inch bolts. The notch thus formed on the corner of the triangle holds the chain in proper location as the post is raised.

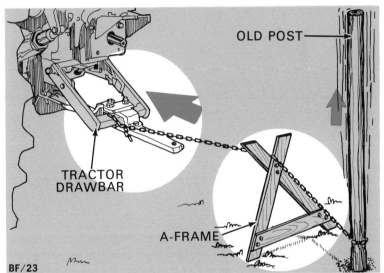

2. *Remove large trees with heavy rope, cable or log chain at least 20 feet long.*

   (1) *Attach rope or chain to drawbar of tractor.*

   (2) *Attach other end to tree.*

   If tree is of a variety that does not break or bend easily, attach rope or cable about six or seven feet above ground. Otherwise you will have to hook closer to base of tree.

   (3) *Move tractor ahead slowly.*

   As tree starts to fall, cut roots with mattock or axe.

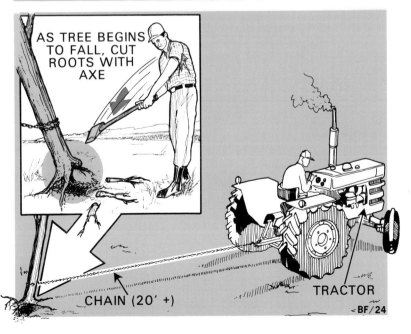

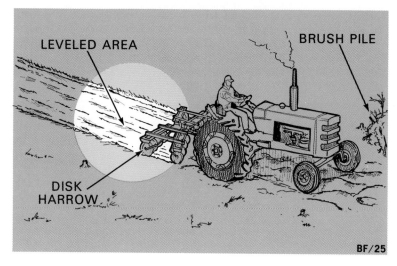

3. *Pile material by hand for rotting or use for filling gully.*

4. *Use disk harrow and drag for leveling.*

# X. Building Barbed-Wire & Woven-Wire Fences.

Barbed wire and woven wire fences are still the most common pasture fence. Most woven wire fences have a strand of barbed wire at the bottom and top to prevent animals from pushing under or over. Therefore, building barbed wire fences is discussed first.

The installation of brace assemblies and posts is very similar for these two types of fences.

Building barbed wire and woven wire fences is discussed under the following headings:

A. Installing Braces and Wood Posts.

B. Installing Braces and Steel Posts.

C. Installing Barbed Wire.

D. Installing Woven Wire.

E. Grounding Wire Fences for Lighting Protection.

# A. Installing Braces & Wood Posts

Most anchor-and-brace assemblies are all wood, all steel, or a combination of wood posts and steel braces. Wood-and-steel assemblies are discussed first.

From your study of this section you will be able to **describe the types of wood-and-steel brace assemblies, tell where to locate them** and **install them properly.**

Before you start to erect your anchor-and-brace assemblies, be sure to determine where you want each of them to be located. Allow space for gates. Gates should be at least 12 feet wide if wagons, trucks and farm machinery are to pass through. Fourteen feet is a safer width to assure passage of all farm machines.

Installing wood posts and braces is discussed under the following headings:

1. Tools and Materials Needed.
2. Locating Wood-and-Steel, Anchor-and-Brace Assembly.
3. Installing Wood-and-Steel, Anchor-and-Brace Assembly.
4. Installing Brace Wire.
5. Installing Wood Line Posts.

## TOOLS AND MATERIALS NEEDED

Post hole diggers or post auger
Tamping bar
Spud
Axe
Spade
Claw hammer
Handsaw
Wire splicer
Brace and bit ($\frac{3}{8}''$–$\frac{1}{2}''$)
Steel dowels ($\frac{3}{8}''$–$\frac{1}{2}''$ x 4") (2 per brace)
Staples
1 roll brace wire (barbed or smooth wire)
Carpenter's level
6' rule
Marking crayon
Ball of twine

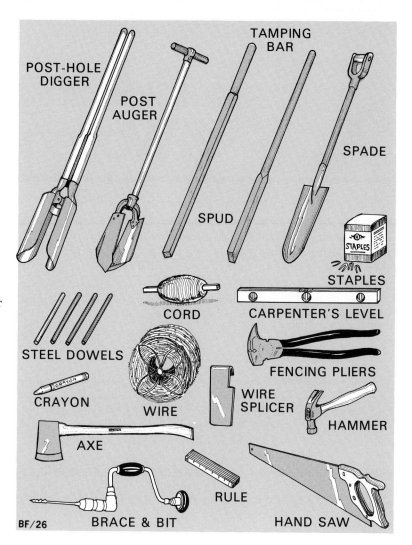

## LOCATING WOOD-AND-STEEL, ANCHOR-AND-BRACE ASSEMBLY

To locate wood-and-steel, anchor-and-brace assembly, procedures vary for the following conditions:

a. For **straight fences on flat land.**

1. For **fence lengths of 10 rods or less,** use single-span end construction.

Note: One rod is 16.5 feet, 20 rods is 330 feet, and 80 rods is 1,320 feet ($\frac{1}{4}$ mile).

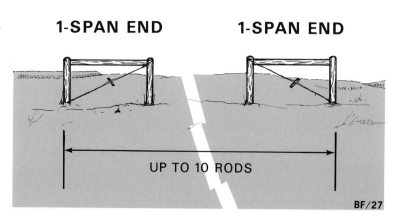

2. For **fence lengths of 10 to 40 rods,** use z-span end construction.

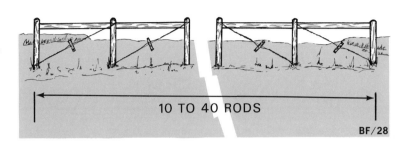

3. For **fence more than 40 rods long,** use a braced-line-post assembly to divide the fence lengths.

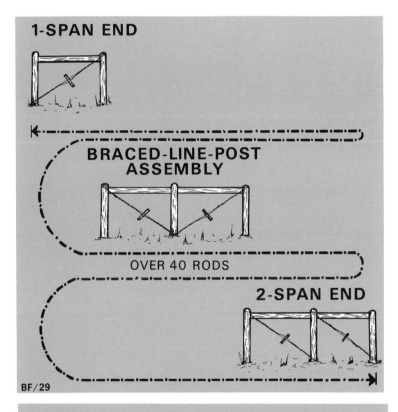

b. For **straight fences on rolling land.**

On rolling land, fence stretching is easier if braced-line-post assemblies are located at the foot and top of each hill.

## c. For **curved fences.**

Contour fences, more than 20 rods long, should have a braced-line-post assembly installed to keep the stretches to 20 rods or less. Install in straight section at least one post span away from a curve. Do not install on a curve. It will not hold well.

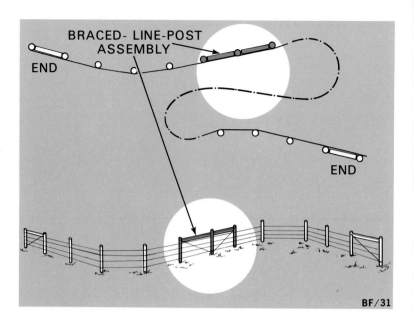

## INSTALLING WOOD-AND-STEEL, ANCHOR-AND-BRACE ASSEMBLY

To install a wood-and-steel, anchor-and-brace assembly, proceed as follows:

1. *Mark ground line on anchor-and-brace posts.*

    Setting depth should be at least 3 feet, 6 inches. If your post is extra long, set at greater depth to further increase strength of your anchor-and-brace assembly.

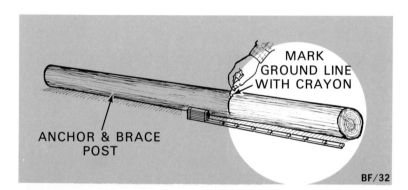

2. *Dig hole for anchor post.*

    Make hole at least 12 inches in diameter.

    Dig to a depth of 3 feet, 6 inches.

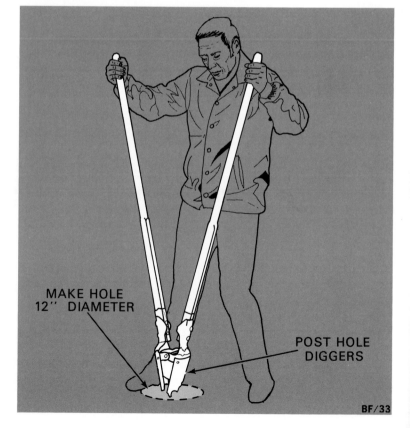

3. *Place post in hole and tamp soil around post.*

Replace small amounts of soil at a time and tamp thoroughly. Plumb post at same time, checking occasionally to see that it is in proper alignment.

If post is too crooked to use carpenter's level, use plumb bob.

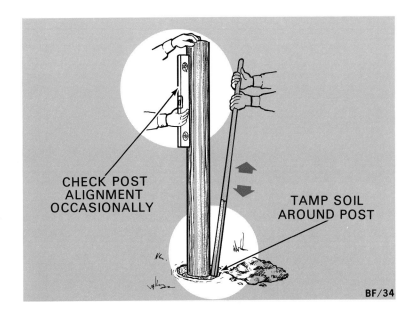

CHECK POST ALIGNMENT OCCASIONALLY

TAMP SOIL AROUND POST

BF/34

4. *Measure from anchor post to first brace post and dig hole for brace post.*

Use post or pipe that you selected for horizontal brace for measuring distance. It should be at least 8 feet long. If you are using 1½-inch pipe or larger, or 2½-inch angle iron or larger, span length may be increased to 10 or 12 feet. The extra brace length further increases the strength of your anchor-and-brace assembly.

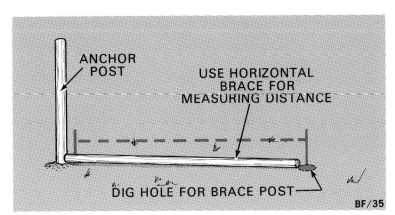

ANCHOR POST

USE HORIZONTAL BRACE FOR MEASURING DISTANCE

DIG HOLE FOR BRACE POST

BF/35

5. *Place brace post in hole but do not tamp.*

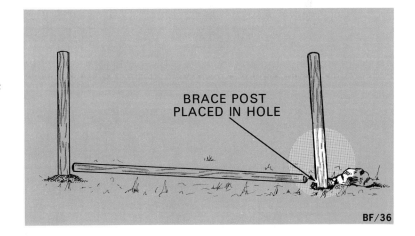

BRACE POST PLACED IN HOLE

BF/36

6. *Mark hole for dowel 8 to 12 inches from top of anchor post.*

If using pipe or angle-iron brace, mark post for notching with member centered 8 to 12 inches from top of post.

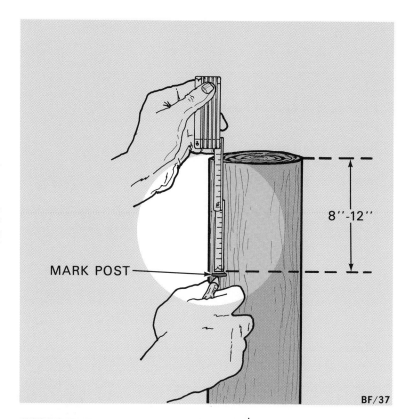

8"-12"

MARK POST

BF/37

7. *Bore hole same size as dowel, two inches deep.*

Be sure to remove all shavings.

For pipe or angle-iron make notch about ½ inch deep.

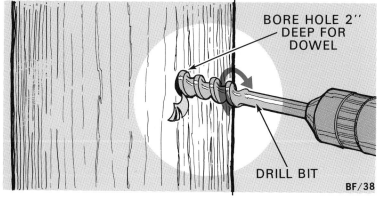

BORE HOLE 2" DEEP FOR DOWEL

DRILL BIT

BF/38

8. *Bore same size holes to same depth in each end of horizontal brace member.*

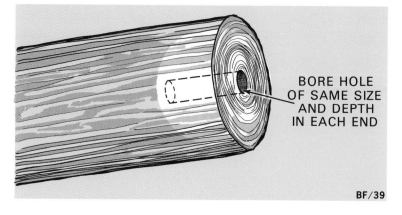

BORE HOLE OF SAME SIZE AND DEPTH IN EACH END

BF/39

9. *Insert dowel in anchor post.*

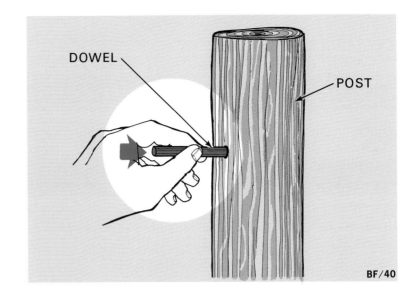

10. *Install brace member on anchor post.*

    Position opposite end on brace post so brace member is parallel with ground line.

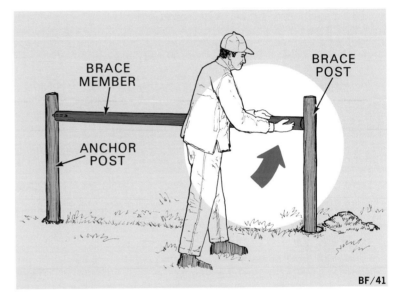

11. *Insert dowel in brace post.*

    Mark hole for dowel in brace post.

    Bore hole in brace post same size as steel dowel, 2 inches deep.

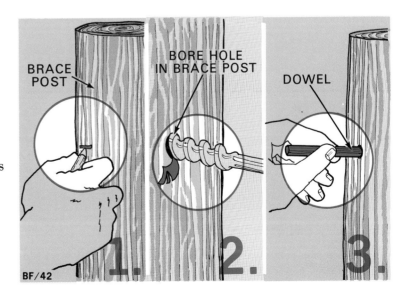

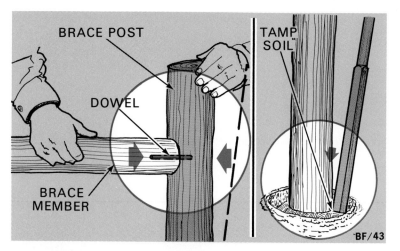

12. *Install brace member between anchor post and brace post.*

    Replace soil around brace post and tamp.

## INSTALLING BRACE WIRE

To install the brace wire, proceed as follows:

1. *Drive staple about half its length into brace post about 4 inches above brace member on opposite side from brace.*

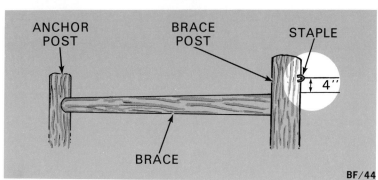

2. *Drive staple in similar manner on anchor post about 4 inches from ground line opposite side from brace.*

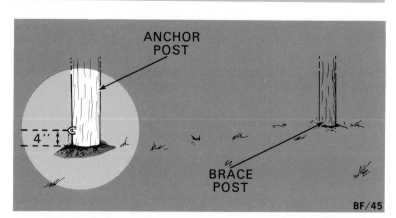

3. *Unroll enough brace wire for two complete loops around anchor and brace post.*

    To determine length required, use cord.

    Do not loop wire off roll. Unroll it to avoid kinks.

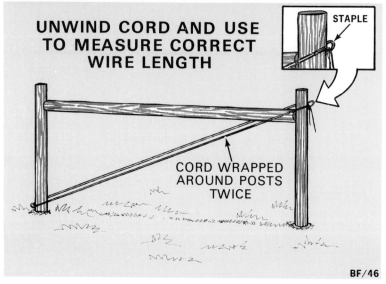

4. *Thread end of brace wire through one staple and then through other. Repeat to form three wire strands.*

Remove rough slack from wire.

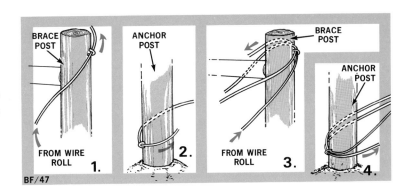

5. *Wrap wire around anchor post and return toward brace post.*

Leave enough wire length so end extends about two-thirds of way back to brace post.

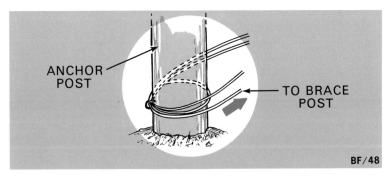

6. *Cut brace wire from roll allowing enough wire to wrap around brace post and extend 6 to 12 inches past other wire end.*

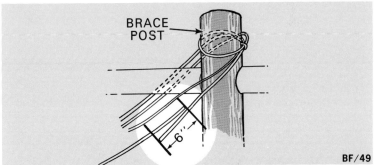

7. *Make splice.*

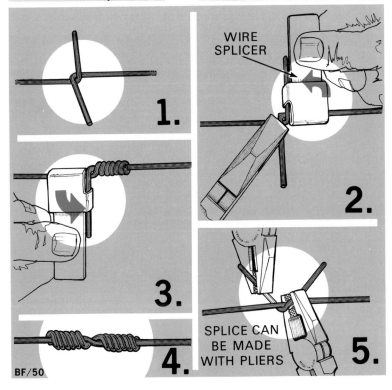

8. *Twist brace wire until whole assembly is rigid.*

Use a good strong stick, rod, or pipe *approximately 18 to 24 inches long.* As wire is tightened, tap with hammer where it wraps around post so it will fit smoothly and remain tight. Leave member, used for twisting, in place.

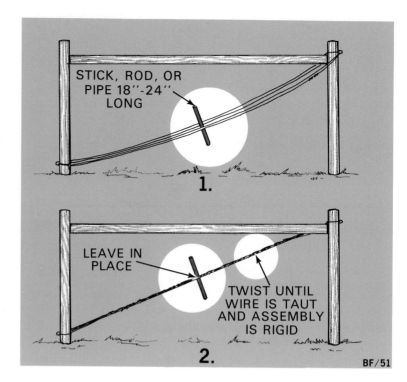

If your fence is over 40 rods in length, or if you have sudden dips and rises in your fence line, you will need to install braced-line-post assemblies. These are sometimes called "stretcher-post assemblies."

Note: One brace wire pulls in the opposite direction from the other. The reason is to provide an assembly that will take fence pull from either direction. There may be such a situation if a tree falls across one section of your fence or if an automobile or tractor damages a section. The fence section on the undamaged side will still remain tight while the damaged portion is repaired and restretched.

Each section of fence must be built separately and each fence end wrapped around the center post. A continuous fence, spliced together and stapled to the braced-line post assembly, will pull loose (staples pull out) if one section is damaged. Then both sections become slack. It will then take more time to get your fence restretched.

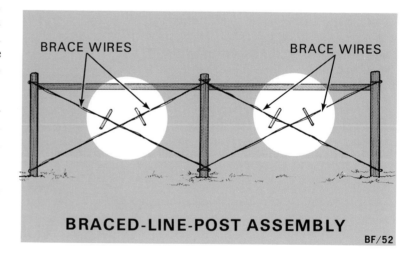

BRACED-LINE-POST ASSEMBLY

106

## INSTALLING WOOD LINE POSTS

To install wood line posts, proceed as follows:

1. *Stretch cord, rope or strand of barbed wire between two anchor-post assemblies (or between anchor-post and stretcher-post assembly).*

   Some fence builders like to use a barbed wire between the bottom of their woven-wire fence and the ground. If you plan to do this, it will save time to use your barbed wire for the guide line.

2. *Measure line post spacings with gage pole.*

   If you are using a power digger or power post driver, count drive wheel revolutions to determine post location. Post spacings should be about 16 feet for woven-wire fences, 12 to 14 feet for barbed-wire fences and 5 to 8 feet for board fences, depending on board length.

3. *Mark ground line on post or digging tool with chalk or crayon.*

   Ground line is determined by figuring overall height of fence plus about three or four inches to allow for post extending above fence. If this procedure is followed, posts will be a uniform height above ground unless ground surface is irregular.

4. *Dig or bore hole for post and check hole depth to determine when hole is deep enough.*

   A power hole digger or post driver will save lots of time and hard work, if one is available.

   (Small wood posts—2½ to 3 inches in diameter—may be sharpened and driven into moist ground. Use a driver made of 5-inch pipe and 2 feet long with handles welded on opposite sides.)

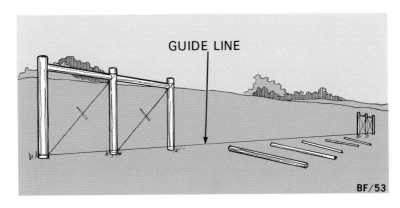

GUIDE LINE

BF/53

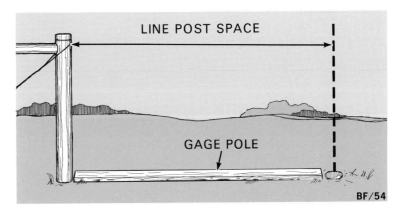

LINE POST SPACE

GAGE POLE

BF/54

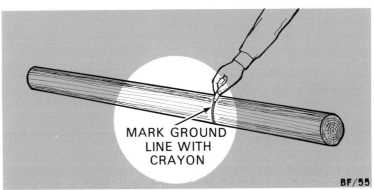

MARK GROUND LINE WITH CRAYON

BF/55

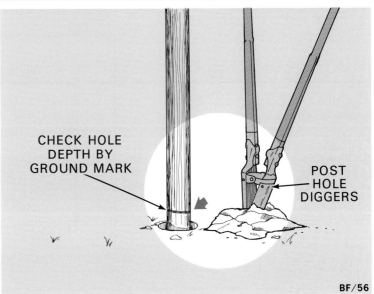

CHECK HOLE DEPTH BY GROUND MARK

POST HOLE DIGGERS

BF/56

5. *Set post and align as dirt is backfilled in hole.*

When you have marked to within five or six post spacings from end, divide remaining distance to give post line an appearance of even spacing.

Some fence builders like to align every tenth post between two anchor-and-brace assemblies, then align other posts between these.

If you are contour fencing, lean top of post to outside of curve about 2 inches. Tamp each shovelful of dirt as it is placed in the hole around post.

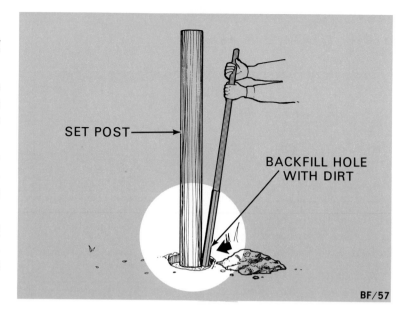

SET POST

BACKFILL HOLE WITH DIRT

BF/57

If you have a low place in your field with a gentle rise on each side, you will have trouble with the lowest line posts staying in the ground. Dig the hole larger and pour concrete around the base of the post. If water flows under the fence in wet weather, use two of these posts—one on each side of the depression.

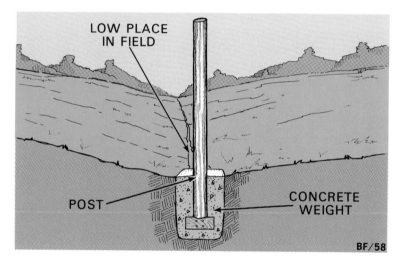

LOW PLACE IN FIELD

POST

CONCRETE WEIGHT

BF/58

If your fence crosses a low wet place such as the edge of a pond or lake, use concrete-weighted posts or metal posts (pipe) weighted with stone or rock.

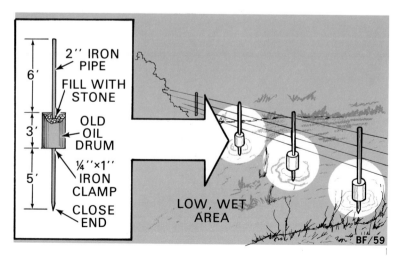

6'

3'

5'

2'' IRON PIPE

FILL WITH STONE

OLD OIL DRUM

¼''×1'' IRON CLAMP

CLOSE END

LOW, WET AREA

BF/59

Do not try to set posts in a gully or stream.

If gully or stream is less than 16 feet wide—set line post on each side and continue your fence across it.

If your gully or stream is more than 16 feet wide—use anchor-and-brace assembly on each side and stretch fence as separate units.

See Part 1 for kinds of floodgates to use over a stream.

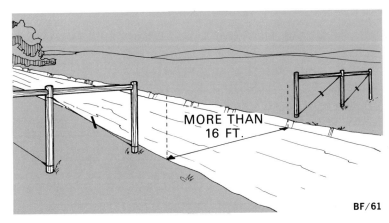

You may have a few low places where hogs, calves or lambs can get out. If there is little or no water flowing through any of them in wet weather, a few shovelsful of dirt may be all that is needed. If there is some water passing through the opening in wet weather, or if the space is too large to fill with dirt, either barbed wire or woven wire can be used as a filler, but barbed wire requires less cutting and fitting.

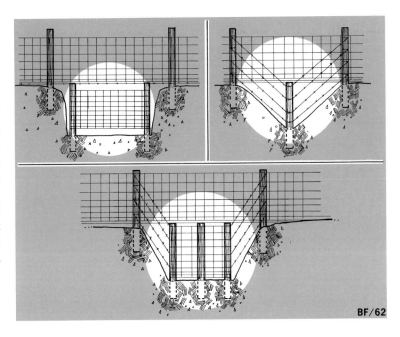

# B. Installing Braces & Steel Posts

The procedures that follow provide for anchoring the post and brace in concrete. There are commercial designs that provide bracing without using concrete.

On completion of your study of this section, you will be able to **install braces and steel posts in concrete.**

Installing steel posts and braces are discussed under the following headings:

1. Tools and Materials Needed.

2. Installing Steel Post-and-Brace Assembly.

3. Installing Steel Line Post.

## TOOLS AND MATERIALS NEEDED

Steel post driver
Adjustable end wrench
Gage stick
Carpenter's level
Cement
Sand
Crushed stone
Water

(If you are building an anchor-and-brace assembly of steel, figure $3\frac{1}{2}$ cubic feet of concrete for an end and $4\frac{1}{2}$ cubic feet for a corner. Mixture should be 1 part cement, 2 parts sand and 4 parts crushed stone.)

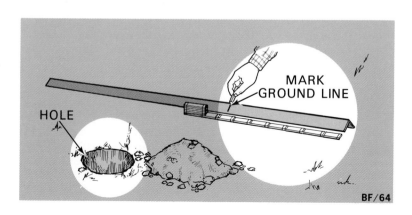

3rd STRAND BARBED WIRE
2nd STRAND BARBED WIRE
1st STRAND BARBED WIRE
TOP OF WOVEN WIRE
CEMENT
WATER
SAND
CRUSHED STONE
STEEL POST DRIVER
CARPENTER'S LEVEL
ADJUSTABLE END WRENCH
GAGE STICK
8″   6″   2″-3″   3″
BF/63

## INSTALLING STEEL POST-AND-BRACE ASSEMBLY

Procedure for installing the steel anchor post-and-brace assembly is given as follows:

1. *Dig anchor post hole and mark ground line on post with crayon or chalk.*

   Make hole about 12 inches in diameter and 3 feet, 6 inches deep.

   You can also mark your digger or auger handle, but a mark on the post will assure setting it at proper depth.

HOLE   MARK GROUND LINE   BF/64

**2.** *Attach brace to anchor post.*

For corner posts, add braces in both directions.

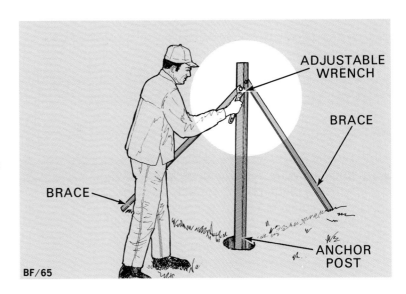

**3.** *Dig hole where brace contacts ground.*

In southern climates, dig hole 15″ X 18″ X 8″.

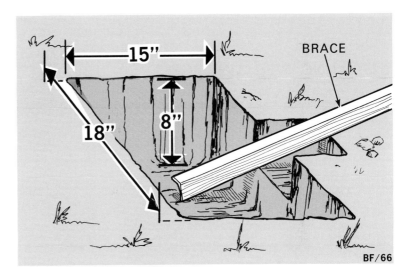

In areas where ground freezes deeply, hole must be deepened to provide 8″ of concrete below frost line. If this is not done, frost may raise concrete pier.

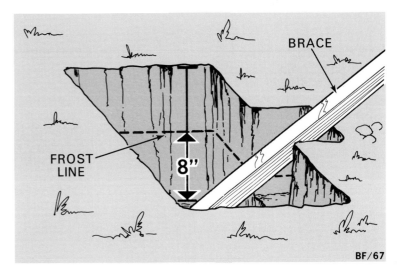

4. *Mix and place concrete around anchor post and brace.*

Tamp concrete while being placed and plumb post with level. Be sure mix is not soupy. A soupy mix is weak and will not hold post in plumb position. Slope concrete away from post to drain away water.

NOTE: Concrete should cure for at least one week before fence is attached.

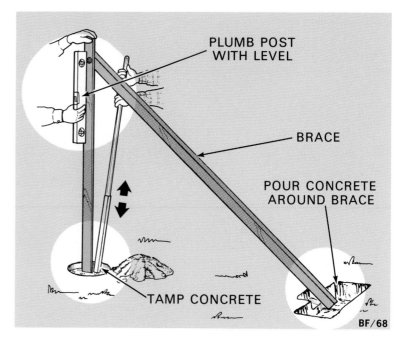

PLUMB POST WITH LEVEL

BRACE

POUR CONCRETE AROUND BRACE

TAMP CONCRETE

BF/68

## INSTALLING STEEL LINE POSTS

To install the steel line posts, use a steel post, proceed as follows:

1. *Align post as with wood post.*

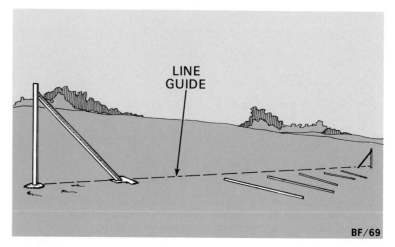

LINE GUIDE

BF/69

2. *Mark ground line on post.*

3. *Position post with wire-holding studs (or grooves) on wire side.*

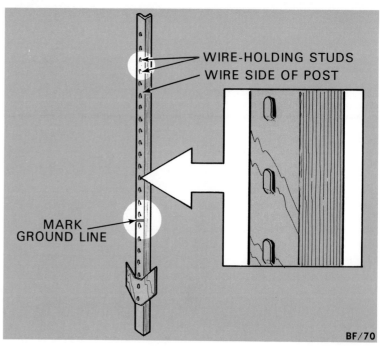

WIRE-HOLDING STUDS
WIRE SIDE OF POST

MARK GROUND LINE

BF/70

4. *Drive posts into ground with tubular, or power operated, fence-post driver.*

If your ground is uneven, you may find it an advantage to leave ground line on post two or three inches out of ground until after fence is attached. Posts can then be driven in far enough to even fence.

If you are contour fencing, lean top of posts to outside of curve about 2 inches.

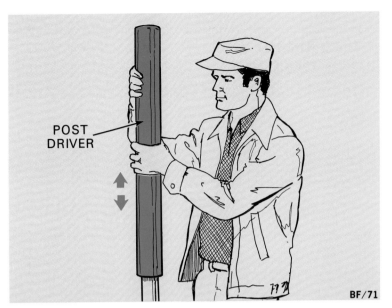

# C. Installing Barbed Wire

The main things you need to learn about installing barbed wire are to stretch it properly and attach it securely to the post.

From your study of this section, you will be able to **become proficient in stretching and attaching barbed wire to posts.**

Installing barbed wire is discussed under the following headings:

1. Tools and Materials Needed.
2. Laying Barbed Wire Along Fence Line.
3. Stretching Barbed Wire.
4. Attaching Barbed Wire to Posts.

## TOOLS AND MATERIALS NEEDED

Fence stretcher
Staples (wood posts)
Wire clamps (steel posts)
18"-24" rod
Claw hammer
Fencing pliers
Wire splicer

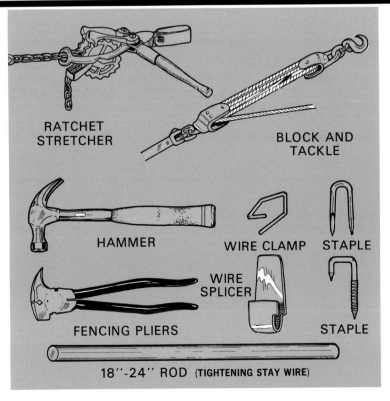

## LAYING BARBED WIRE ALONG FENCE LINE

Common wire spacings are illustrated. You may vary the spacing according to your needs.

Common spacings for short span fences.

Common spacings for suspension fences.

To lay barbed wire along fence line, proceed as follows:

1. *Attach end of wire to end post.*

   If you are using **wood posts,** staple the wire.

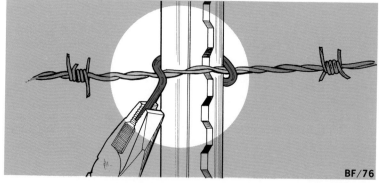

   If you are using **steel posts,** use wire clamps.

2. *Extend wires around post and wrap.*

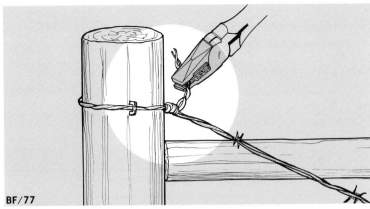

BF/77

3. *Unroll barbed wire to next anchor post,*

Use one of the methods shown.

Do not loop wire off side of roll. This makes it very difficult and dangerous to work, and creates kinks.

Be sure to use leather gloves when working with barbed wire. It will save scratching and cutting your hands which may result in serious injury.

BF/78

## STRETCHING BARBED WIRE

Procedures for stretching barbed wire are as follows:

1. *Erect dummy post for attaching stretcher.*

The dummy post is a temporary structure used only for stretching the fence. Some fence builders stretch their fences directly from the anchor post. That leaves a loose fence end to attach to the anchor post and will permit the fence to "slack off" some when the stretchers are removed. Use of a dummy post will permit the tightened fence to be attached to the anchor post so there is little extra slack when stretchers are removed.

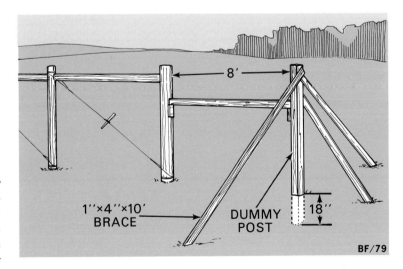

8'

1''×4''×10' BRACE

DUMMY POST

18''

BF/79

2. *Attach fence stretcher rachet or block-and tackle to dummy post.*

3. *Attach barbed wire to fence stretcher rachet, or to block-and-tackle.*

4. *Stretch barbed wire until fairly tight.*

5. *Check wire to make sure it is free.*

   There is no method of knowing when barbed wire is stretched to proper tension. If wire is longer than 20 rods, it should be supported with wire loops from top of the posts at intervals of 8-10 posts.

   Caution: With hand stretchers, it is possible to stretch barbed wire so tightly that it will break. When this happens, anyone standing near stretched wire can be severely cut. If you must handle barbed wire while it is being stretched, keep post between you and wire. Handle with pliers and leather gloves.

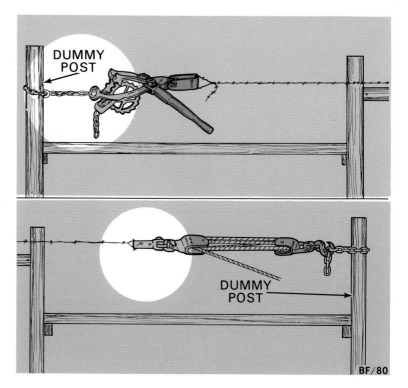

## ATTACHING BARBED WIRE TO POSTS

Attaching wire to post varies with the type of posts (a) wood, (b) steel and (c) concrete,

(a) To attach wire to **wood post,** proceed as follows:

1. *Set staple cross-wise of grain.*

   This procedure permits staple to be held much more tightly and avoids splitting action caused by both prongs of staple being driven into same grain.

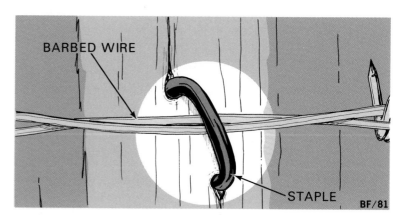

2. *Drive staple into post.*

   Wire should be held closely, not snugly, or tightly.

   Do not bury staple in post. It damages the wire.

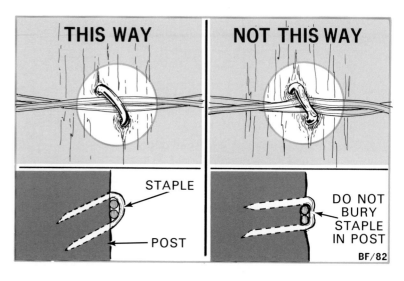

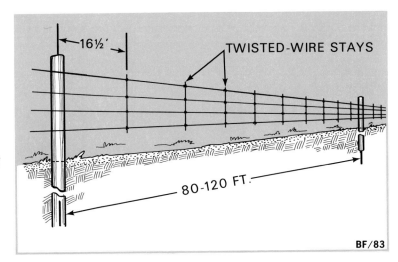

3. *Attach stay wires if you are building a suspension fence.*

(b) To attach wire to **steel posts,** proceed as follows:

1. *Hook post clamp over wire and snap into position around post.*

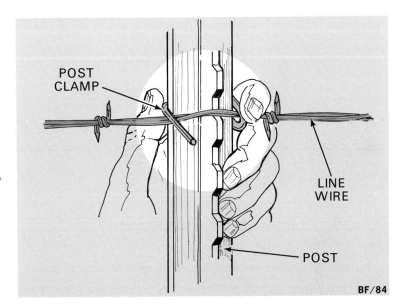

2. *Bend other side over wire to form hook.*

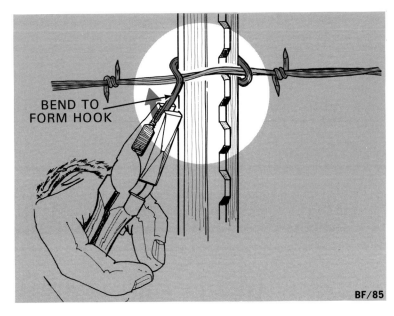

If your post is equipped with lugs, hook wire in lug and close with fencing pliers or hammer.

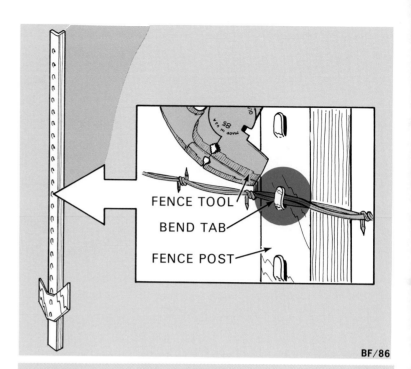

FENCE TOOL
BEND TAB
FENCE POST

BF/86

(c) To attach wire to **concrete posts,** proceed as follows:

1. *Extend wire around post to form loop and cut wire ends to desired length for wrapping.*

   Use 12-gage, galvanized wire or larger.

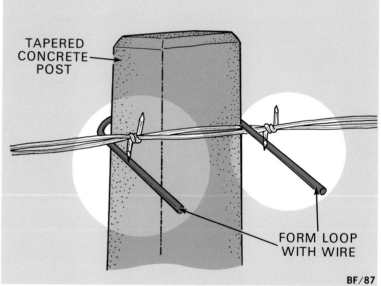

TAPERED CONCRETE POST

FORM LOOP WITH WIRE

BF/87

2. *Pull fence against post and wrap loop ends around wire.*

   To get a snug fit, tap wire loop with hammer before second wire end is wrapped.

   Wrap wire with pliers or wire splicer.

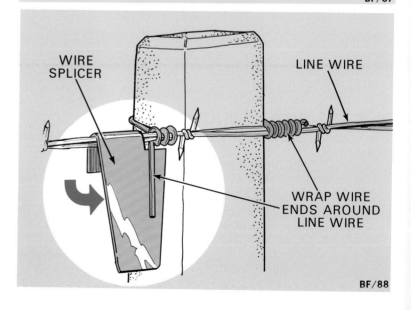

WIRE SPLICER

LINE WIRE

WRAP WIRE ENDS AROUND LINE WIRE

BF/88

118

# D. Installing Woven Wire

Procedures for installing woven wire fences vary somewhat from those for installing barbed wire.

From your study of this section you will be able to **lay out woven wire, stretch it** and **attach it to posts.**

Procedures for installing woven wire are given under the following headings:

1. Tools and Materials Needed.
2. Laying Woven Wire Along Fence Line.
3. Stretching Woven Wire.
4. Attaching Woven Wire to Posts.

## TOOLS AND MATERIALS NEEDED

Stretcher
Double jack, or block and tackle
18″ rod
Wire clamps, or staples
Compression fittings
Splicing tool
Hammer
Pliers or fence tool
Crimper

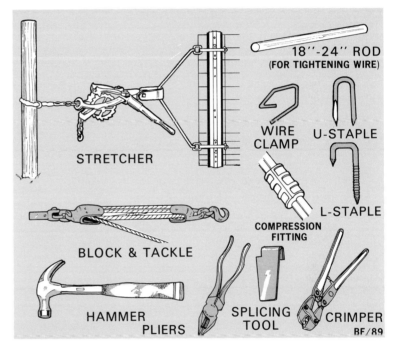

STRETCHER
BLOCK & TACKLE
HAMMER
PLIERS
SPLICING TOOL
CRIMPER
18″-24″ ROD (FOR TIGHTENING WIRE)
WIRE CLAMP
U-STAPLE
L-STAPLE
COMPRESSION FITTING
BF/89

## LAYING WOVEN WIRE ALONG FENCE LINE

Procedures for laying woven wire along fence line are given as follows:

1. *Examine fence roll to determine from which end of fence line fence should be unrolled.*

When your fence is in proper unrolling position, the bottom of the roll—close mesh end—is next to post line. If top of roll is next to post line, it will cause you considerable work in putting the fence into position after it is unrolled.

If livestock pressure is mostly from one side of fence—as along a public road—put fence on side of posts where most pressure will be. Posts on road side of fence will not look as well as on field side, but maintenance will be less. Posts will take pressure rather than staples when livestock presses against fence.

If you are fencing on the contour, start unrolling fence from end with least curvature.

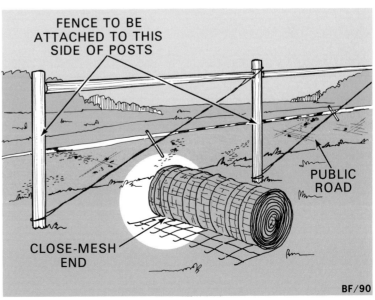

FENCE TO BE ATTACHED TO THIS SIDE OF POSTS
PUBLIC ROAD
CLOSE-MESH END
BF/90

2. *Starting ahead of anchor post (at least two feet), unroll fence about one or two line-post spacings and set on end.*

BF/91

3. *Remove one stay wire from top to bottom.*

   Cut stay wire between line wires, loosen joint and slip joint off end of line wires.

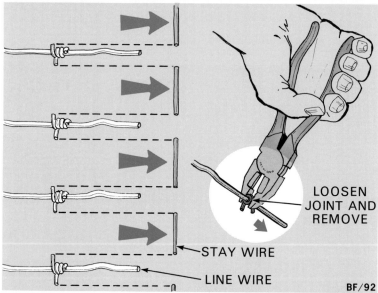

LOOSEN JOINT AND REMOVE

STAY WIRE

LINE WIRE

BF/92

4. *Stand fence against anchor post and adjust to desired height.*

   Lift about 3 inches if barbed wire is to be used under woven wire. If barbed wire is not used under fence, lower to height of about 1/2 inch above ground.

ADJUST FENCE TO DESIRED HEIGHT

BF/93

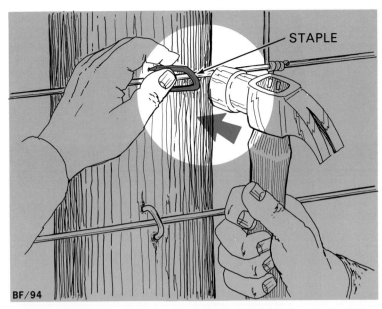

5. *Staple fence in position.*

6. *Extend end of each line wire around post and wrap on itself.*

   Do not depend on staples to hold your fence tightly enough to take the fence pull. The fence is damaged and staples will not hold.

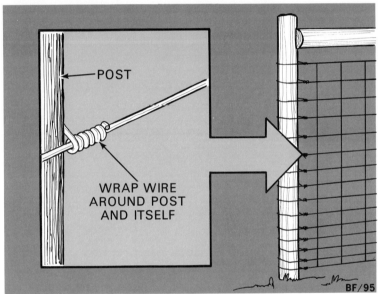

POST

WRAP WIRE AROUND POST AND ITSELF

7. *Complete unrolling of fence to next anchor-post assembly (or braced-line post assembly.)*

   If you are building a contour fence, unroll so fence is on outside of post-line curvature. This will mean that fence will have to be changed from one side of post line to other depending on direction of curvature.

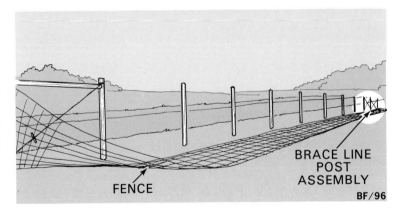

BRACE LINE POST ASSEMBLY

FENCE

If it is necessary for you to splice two sections of fence together, use (a) a splicer, or (b) a crimper.

**(a)** If you use a **splicer,** proceed as follows:

(1) *Cut ends of line wires on each section so about 4 inches of each line wire extends beyond stay wire.*

(2) *Pull ends of fence sections together until stay wires meet.*

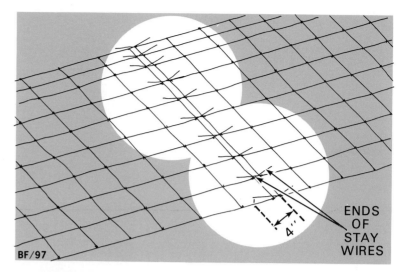

(3) *Bend top line wire of one fence section around top line wire of other fence section and wrap.*

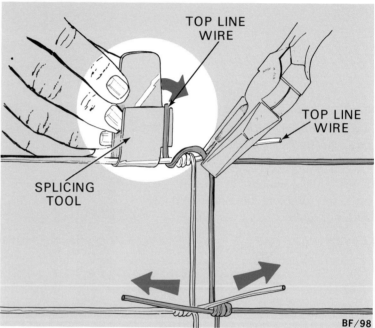

(4) *Wrap remaining top line wire in opposite direction.*

122

(b) If you use a **crimper**, proceed as follows:

  (1) *Overlap ends of top wire about two inches.*

  (2) *Place compression fitting over both wires.*

  (3) *Crimp fitting.*

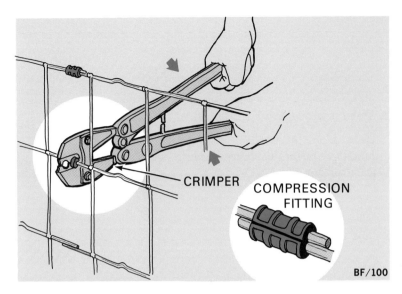

CRIMPER
COMPRESSION FITTING

BF/100

## STRETCHING WOVEN WIRE

The procedures given here are for double-jack, single-jack, or block-and-tackle fence stretchers.

Some fence builders use a tractor to stretch woven wire or barbed wire. In spite of the fact that time may be saved, tractor stretching is not recommended. Here are the reasons:

The tractor operator is in great danger. It is easy to break either woven or barbed wire without the operator knowing that it has reached the breaking point. When the fence breaks, the recoil is sometimes sufficient to throw the clamp bar and chain against the tractor and operator. With barbed wire, the wire itself may recoil on the operator adding further to the injury. So many people have been hurt or killed that the National Safety Council recommends strongly against the practice.

BARBED WIRE

BF/101

To **stretch woven wire,** proceed as follows:

1. *Erect dummy post for attaching stretchers.*

The dummy post is a temporary structure used only for stretching the fence. Sometimes a fence is stretched directly from the anchor post. That leaves a loose fence end to attach to the anchor post and will permit the fence to "slack off" some when the stretchers are removed. Use of a dummy post will permit the tightened fence to be attached to the anchor post so there is little extra slack when stretchers are removed.

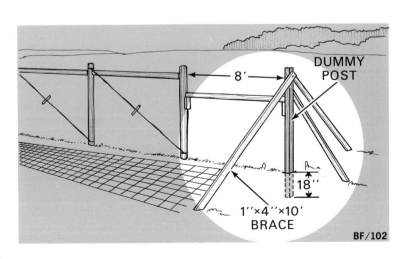

8'
DUMMY POST
18"
1"×4"×10' BRACE

BF/102

2. *Stand fence against line posts.*

   Hold fence in position with props or loops of wire or string—about every third or fourth post.

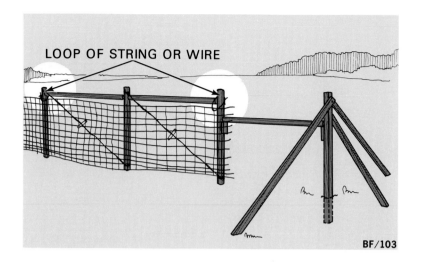

LOOP OF STRING OR WIRE

BF/103

3. *Attach chain (or cable) of stretchers to dummy post.*

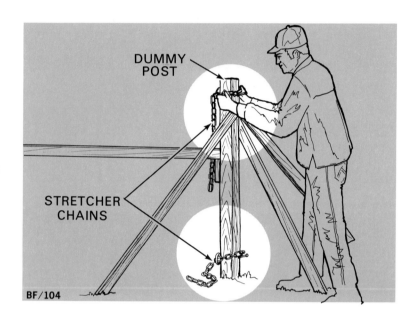

DUMMY POST

STRETCHER CHAINS

BF/104

4. *Attach clamp bar to fence at a position about opposite anchor post.*

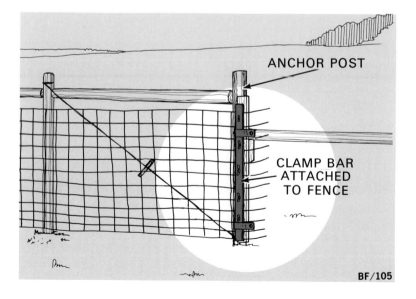

ANCHOR POST

CLAMP BAR ATTACHED TO FENCE

BF/105

5. *Attach rachets to clamp bar.*

In attaching rachets to clamp bar, be sure they are connected at a lower position on bar than where chain or cable attaches to dummy post. When fence is pulled, it will lift off ground rather than drag.

These instructions are for a double-jack stretcher. If you have a single-jack stretcher, be sure there are as many line wires above point of attachment as there are below. This keeps the tension about the same on all wires.

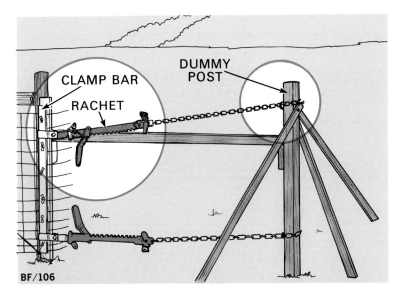

CLAMP BAR

DUMMY POST

RACHET

BF/106

6. *Tighten fence slowly by turning top rachet, then lower rachet, alternating back and forth to maintain even wire tension at top and bottom.*

It is important that fence be tightened slowly so that tension can be distributed evenly over length of fence. It will help if a second person shakes fence loose from posts and other obstructions as it is being stretched. Grasp top of fence and bounce it.

7. *Continue stretching until tension curves are approximately one-third removed.*

Recent studies indicate that removing as much as one-half of the tension curve, as formerly recommended, is too much. The tension curve is over stretched and it loses some of its spring effect.* The fence tends to loosen.

Stay wires should be as nearly plumb as possible.

If you are building fences in summer, don't pull out as much tension curve as in winter. Cold weather will cause the fence to tighten.

If you are building a contour fence, stretch from ⅓ to ⅔ as much as for straight fence. Your fence will appear loose, but it will retain satisfactory tension. A straight fence stretched in this manner will not retain satisfactory tension.

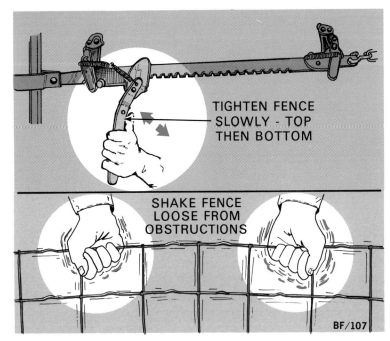

TIGHTEN FENCE SLOWLY - TOP THEN BOTTOM

SHAKE FENCE LOOSE FROM OBSTRUCTIONS

BF/107

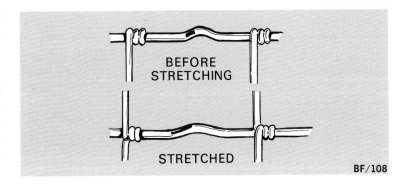

BEFORE STRETCHING

STRETCHED

BF/108

---

*Boyd, J. S. and Wilson, J. D.; *Effect of Temperature on Tightness of Fences;* Transaction of the American Society of Agricultural Engineers, 1960.

## ATTACHING WOVEN WIRE TO POSTS

To attach woven wire to posts, proceed as follows:

1. *Attach wire to anchor post.*

   Procedures vary for (a) wood, (b) steel, or (c) concrete posts.

   (a) If you are using **wood posts,** proceed as follows:

   (1) *Set staple cross-wise of grain.*

   This procedure permits staple to be held much more tightly and avoids splitting action caused by both prongs of staple being driven into same grain. Do not staple stay wire.

   (2) *Drive staple into post.*

   Wire should be held closely, not snugly, or tightly.

   Do not bury staple in post. It damages the wire.

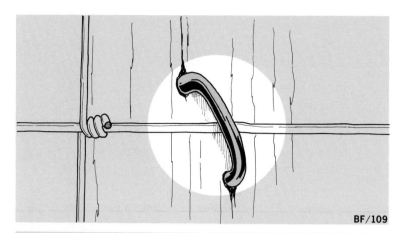

BF/109

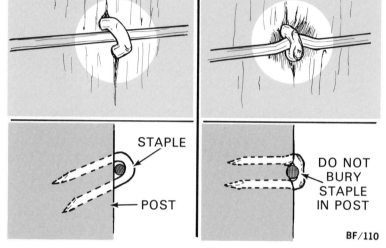

THIS WAY    NOT THIS WAY

STAPLE

POST

DO NOT BURY STAPLE IN POST

BF/110

   (b) If you are using **steel posts,** proceed as follows:

   (1) *Hook post clamp over line wire and snap into position around post.*

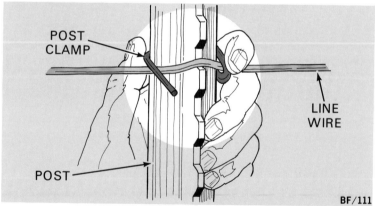

POST CLAMP

LINE WIRE

POST

BF/111

   (2) *Bend other side over line wire to form hook.*

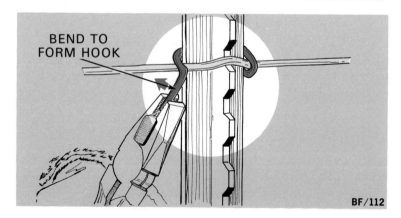

BEND TO FORM HOOK

BF/112

(c) If you are using **concrete posts**, proceed as follows:

  (1) *Extend wire around post to form loop.*

  Use 12-gage, galvanized wire or larger.

  (2) *Cut wire ends to desired length for wrapping.*

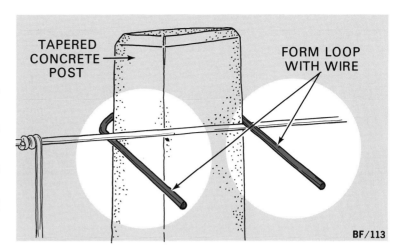

TAPERED CONCRETE POST

FORM LOOP WITH WIRE

BF/113

  (3) *Pull fence against post and wrap loop ends around line wire.*

  To get a snug fit, tap wire loop with hammer before second wire end is wrapped.

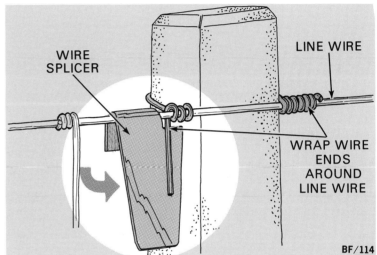

WIRE SPLICER

LINE WIRE

WRAP WIRE ENDS AROUND LINE WIRE

BF/114

2. *Remove (or drive back) stay wires for a distance sufficient to extend around anchor post and to wrap back on itself.*

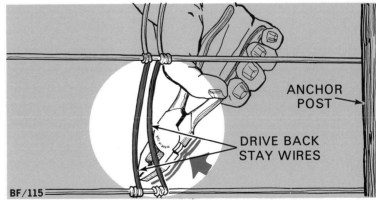

ANCHOR POST

DRIVE BACK STAY WIRES

BF/115

3. *Cut middle line wire, extend around post and wrap back on itself.*

4. *Do same with every other wire working toward top and bottom.*

5. *Cut and wrap remaining wires leaving top wire until last.*

  Caution: Before cutting top wire, make sure stretcher will not fall and injure anyone.

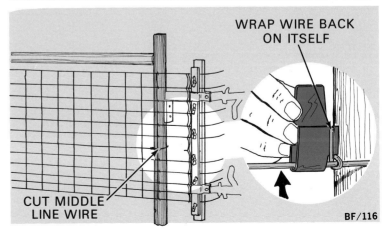

WRAP WIRE BACK ON ITSELF

CUT MIDDLE LINE WIRE

BF/116

**6.** *Attach top of wire to other line posts.*

Begin at point farthest from stretcher. Attach top wire first.

If barbed wire is used under woven-wire fence, allow about 3 inches between bottom wire and ground line. If barbed wire is not used, bottom wire of fence should clear the ground by approximately ½ inch.

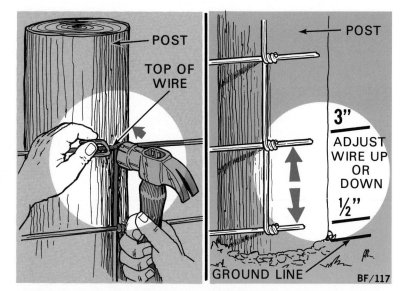

**7.** *Attach bottom wire next.*

You can do this easily by putting your foot on bottom line wire to hold it in position until staple is driven into place.

**8.** *Attach every other wire on remainder of post.*

If fencing has close spacing of line wires at bottom of fence, fasten every third line wire until spacing between line wires is approximately six inches.

**9.** *Add barbed wire if needed.*

Follow procedures given for stretching and attaching barbed wire.

Attach first strand of barbed wire 2″ above top of woven wire. Additional strands should be spaced 6″ to 8″ apart.

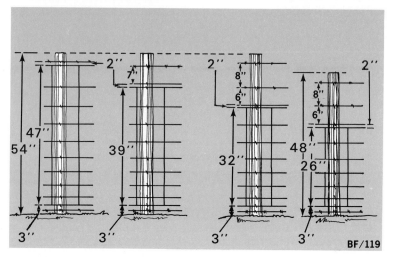

# E. Grounding Wire Fences for Lightning Protection

According to the USDA Bulletin No. 2136 by Harry L. Garver:

Livestock are usually killed instantly when they are near a fence that receives a lightning discharge. An ungrounded or improperly grounded wire fence can carry some of the electric current from the lightning discharge along its wires as far as 2 miles. Wire fences that are attached to trees or buildings are most likely to receive and carry lightning discharges, but any ungrounded wire fence with wooden posts, or steel posts set in concrete, is a hazard to livestock.

If you are using all steel posts, they provide a good means of grounding fences in humid areas. During even the driest periods, you can usually depend on some of them being in contact with moist soil. If the soil dries beyond post depth, either use extra long steel posts or install special ground rods as recommended for wood or concrete posts.

If you are using wood or concrete posts, you have a very poorly grounded fence, even in humid areas. You may alternate wood and steel posts which usually provides satisfactory grounding in humid areas. However, you are much more certain of providing good grounding if you install specially-driven ground rods in accordance with the procedures that follow. They extend into the soil twice as far as the average post.

From your study of this section, you will be able to **install a ground rod** and **connect the fence wire to it.**

Grounding wire fences are discussed under the following headings:

1. Tools and Materials Needed.
2. Installing Ground Rod.
3. Connecting Wire to Ground Rod.
4. Grounding an Electric Fence.

## TOOLS AND MATERIALS NEEDED

Hammer
Post Driver
Material for each ground installation:
   1 8 to 10-foot length of ½-inch galvanized pipe
      Use a 10-foot length for 47″ fences or an 8-foot length for a 32″ fence.
   4 pipe straps
   8 10-penny nails

For electric fence:
   No. 6 copper wire
   Lightning arrester
   Solderless connector clamp
   Metal clamp
   1 8′ length of ½-inch galvanized pipe.

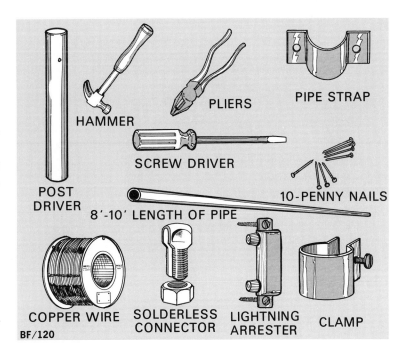

POST DRIVER    HAMMER    PLIERS    PIPE STRAP    SCREW DRIVER    10-PENNY NAILS    8′-10′ LENGTH OF PIPE    COPPER WIRE    SOLDERLESS CONNECTOR    LIGHTNING ARRESTER    CLAMP

BF/120

## INSTALLING GROUND ROD

To install a ground rod, proceed as follows:

1. *Pound end of pipe into a wedge shape.*
2. *Select location for driving ground rod.*
   If there is a low place along the fence line (within 150 feet of both ends of the fence, or within 150 feet of one end of the fence and within 300 feet of the next ground rod), it will probably be your best location. The ground rod is more likely to be in moist soil all of the time. Set ground rod on fence side of post and as close to fence as possible.
3. *Drive pipe in ground with post driver.*
   Allow about 4 to 6 inches of the pipe to extend above the fence.

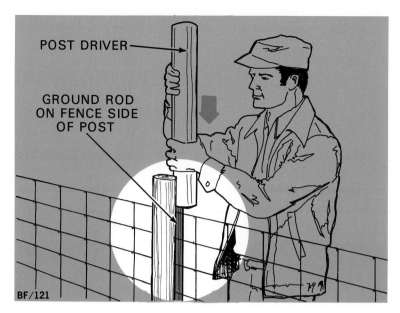

## CONNECTING WIRE TO GROUND ROD

To make contact between the fence and the ground rod, proceed as follows:

1. *Place pipe strap over pipe, above top line wire and nail.*
2. *Nail remaining straps.*

## GROUNDING AN ELECTRIC FENCE

Electric fences should be grounded for protection from lightning, yet must be insulated to permit the system to work. Lightning arresters are used to bleed off severe electrical surges in the fence caused by lightning.

To ground an electric fence, proceed as follows:

1. *At intervals of 300 feet, drive an 8' length of pipe into the ground.*
   Leave about 6″ exposed. Locate this on the side of the post opposite the fence wire.
2. *Install a lightning arrester on the electric fence post.*
   If the fence has two wires, attach a colored lead to each. If there is only one wire, attach both colored leads to it.
3. *Attach the middle (white) wire to a short length of No. 6 copper wire with a solderless connector.*
4. *Attach the No. 6 copper wire to the exposed ½″ pipe with a metal clamp.*
5. *Check the No. 6 wire to insure that it is not touching the electric fence.*

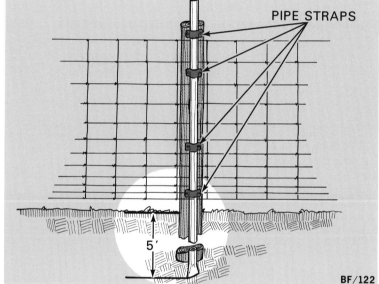

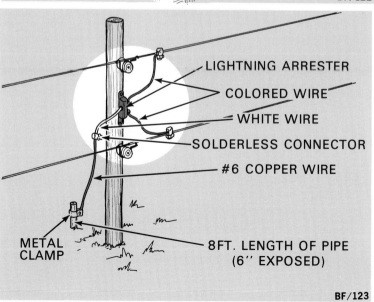

# XI. Building Electric Fences.

Electric fences are generally considered temporary. Generally one strand of smooth or barbed wire is used. Posts are small and require very little bracing.

From your study of this section, you will be able to **construct an electric fence; install the posts, insulator and wire.**

Procedures are discussed under the following headings:

A. Installing Posts and Braces.

B. Installing Wire for Electric Fences.

C. Building Gates for Electric Fences.

# A. Installing Posts and Braces

Posts and braces need not be as sturdy as for permanent fences.

From your study of this discussion you will be able to **install anchor and brace assemblies and line posts.**

Installing posts and braces are discussed under the following headings:

1. Tools and Materials Needed.

2. Installing Posts and Braces for Electric Fences.

## TOOLS AND MATERIALS NEEDED

Post Driver:
    Capped 1½″ steel pipe, or larger, for steel posts
    Sledge Hammer for wood posts
Axe
Pliers
Hammer

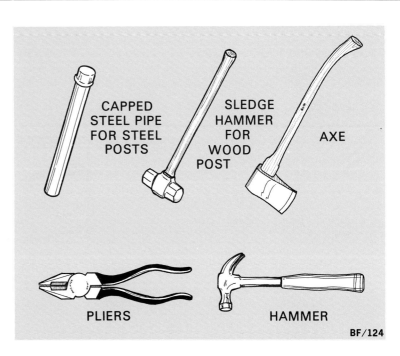

CAPPED STEEL PIPE FOR STEEL POSTS

SLEDGE HAMMER FOR WOOD POST

AXE

PLIERS

HAMMER

BF/124

## INSTALLING POSTS AND BRACES FOR ELECTRIC FENCES

To install posts and braces, proceed as follows:

1. *Use a permanent fence post if available.*

   If you have a permanent fence at one end, you may be able to use one of the line posts already installed.

PERMANENT FENCE

LINE POST TO BE USED

BF/125

2. *Sharpen post on one end and drive into ground until reasonably firm.*

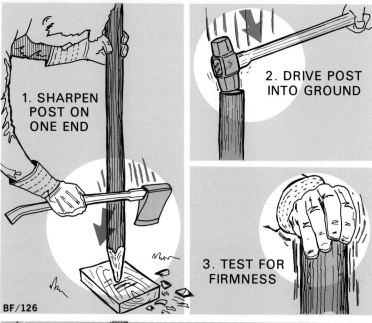

1. SHARPEN POST ON ONE END

2. DRIVE POST INTO GROUND

3. TEST FOR FIRMNESS

BF/126

3. *Cut brace to fit against top of anchor post.*

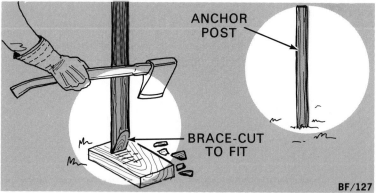

ANCHOR POST

BRACE-CUT TO FIT

BF/127

4. *Mark point where brace rests on ground.*

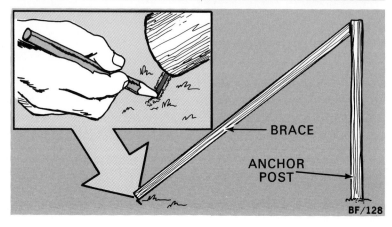

BRACE

ANCHOR POST

BF/128

5. *Set first line post on mark and drive in ground.*

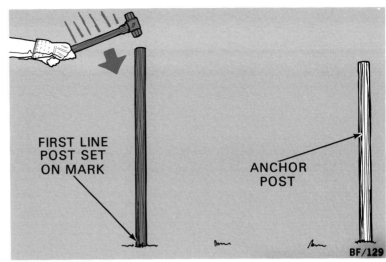

6. *Wedge brace between base of line post and top of anchor post.*

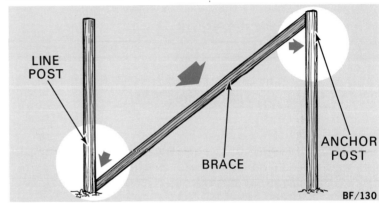

7. *Toe nail (if wood), or wire top of brace in position.*

8. *Install similar anchor-and-brace assembly at opposite end of fence.*

9. *Space line posts to fit needs of your fence and drive into ground.*

Posts can be 40′ to 50′ apart.

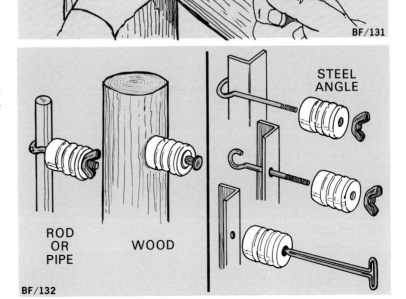

10. *Attach insulators.*

Insulator height should be about ⅔ the height of the animals to be contained—usually about as follows:

Horses and cattle, 30″ to 36″.

Large hogs, 14″ to 16″.

Pigs, 6″ to 8″.

Sheep 2 wires, 8″ and 22″.

# B. Installing Wire for Electric Fences

Wire for electric fences is generally smooth wire.

Barbed wire can be used. Hand stretching is usually sufficient.

From your study of this section you will be able to **lay out wire for the electric fence,** and **attach it to the insulators.**

Procedures for installing wire for an electric fence are given under the following headings:

1. Tools and Materials Needed.

2. Laying Wire Along Fence Line.

3. Attaching Wire to Insulators.

## TOOLS AND MATERIALS NEEDED

Claw Hammer
Pliers (wire cutting)
Line posts (small sharpened wood posts; stakes; steel posts, pipe or steel rods)
Braces (wood)
Line post insulators
Strain insulators (for ends and corners)
Special wire clips or roll of 12- or 14-gage wire (for attaching line wire to insulators)
Insulated gate handle (if gate is needed)
Barbed or smooth line wire
Insulator fasteners

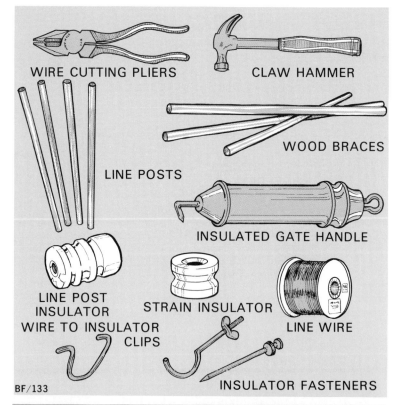

WIRE CUTTING PLIERS  CLAW HAMMER

LINE POSTS  WOOD BRACES

INSULATED GATE HANDLE

LINE POST INSULATOR

STRAIN INSULATOR

LINE WIRE

WIRE TO INSULATOR CLIPS

INSULATOR FASTENERS

BF/133

## LAYING WIRE ALONG FENCE LINE

Procedures for laying out wire are given as follows:

1. *Fasten end of wire roll to end post strain insulator.*

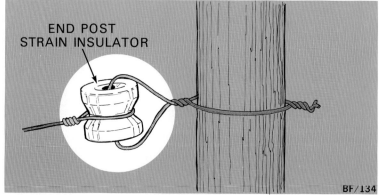

END POST STRAIN INSULATOR

BF/134

2. *Unroll wire along the fence line.*

Do not loop wire off side of roll. This makes it very difficult and dangerous to work, and creates kinks.

Be sure to use leather gloves when working with barbed wire. It will save scratching and cutting your hands which may result in serious injury.

## ATTACHING WIRE TO INSULATORS

To attach wire to insulators, proceed as follows:

1. *Pull wire by hand and attach to insulator on first line post using any one of the following procedures:*

   (a) Wrap wire around insulator, or...

   (b) Use commercial-type, line-wire clip or . . .

   (c) Use a short length of No. 12 galvanized wire, or smaller.

Stretch and attach to remaining posts in same manner.

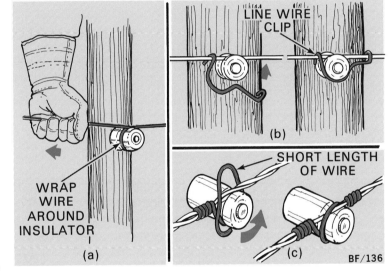

2. *Attach to strain insulator on end or corner post.*

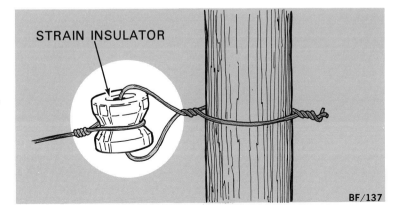

3. *Splice wire if needed.*

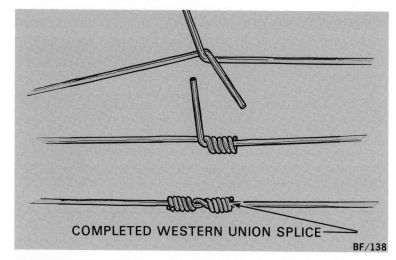

COMPLETED WESTERN UNION SPLICE

BF/138

4. *Place an extra loop of wire in sharp gullies or ditches to prevent animals from slipping under the wire.*

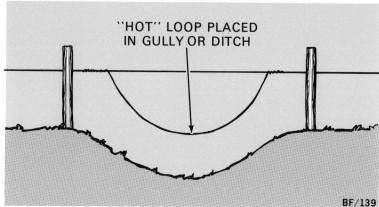

"HOT" LOOP PLACED IN GULLY OR DITCH

BF/139

5. *Attach signs*

Some states do not recognize an electric fence as a boundary or roadside fence; but where used as such, it should be plainly marked. Approval agencies state that a 4 x 8-inch yellow sign with "ELECTRIC FENCE" printed in black on both sides in letters of not less than one inch in height shall be attached to posts at intervals of not more than 200 feet.

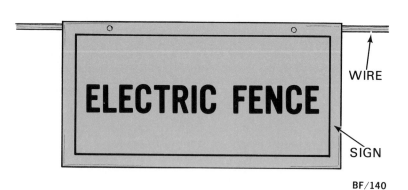

ELECTRIC FENCE

WIRE

SIGN

BF/140

# C. Building Gates For Electric Fences

For an electric fence it may be desirable or necessary to build a gate.

From your study of this section you will be able to **build an insulated gate for an electric fence.**

Building gates for electric fences are discussed under the following headings:

1. Tools and Materials Needed.
2. Building the Gate.

## TOOLS AND MATERIALS NEEDED

Pliers (wire cutting)
Line post insulators
Special wire clips or roll of 12-or 14-gage
    wire (for attaching line wire to in-
    sulators)
Screen door spring
Insulated gate handle
Barbed or smooth line wire
Fasteners (insulator)

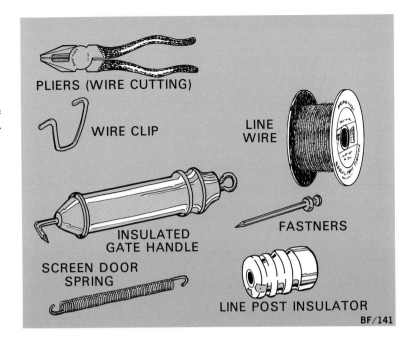

## BUILDING THE GATE

To construct an insulated gate for an
electric fence, proceed as follows:

1. *Attach line post insulator to end post.*

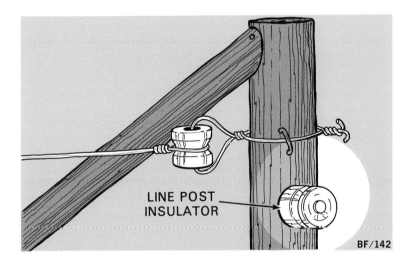

2. *Splice barbed (or smooth) wire to line
wire.*

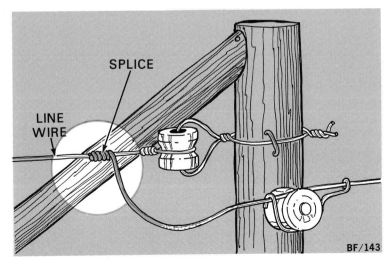

137

3. *Form about 6-inch loop in wire and attach screen door spring.*

Some gate hooks are equipped with a spring. If yours is of this type, omit this step.

4. *Repeat steps 1 and 2 at opposite post.*

Allow enough extra wire to more than reach across gate width.

5. *Attach wire to gate hook.*

Attach so spring will put small amount of tension in gate wire when handle is hooked to loop.

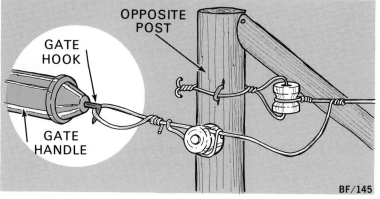

# XII. Building Cable Fences.

Cable fences are used in high confinement areas for livestock. They may be used for cattle holding pens, feed lots, and horse corrals. Cable fences are expensive at first but are very durable and relatively maintenance free.

From your study of this section you will be able to **lay out cable fence lines, install cable fence springs,** and **stretch the cable** and **secure it.**

Procedures for installing cable fences are given under the following headings:

A. Laying Out Fence Lines.

B. Installing Posts.

C. Installing and Stretching Cables and Springs.

## A. Laying Out Fence Lines

(Follow procedures under "IX. Laying Out and Clearing Fence Lines.")

## B. Installing Posts

Use heavy wood or steel posts. Corner post should be 6″ top diameter, pressure treated wood (9′ long for a 5′ fence - 10′ long for a 6′ fence). Or if steel posts are preferred, use 3″ outside diameter galvanized steel pipe set in concrete (7′-6″ long for 5′ fence and 8′-6″ long for 6′ fence).

Line posts should be either 5″ top diameter, treated wood (8′ long for 5′ fence) or 6″ top diameter treated wood (9′ long for 6′ fence). If steel posts are used, a 3″ outside diameter galvanized steel pipe should be used.

(For installing wood posts, follow procedures under "X. A. Installing Braces and Wood Posts." For installing steel posts, follow procedures under "X. B. Installing Braces and Steel Posts.")

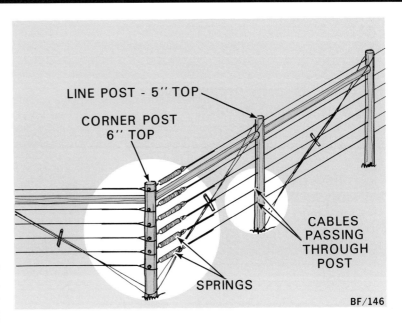

LINE POST - 5″ TOP

CORNER POST 6″ TOP

CABLES PASSING THROUGH POST

SPRINGS

BF/146

# C. Installing and Stretching Cables and Springs

Cables are heavy and require quite a bit of tension. They are not fastened to each line post. They are fastened to corner post with a tension spring installed at one end.

From your study of this section you will be able to **stretch** and **install the cables.**

Procedures are discussed under the following headings:

1. Tools and Materials Needed.

2. Installing and Stretching the Cable and Spring.

## TOOLS AND MATERIALS NEEDED

Cable stretcher
Adjustable wrench
Drill or brace and bits
Drill bits, $\frac{1}{2}$" and 9/16"
5" or 7" eye bolts
$\frac{3}{8}$" wire rope thimbles
Cable fence springs
$\frac{3}{8}$" wire rope
$\frac{3}{8}$" cable clamps

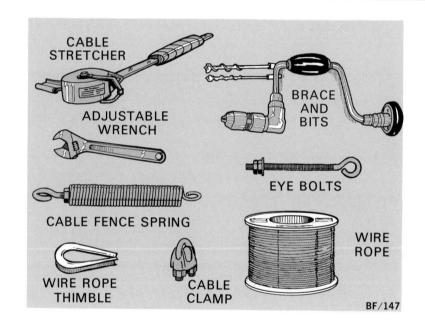

## INSTALLING AND STRETCHING THE CABLE AND SPRING

Proceed as follows:

1. *Mark posts for drilling holes.*

   Cables should be the following heights from the feed lot surface:

   16", $23\frac{1}{2}$, 31", $38\frac{1}{2}$", 46", and 57".

   Measure the corner posts and stretch a string between them at the 57" height.

   Measure the distances of the remaining holes from the top string:

   11", $7\frac{1}{2}$", $7\frac{1}{2}$", $7\frac{1}{2}$", and $7\frac{1}{2}$".

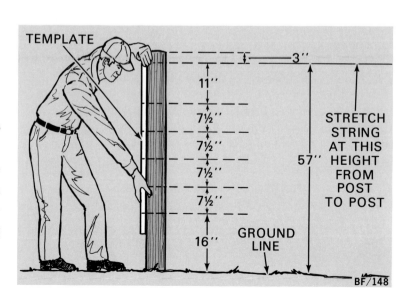

2. *Drill holes in posts.*

For wood posts, drill 9/16″ holes in corner posts parallel to fence for eye bolts. Drill ½″ hole in line posts to thread cable through — parallel to fence.

For steel posts, drill ⅜-inch holes parallel to fence in corner posts, for eyebolts. Drill ⅜-inch holes in line posts at right angles to fence for eye-bolts.

(For steel posts, it is recommended that the posts be marked for the holes and that the holes be drilled in the shop before going to the site.)

3. *Thread the cable through the holes or eye bolts.*

Insert the eye bolt into the corner post with the threaded end pointed away from the enclosure.

Place a flat washer and two nuts on the threaded end of the eye bolt.

4. *Hook spring into the eye bolt at the corner of the fence.*

5. *Make a loop in the cable at the spring end by bending the cable around the ⅜″ thimble.*

DRILL HOLE THROUGH POST

DRILL BIT

BF/149

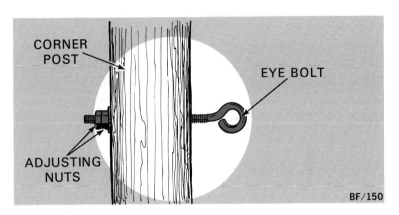

CORNER POST

EYE BOLT

ADJUSTING NUTS

BF/150

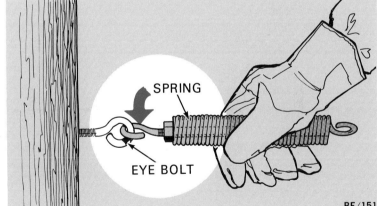

SPRING

EYE BOLT

BF/151

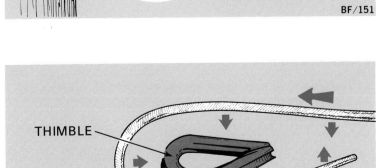

THIMBLE

LOOP IN CABLE

BF/152

6. *Secure the loop by installing two ⅜″ cable clamps.*

   Be sure the tightening nuts are on the long strand. Tighten the nuts on the cable clamps.

7. *Hook the loop just completed to the spring.*

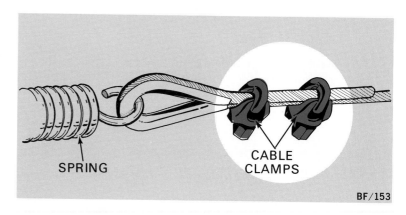

SPRING

CABLE CLAMPS

BF/153

8. *Go to the other end of the fence line and attach the cable stretcher to the corner post and to the cable.*

   Stretch the cable until the spring hooked to the cable begins to open.

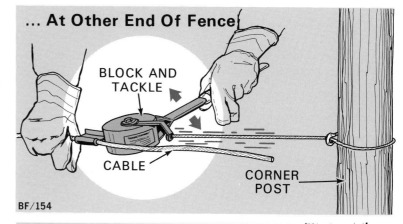

**... At Other End Of Fence**

BLOCK AND TACKLE

CABLE

CORNER POST

BF/154

9. *With the cable tight, wrap the loose end of the cable around the terminal post.*

   Secure the cable as in step 6 with cable clamps. Remove the cable stretcher.

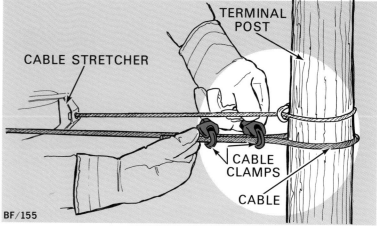

TERMINAL POST

CABLE STRETCHER

CABLE CLAMPS

CABLE

BF/155

10. *Adjust tension on the cable.*

    Tighten or loosen cable spring by adjusting the two nuts on the eye bolt. The spring should just start to open for the proper tension.

11. *Repeat the above steps on all cables.*

CHECK SPRING TENSION

ADJUST TWO EYE BOLT NUTS

BF/156

142

# XIII. Building Welded-Wire Panel Fences.

Welded wire fences are used to enclose farm animals in feed lots and stockades where the animals are in close confinement. The 16-foot-long panels are constructed of one-quarter inch steel wire running both vertical and horizontal. The vertical wires are on 8-inch centers. Horizontal wires are on either two-or four-inch centers depending upon the use of the fence.

The wires are welded at the intersections making the panel rigid and quite strong. The panels are completely self-supporting. Hog panels are generally 34 inches high while cattle and combination panels are 52 inches high.

Procedures for building a welded wire panel fence are given under the following heading:

A. Laying Out Fence Lines and Installing Posts.

B. Hanging and Fastening Panels.

# A. Laying Out Fence Lines and Installing Posts

Heavy treated wood posts are recommended. A minimum diameter of 5″ at the top and a minimum length of 8′ is recommended. No corner braces are needed with this type fence. Posts are usually set in concrete.

From your study of this section you will be able to **lay out the fence line** and **install the posts.**

Procedures for laying out fence lines and setting posts for welded wire panel fences are given under the following headings:

1. Tools and Materials Needed.

2. Laying Out the Fence Line.

3. Installing the Posts.

## TOOLS AND MATERIALS NEEDED

Post hole digger or auger
Tamping bar
Shovel
Axe
Stakes
String
Wood posts
Cement
Sand
Crushed stone or gravel
Water
Steel tape

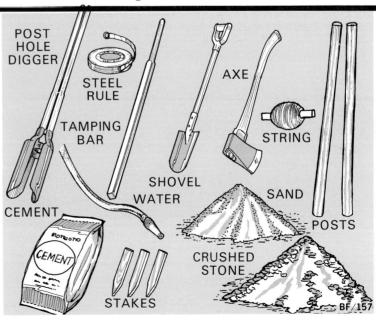

POST HOLE DIGGER

STEEL RULE

AXE

TAMPING BAR

STRING

SHOVEL

WATER

SAND

CEMENT

POSTS

CRUSHED STONE

STAKES

BF/157

## LAYING OUT THE FENCE LINE

Proceed as follows:

1. *Drive stake at one corner.*

   If fence is to be connected to a building, start at the building.

2. *Measure from the first stake to the next corner stake.*

   Use a steel tape. Align the fence with the building.

   Make the distance equally divisible by 16 feet if possible. The panels are difficult to cut.

3. *Drive a stake.*

4. *Proceed to the other corners and drive stakes.*

5. *Check to see if the lot is square or rectangular.*

   Measure the distance between corners (diagonally).

   The diagonal distances should be the same.

6. *Stretch a string between the corner stakes for aligning posts.*

7. *Measure increments of 8 feet, or 5⅓ feet and drive stakes for post holes.*

## INSTALLING THE POSTS

Proceed as follows:

1. *Dig post holes.*

   It is important that you dig the holes at the exact spot because the panel length cannot be altered. The usual procedure of placing the fence on the inside of the posts has one exception at each corner. Since stockade panels can-

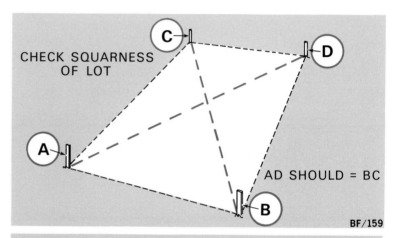

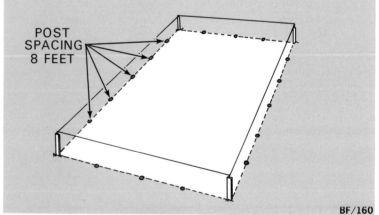

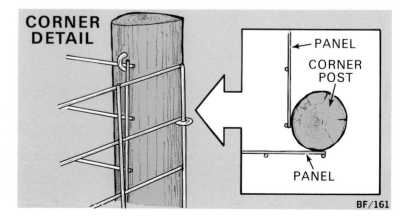

not be crossed at corners, it is necessary to place corner posts on the outside of one line of fence and inside of the other.

2. *Set the post and re-check distance.*

3. *Pour concrete around posts.*

Be careful not to move the posts out of line.

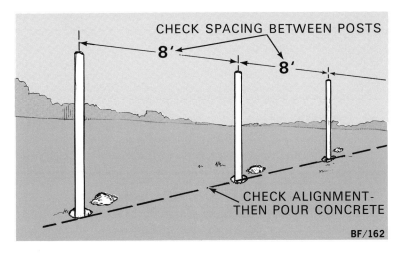

CHECK SPACING BETWEEN POSTS

8'  8'

CHECK ALIGNMENT—THEN POUR CONCRETE

BF/162

# B. Hanging and Fastening Panels

Hanging the panels is easy, if the posts are set in the proper position.

From this section you will be able to **hang the panels** on the posts and **fasten them to the posts.**

Hanging and fastening panels are discussed under the following headings:

1. Tools and Materials Needed.
2. Hanging the Panels.
3. Fastening the Panels to the Posts

## TOOLS AND MATERIALS NEEDED

Claw hammer
10d nails
Adjustable end wrench
J bolts ⅜″ x 7″, nuts and washers
Brace and bit, ⅜″ diameter
Welded wire panels, ¼″ wire welded in 16′ - long panels,
    34 inches high for hogs,
    52 inches high for cows.

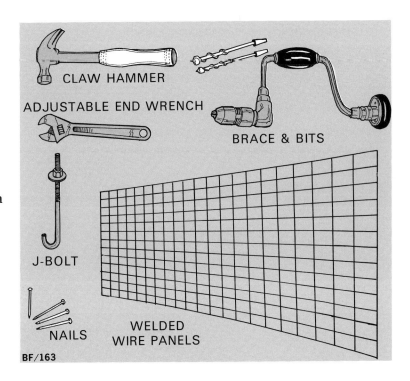

CLAW HAMMER
ADJUSTABLE END WRENCH
BRACE & BITS
J-BOLT
NAILS
WELDED WIRE PANELS

BF/163

## HANGING THE PANELS

Proceed as follows:

1. *Drive nails near top of posts where the panels meet.*

   Drive nails so that the panel will hang 6 inches off the ground.

   Note: Be sure to place panel on the inside of the line posts. On corner posts, place one panel on the inside of the post and the other panel on the outside of the post.

TOP OF POST

NAIL

AREA WHERE PANELS MEET

BF/164

2. *Hang the panels loosely on the nails and position the panels.*

   Turn the vertical wires on the first panel to the inside. Turn the vertical wires on the second panel to the outside. Continue alternating the panels in this manner along the entire fence.

   Mark each post at the top, center, and bottom horizontal wire to locate holes for the J-bolt fasteners. Place the mark at the intersection of the vertical and horizontal wire.

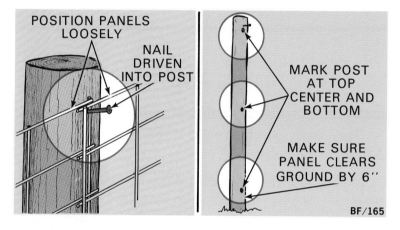

POSITION PANELS LOOSELY

NAIL DRIVEN INTO POST

MARK POST AT TOP CENTER AND BOTTOM

MAKE SURE PANEL CLEARS GROUND BY 6"

BF/165

3. *On sloping land, step down adjacent panels one horizontal wire.*

   Small variations in slope can be accommodated by tilting the panel slightly.

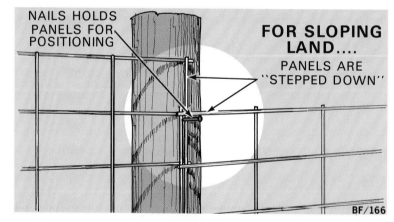

NAILS HOLDS PANELS FOR POSITIONING

FOR SLOPING LAND....

PANELS ARE "STEPPED DOWN"

BF/166

## FASTENING THE PANELS TO THE POSTS

Proceed as follows:

1. *Drill a ⅜" hole for each fastener.*

   Place one at the top, center, and bottom of each post.

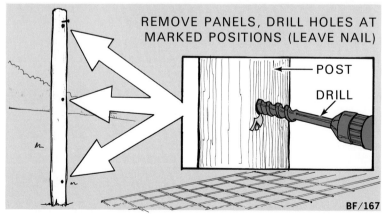

REMOVE PANELS, DRILL HOLES AT MARKED POSITIONS (LEAVE NAIL)

POST

DRILL

BF/167

2. *Notch the post over the hole on the outside to give a flat surface for the washer that goes over the bolt.*

3. *Place the J-bolts into the holes.*

   Alternate hooking the J-bolts to the vertical and horizontal wires.

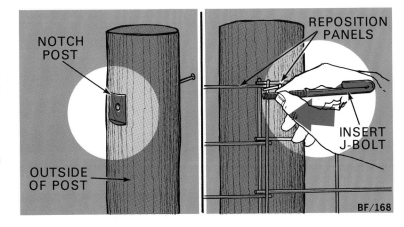

4. *Firmly imbed the hook end of the J-bolt into the wood post with a sharp blow of the hammer.*

5. *Place a washer over the threaded end of the bolt.*

   Thread the nut on the bolt and tighten securely with the wrench.

6. *Cut projecting ends of bolts off.*

   To do this, score with a chisel or hack saw and break off with a hammer.

7. *Hang and fasten remaining panels using same procedures.*

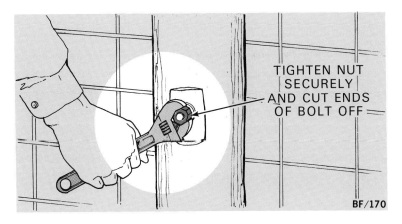

# XIV. Building Board Fences.

Board fences can be built in a wide variety of designs. Two of the more popular designs—the diamond panel and straight panel—are explained in the procedures that follow.

You can vary these designs if you wish by increasing or decreasing the number of boards, the width of the boards and the spacing between them.

Building board fences is discussed under the following headings:

A. Installing Posts and Braces.

B. Installing Boards.

## A. Installing Posts and Braces

For board fences, corner anchors and braces are not necessary as in wire fences.

From your study of this section, you will be able to **install posts** and **attach boards to the posts.**

Installing posts is discussed under the following headings:

1. Tools and Materials Needed.

2. Staking Out the Fence Line.

3. Installing the Posts.

### TOOLS AND MATERIALS NEEDED

Round pointed shovel
Post hole digger
Tamping bar
Carpenter's level
Six-foot rule
Heavy cord
Gage pole (for post spacing)
Posts, 4" x 4" x 7' (or ½-round, or split, posts with 4" flat face)
(Use 8' posts for barn lots or corral fences)
Axe
Stakes

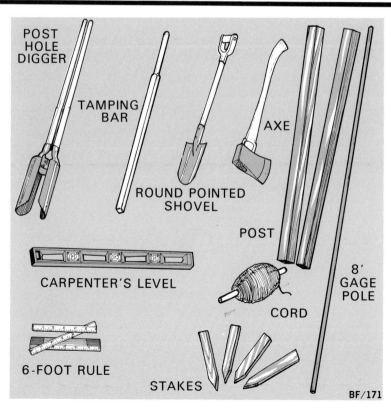

POST HOLE DIGGER

TAMPING BAR

AXE

ROUND POINTED SHOVEL

POST

8' GAGE POLE

CARPENTER'S LEVEL

CORD

6-FOOT RULE

STAKES

BF/171

## STAKING OUT THE FENCE LINE

Proceed as follows:

1. *Drive stake at each end of proposed fence line and stretch cord between stakes.*

   If your fence is to have a slight curve, outline curve with additional stakes. If your fence is to be angular, drive additional stakes at corners.

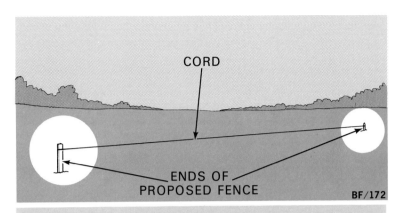

CORD

ENDS OF PROPOSED FENCE

BF/172

2. *Measure off post spacings.*

   The spacing between your first two posts should be about 7' 10" from post center to post center. That allows your 8-foot boards to extend across the face of the end post to the center of the second post.

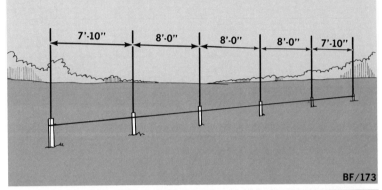

7'-10"  8'-0"  8'-0"  8'-0"  7'-10"

BF/173

3. *Using the 8' gage pole for rest of spacing, drive stake, or make mark in ground, next to string.*

   If your post spacing does not come out even, shorten post spacings from 6 to 12 inches at one end until provision is made for last panel to be almost full length.

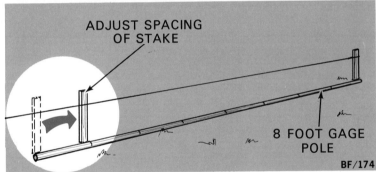

ADJUST SPACING OF STAKE

8 FOOT GAGE POLE

BF/174

## INSTALLING THE POSTS

Proceed as follows:

1. *Dig hole approximately 2½ feet deep, for 7-foot end post.*

   Be sure there is enough post above ground for the height of fence you have planned, plus about one inch. A 2½-foot setting will leave about one inch. Extra length allows for minor irregularities in height of fence.

   Fences are generally about 50" to 60" high.

2. *Place post in ground with flat surface on side where boards will be nailed.*

3. *Set post.*

   Tamp dirt firmly around post, checking occasionally with level to make sure post is plumb.

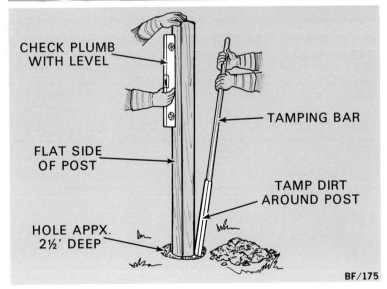

CHECK PLUMB WITH LEVEL

TAMPING BAR

FLAT SIDE OF POST

TAMP DIRT AROUND POST

HOLE APPX. 2½' DEEP

BF/175

4. *Set other end post in same manner.*

5. *Set a line post on each major rise or depression.*

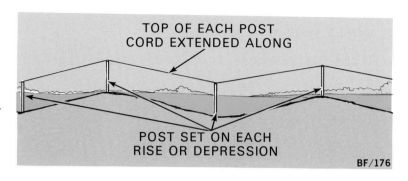

TOP OF EACH POST
CORD EXTENDED ALONG

POST SET ON EACH
RISE OR DEPRESSION

BF/176

6. *Extend cord along top of each post.*

7. *Set remaining posts so that top edge of post touches string.*

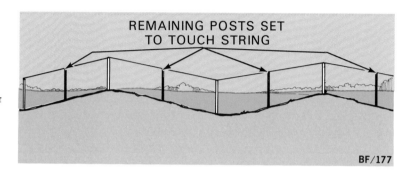

REMAINING POSTS SET
TO TOUCH STRING

BF/177

# B. Installing Boards

Boards are nailed to post end to end.

From this discussion you will be able to **lay out boards, saw them to the correct length,** and **nail them to the post.**

Installing boards are discussed under the following heading:

1. Tools and Materials Needed.
2. Laying Out, Sawing and Attaching Boards to Posts.

## TOOLS AND MATERIALS NEEDED

Hand saw or power saw
Claw hammer
Try square
Pencil
Boards
For two 8-foot fence panels
(16 feet long):
½ lb. 10-penny common nails (preferably galvanized)

Straight Panel:
    4 pcs. 1″ x 6″ (for barn lots or corrals use 2″ x 6″) x 16′
    (If top fascia board is used, add one more board)

Diamond Panel:
    3 pcs. 1″ x 6″ x 16′
    4 pcs. 1″ x 4″ x 10′ for cross members.
    2 pcs. 1″ x 4″ x 3′5″ vertical fascia boards

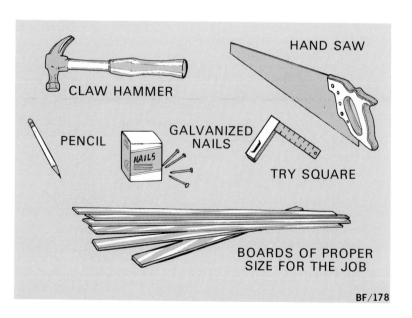

HAND SAW

CLAW HAMMER

PENCIL

NAILS

GALVANIZED
NAILS

TRY SQUARE

BOARDS OF PROPER
SIZE FOR THE JOB

BF/178

## LAYING OUT, SAWING AND ATTACHING BOARDS TO POSTS

1. *Lay out boards along fence line.*

   Place the correct number of boards for each panel. Do not stack them against the post. They will get in the way of installation.

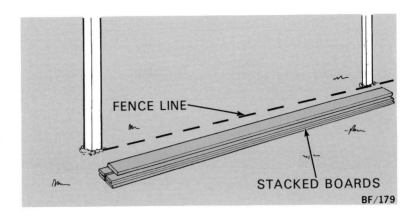

2. *Place 16-ft, board (6″ width) at top of first two spans for rough measurement and mark for sawing.*

   Board should be even with outer edge of end post and extend to center of third post. With other line posts, measurement is taken from center to center.

3. *Saw ends of board.*

   Since joints between ends of boards will be covered with a finishing (fascia) board, a close fit is not necessary.

4. *Apply wood preservative generously to freshly cut surfaces if using treated lumber.*

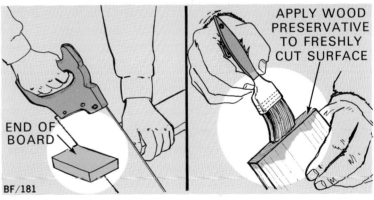

5. *Nail board to all three posts with at least two nails in each post. (Three nails are better.)*

   Stagger nails to avoid splitting.

**6.** *Measure second board from first post to center of second post.*

The second and fourth boards are only one panel long at the start. This keeps from having all of the joints on one post and none on the next. This arrangement saves construction time and makes a stronger fence.

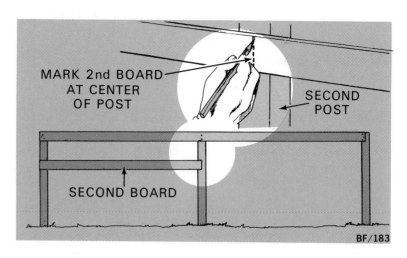

**7.** *Space and nail board.*

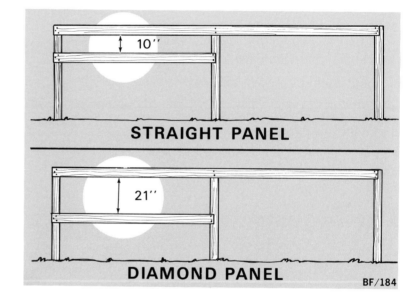

**8.** *Measure, saw (apply preservative) and nail remaining boards in same manner.*

Measurements are based on boards 6 inches wide. Narrower boards will require wider spacings.

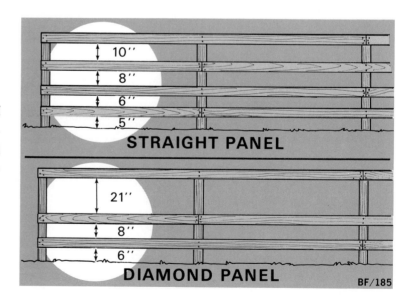

152

If you are installing a diamond panel:

(1) *Place 4-inch board in position on fence and mark for sawing.*

(2) *Saw as marked.*

(3) *Paint preservative generously on freshly cut surface if using treated lumber.*

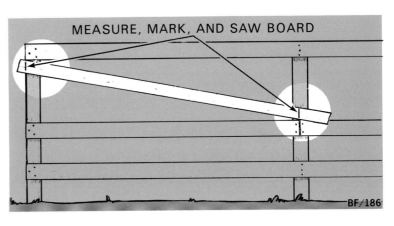

MEASURE, MARK, AND SAW BOARD

BF/186

(4) *Nail boards in position.*

(5) *Measure, saw (apply preservative) and nail remaining boards in same manner.*

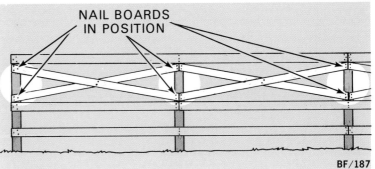

NAIL BOARDS IN POSITION

BF/187

9. *Install fascia boards.*

Fascia boards are mostly for improving overall appearance. However, the top fascia board can be of value in protecting and strengthening the top of your fence if used around a horse pasture.

(1) *Saw top of posts even with top board.*

If top fascia board is used, bevel top of post slightly so it will slope toward side where boards are attached.

(2) *Apply preservative generously to top of post.*

(3) *Place top (16-ft.) fascia board (if used) on top of posts and mark for saw lines.*

Plan to stagger fascia-board joints so that both don't come on same post.

(4) *Square and saw ends.*

(5) *Nail board in position.*

Board should overlap both top fence board and end of vertical fascia board.

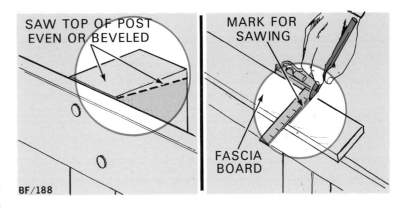

SAW TOP OF POST EVEN OR BEVELED

MARK FOR SAWING

FASCIA BOARD

BF/188

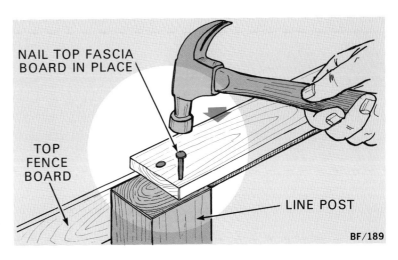

NAIL TOP FASCIA BOARD IN PLACE

TOP FENCE BOARD

LINE POST

BF/189

153

(6) *Measure and mark vertical fascia board.*

(7) *Square and saw board.*

(8) *Apply preservative generously to freshly cut surface.*

(9) *Nail in position.*

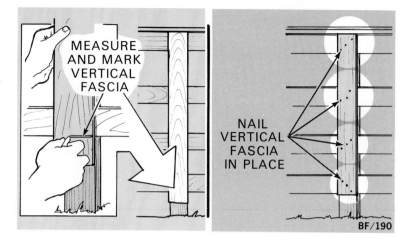

154

Wood rail fences are popular with many home owners who have limited acreage. Some fences consist of split wood rails stacked atop each other. Adjacent sections are set at an angle giving a zig-zag shape. The rails are stacked to the height desired.

Fences consisting of two or three rails supported by posts are quite popular. These are usually chosen for their charm. The distance between the posts vary from 8' to 16'.

Building wood rail fences are discussed under the following headings:

A. Installing Posts and Rails.

B. Installing Zig-Zag Rail Fences.

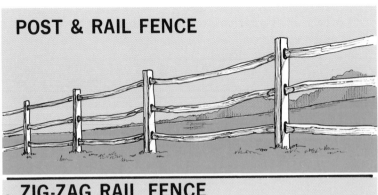

**POST & RAIL FENCE**

**ZIG-ZAG RAIL FENCE**

BF/191

# A. Installing Posts and Rails

A post and rail fence does not require as many rails as an all rail fence.

From your study of this section, you will be able to **drill holes in posts for inserting rails, taper ends of rails** and **set the posts and rails.**

Installing posts and rails are discussed under the following headings:

1. Tools and Materials Needed.

2. Staking Out Fence Line.

3. Drilling Holes in Posts.

4. Tapering Rail Ends.

5. Setting Posts and Rails.

## TOOLS AND MATERIALS NEEDED

Round pointed shovel
Post hole digger
Tamping bar
Carpenter's level
Six-foot rule
Heavy cord
Gage pole (for post spacing)
Large wood drill
Large wood chisel or rasp
Materials for a two rail fence span:
    Two post 6"-8" diameter
    Two rails approximately 5" diameter
    4-16 d. nails
For a three-rail fence:
    Add 1 rail and 2-16d nails.

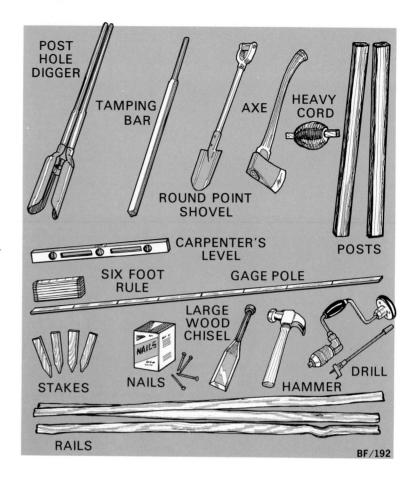

## STAKING OUT FENCE LINE

To stake out fence line, proceed as follows:

1. *Drive stake at each end of proposed fence line and stretch cord between stakes.*

If your fence is to have a slight curve, outline curve with additional stakes. If your fence is to be angular, drive additional stakes at corners.

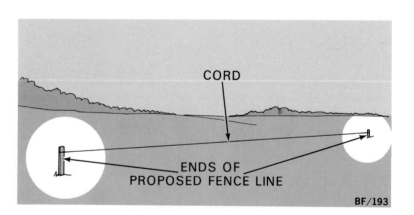

2. *Measure off post spacings.*

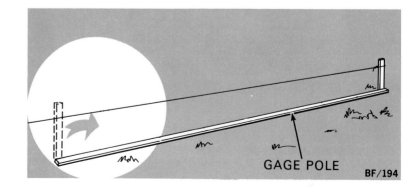

3. *Using gage stick for rest of spacing, drive stake, or make mark in ground, next to string.*

If your post spacing does not come out even, shorten post spacings from 6 to 12 inches at one end until provision is made for last span to be almost full length.

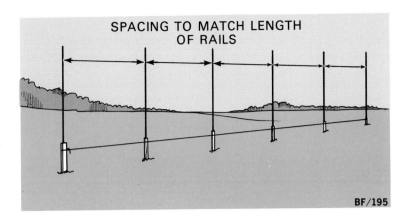

SPACING TO MATCH LENGTH OF RAILS

BF/195

## DRILLING HOLES IN POSTS

To drill holes in posts, proceed as follows:

1. *Locate place for drilling holes.*

Determine where you will need holes in your posts. Plan to insert about $2\frac{1}{2}'$ of post into ground. Space the rails so that you have about as much space between the ground and the first rail as you have between rails. Allow the post to extend about 6 inches above the top of the top rail.

Be sure to keep all holes in the same post in line.

Note: *Use your largest posts for corners.*

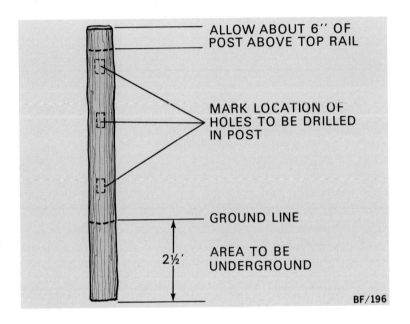

ALLOW ABOUT 6" OF POST ABOVE TOP RAIL

MARK LOCATION OF HOLES TO BE DRILLED IN POST

GROUND LINE

AREA TO BE UNDERGROUND

$2\frac{1}{2}'$

BF/196

2. *Drill holes in posts.*

Make holes through the post large enough to accept over-lapped rails.

Start the hole by drilling circular holes.

POST

DRILLED HOLES

MARKS TO DRILL HOLES BY

DRILL

BF/197

3. *Chisel out hole to accommodate rail.*

Smooth uneven sides with wood chisel or wood rasp. Corner posts will have two holes drilled at 90 degrees to each other at each rail position. Do not drill all the way through the post. End posts are not drilled all the way through.

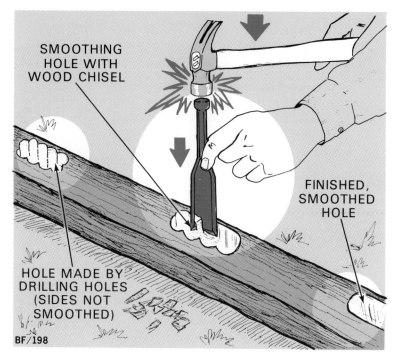

SMOOTHING HOLE WITH WOOD CHISEL

FINISHED, SMOOTHED HOLE

HOLE MADE BY DRILLING HOLES (SIDES NOT SMOOTHED)

BF/198

## TAPERING RAIL ENDS

To taper rail ends, proceed as follows:

1. *Mark end of rail to approximate size of hole in post.*

2. *Taper rail*

   With the axe, taper the end of the rail to about 1½ to 2″ across, starting about 10″ from the end of the rail. Trim from both sides of the rail along the vertical face. Be sure the rail is trimmed on both ends so the trimmed faces are in line.

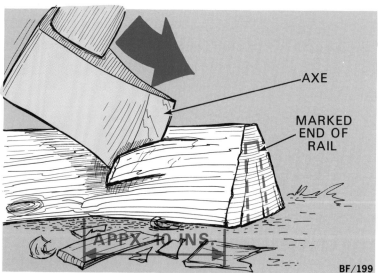

AXE

MARKED END OF RAIL

APPX. 10 INS.

BF/199

## SETTING POSTS AND RAILS

To set posts and rails, proceed as follows:

1. *Dig hole approximately 2½′ deep, for a 7′ end post.*

   Set the end post with the slots turned in the direction of the fence line.

2. *Plumb the post and tamp while back filling the hole.*

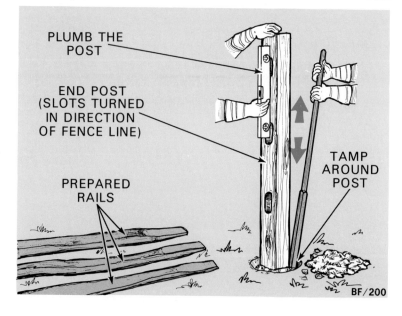

PLUMB THE POST

END POST (SLOTS TURNED IN DIRECTION OF FENCE LINE)

PREPARED RAILS

TAMP AROUND POST

BF/200

3. *Insert rails loosely into end post and locate next post hole.*

4. *Dig the next post hole, insert the post and slide the rails into the slots.*

5. *Plumb the post and back fill, being sure to tamp the soil around the post.*

6. *Secure the rails in position by nailing through the side of the post.*

# B. Installing Zig-Zag Rail Fences

The zig-zag rail fence (Virginia or stacked split rail) is one that is easy to build. Generally, it is not used for containing animals any longer. It is used for decorative purposes.

From your study of this section you will be able to *stack rails in a zig-zag pattern* that will be sturdy and have a pleasing appearance.

Installing rail fences is discussed under the following headings:

1. Tools and Materials Needed.

2. Staking Out Fence Lines.

3. Stacking Rails.

## TOOLS AND MATERIALS NEEDED

Axe
2' stakes
Cord
Rails
Chalk
5' stakes
Tape

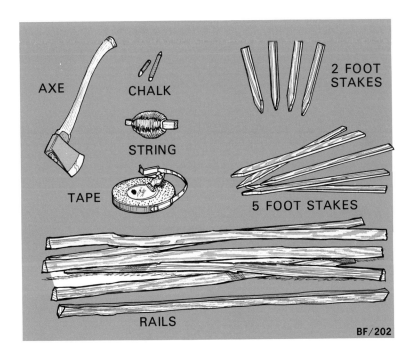

## STAKING OUT FENCE LINES

To stake out fence lines, proceed as follows:

1. *Determine the critical boundary of one side of the fence.*

   You may be building the fence along a property line, a hedge row, or a wooded area.

2. *Clear fence area.*

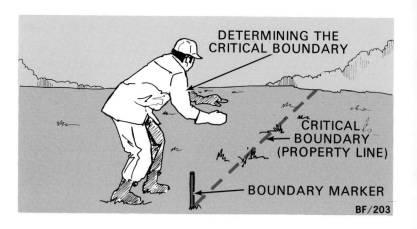

DETERMINING THE CRITICAL BOUNDARY

CRITICAL BOUNDARY (PROPERTY LINE)

BOUNDARY MARKER

BF/203

3. *Drive stakes one foot inside critical boundary of fence line.*

   This is to allow for overhang of rail ends.

4. *Stretch a cord between the stakes.*

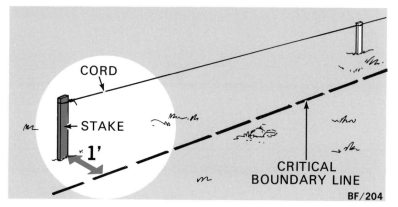

CORD

STAKE

1'

CRITICAL BOUNDARY LINE

BF/204

5. *Establish the width of the fence.*

   (1) *Measure average length of rails.*

   (2) *Subtract two feet.*

   This is the "effective" length of the rail. it provides for overhang when stacked.

   (3) *Divide by two.*

   For example, if your rails are 12 feet long, the width of the fence line would be 5 feet.

   $$\frac{12-2}{2} = 5 \text{ feet}$$

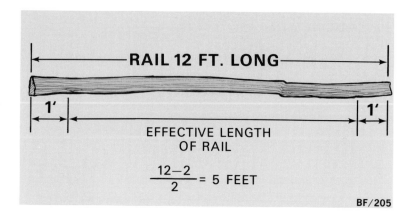

**RAIL 12 FT. LONG**

1'    1'

EFFECTIVE LENGTH OF RAIL

$$\frac{12-2}{2} = 5 \text{ FEET}$$

BF/205

This is the minimum width for stacking rails without support. You can extend the width to ⅔ of the "effective" length of the rails. If you make the width narrower, use posts or stakes to support it. The fence will be stronger, but it will require more rails.

6. *Drive stakes along the second fence boundary opposite the line established in steps 3 and 4.*

7. *Stretch a cord between the stakes in step 6.*

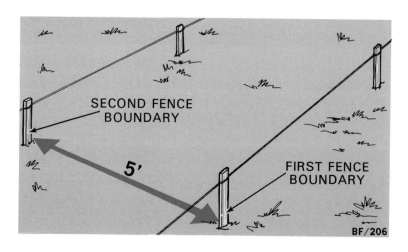

SECOND FENCE BOUNDARY

5'

FIRST FENCE BOUNDARY

BF/206

## STACKING RAILS

Lay out bottom rails first. Proceed as follows:

1. *Mark rails one foot from each end.*

   Starting at one end of the fence, lay the first rail.

2. *Lay rail on one cord line at the point marked.*

3. *Lay rail on the opposite cord line at the point marked on that end.*

4. *Lay the second rail over the first rail at the point marked.*

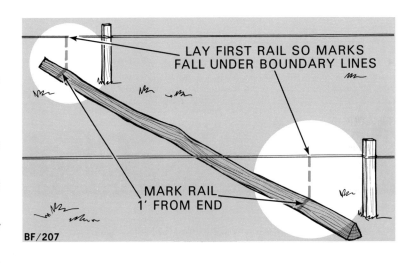

LAY FIRST RAIL SO MARKS FALL UNDER BOUNDARY LINES

MARK RAIL 1' FROM END

BF/207

5. *Lay the other end of the second rail on the opposite line at the point marked.*

6. *Continue laying bottom rails in the same manner.*

7. *Drive 5 foot stakes in the outside of the crossover points.*

   Plumb stakes. These are to be used as guides when stacking the rails.

8. *Stack remaining rails.*

   Overlay ends at crossover points.

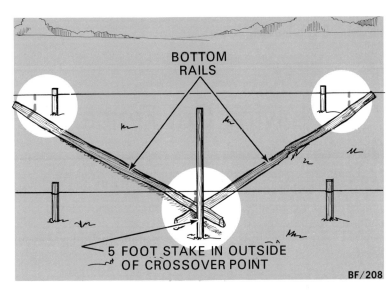

BOTTOM RAILS

5 FOOT STAKE IN OUTSIDE OF CROSSOVER POINT

BF/208

# XVI. Building Chain Link Fences.

Chain link fencing is used extensively for security and containment of small animals. It gives a good appearance and it is relatively easy to install. Usually the fencing fabric is supported on round metal posts with metal rails along the top of the fence. Security fences have from one to four strands of barbed wire on top of the fencing fabric.

Procedures for installing chain link fences are given under the following headings:

A. Laying Out Fence Lines and Setting Posts.

B. Stretching Fencing Fabric and Attaching It To Posts.

# A. Laying Out Fence Lines and Setting Posts

Chain link fences are frequently used in highly populated and extensively developed areas where fences must be located along the property line. The concrete foundation, if used, for the metal posts is located within the property of the person building the fence. This makes it necessary to offset the fence line six inches inside the property line. Accurate placement of all posts requires a string line to be run along the property lines. The string line is extended past the fence corner end a short distance so it can remain intact while the fence is being constructed.

From your study of this section you will be able to **lay out the fence lines** and **set the posts.**

The procedures are described under the following headings:

1. Tools and Materials Needed.
2. Laying Out the Fence Line.
3. Setting the Posts.

## TOOLS AND MATERIALS NEEDED

Post hole digger or auger
Tamping bar
Carpenters level
Axe
Stakes
String
For concrete settings:
    Gravel
    Sand
    Cement
For driven posts:
    Steel anchors
    Post driver
    Sledge hammer
Posts (see table)

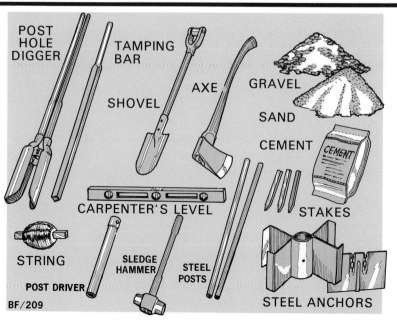

| POST HEIGHT IN RELATION TO FENCE HEIGHT | | |
| --- | --- | --- |
| Fence Height (Inches) | Terminal Post Height* | Line Post Height |
| 36 | 38 | 34 |
| 42 | 44 | 40 |
| 48 | 50 | 46 |
| 60 | 62 | 58 |
| 72 | 74 | 70 |

*Terminal posts are those posts at corners and at gates, or at the end of the fence.

## LAYING OUT THE FENCE LINE

Proceed as follows:

1. *Locate property lines if fence is to be erected near one.*

2. *Drive stakes on line and stretch a string between them.*

3. *Locate the end, corners and gate.*

   Terminal posts must be located 6 inches from the property line if concrete setting is used.

   Be sure gate post locations are accurate for the dimensions of the gates.

4. *Determine the line posts locations.*

   Measure the distance between the terminal posts and divide it into equal spaces. Spacing for fences without top rails, should be a minimum of 8 feet. Minimum spacing for fences with top rails is 10 feet.

5. *Drive stakes at post locations.*

## SETTING THE POSTS

Proceed as follows:

1. *Determine the height of posts above ground.*

   The top of the terminal posts should extend two inches above the fence fabric height.

   The tops of the line posts should be about two inches below the fence fabric height.

   For example, when using 48-inch fencing, terminal post should be 50 inches above the ground. Line posts should be 46 inches above the ground.

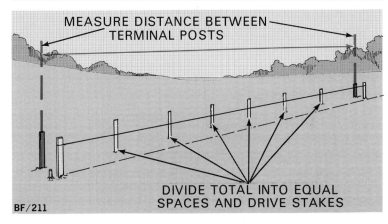

STAKE FOR TERMINAL POST
STRING
STAKE (ON PROPERTY LINE)
BF/210

MEASURE DISTANCE BETWEEN TERMINAL POSTS
DIVIDE TOTAL INTO EQUAL SPACES AND DRIVE STAKES
BF/211

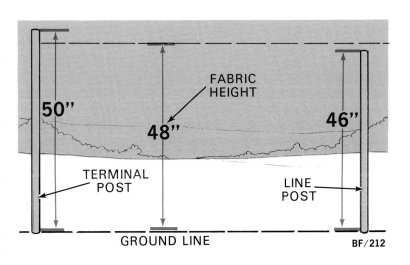

50"
48"
46"
FABRIC HEIGHT
TERMINAL POST
LINE POST
GROUND LINE
BF/212

2. *Mark each post at ground level with chalk.*

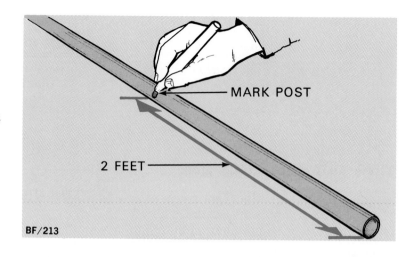

3. *Set posts.*

Two methods are given here for setting posts: (a) setting posts in concrete and (b) setting posts with steel anchors.

a. If you plan to **set your posts in concrete,** proceed as follows:

(1) *Dig post holes.*

The hole should have the same diameter at the bottom as at the **top.**

(2) *Try posts in hole to check depth to chalk mark and remove the post.*

(3) *Pour concrete to a depth of one foot.*

(4) *Set post.*

Set line posts about one-fourth inch inside a line from the outside of the terminal posts. This allows for the width of the fence fabric.

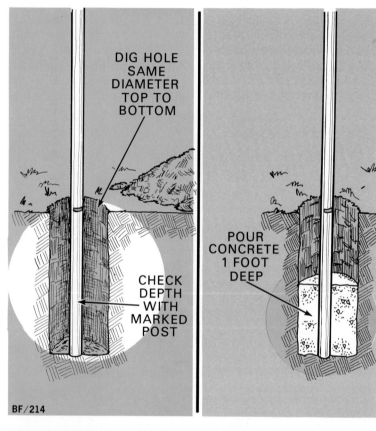

(5) *Check post for vertical alignment with a level.*

(6) *Fill hole with concrete.*

Post footings may be capped with a rich cement mortar and crowned 1½ inches above ground level at the post for water drainage.

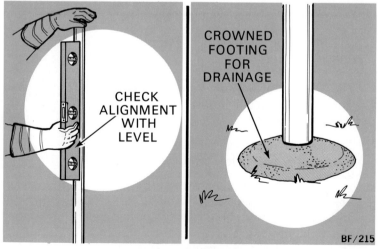

b. If you are **setting post with steel anchors,** proceed as follows;

(1) *Set steel post in position as determined by post stake.*

(2) *Place the post driver over the post.*

(3) *Start the post into the ground.*

(4) *Check post for alignment.*

Check for alignment with the fence and also for vertical alignment.

(5) *Complete driving of post.*

Drive to the chalk mark.

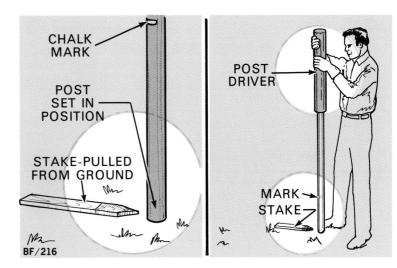

(6) *Remove soil from around post about 4 inches away from the post and 4 inches deep.*

(7) *Drop the metal locking ring over the post.*

Be careful to place the correct side up as noted on the ring.

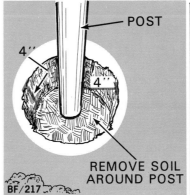
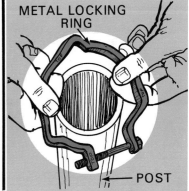

(8) *Place the three anchors straight up between the ring and the post.*

They fit in notches on the ring. Place the anchors evenly around the post with the corner of the anchors away from the posts.

(9) *Tilt each anchor away from the post as far as it will go into the lock ring notch.*

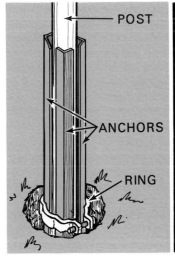
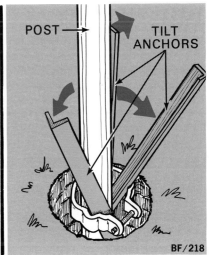

(10) *Drive anchors into the ground.*

Strike each anchor a few times with a sledge hammer and move around the post.

Sink anchors to about 1½ inches above the top of the locking ring.

(11) *Tighten the nut on the locking ring bolt.*

This locks the anchor to the post.

(12) *Cover anchor assembly with dirt.*

BF/219

# B. Stretching Fencing Fabric and Attaching It to Posts

Chain link fencing is heavy. You must have a smooth place to lay it out. Start at one end and unroll the fabric along the fence line.

From your study of this section you will be able to **stretch the fencing and fasten it to the posts.** You will **also be able to hang the gates.** The steps are given under the following headings:

1. Tools and Materials needed.

2. Preparing the Posts for Hanging Fencing Fabric.

3. Hanging, Stretching and Fastening Fencing Fabric.

4. Hanging the Gate.

## TOOLS AND MATERIALS NEEDED

Tension bands
Tie wires
Gate hinges
Gate latch
Post caps
Rail end bands
Top rail ends
Loop caps
Top rail couplings if needed
Fence stretcher and stretcher bar
Pliers
Adjustable wrench
Socket wrench and sockets to fit nuts
Hacksaw
Bolt cutters

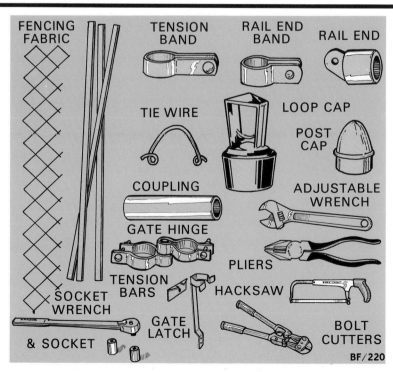

BF/220

166

## PREPARING THE POSTS FOR HANGING FENCING FABRIC

Proceed as follows:

1. *Attach tension bands to terminal posts.*

    Do not spread or distort the bands. Place them at equal distances on the posts. When a top rail is used, add a rail end band at the top of the post.

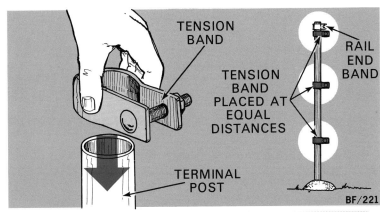

2. *Attach the rail end fittings to the rail end bands.*

    All bolt heads should be toward the outside of the fence.

3. *Install post caps.*

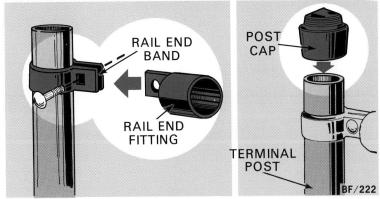

4. *Attach loop caps to top of line posts.*

    Set loop caps with the top rail hole offset toward the outside face of the top rail and line post.

5. *Thread the top rail through the loop caps.*

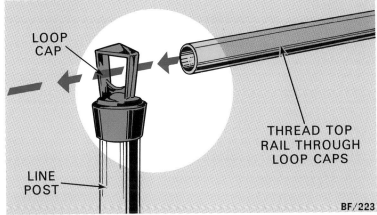

6. *Join top rail sections as needed.*

    Procedures are different for (a) swedged-end top rails and for (b) plain-end top rails.

    a. If you have **swedged-end top rails,** proceed as follows:

    Insert the male ends into the female ends of each rail. No special connection is required.

    b. If you have **plain-end joints** on top rails, proceed as follows:

    Use coupling which slides over the two end rails as they join.

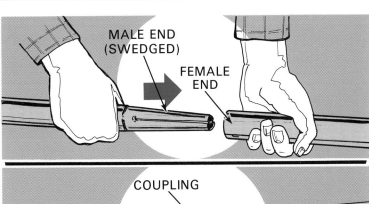

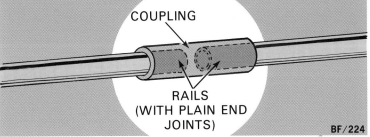

7. *Insert the end of the top rail into the recess in the rail end fitting to the terminal post.*

   If the last section of the top rail is too long to reach the rail end fitting, cut the top rail to the desired length with a hacksaw.

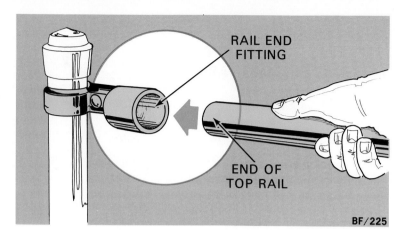

## HANGING, STRETCHING AND FASTENING FENCING FABRIC

Proceed as follows:

1. *Unroll fabric along the fence line.*

2. *Thread tension bar through the end of the fabric and the tension bands.*

   Check to be sure the tension bands are placed equal distances apart on the posts.

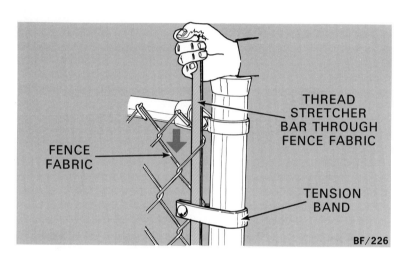

3. *Tighten bolts on the tension bands.*

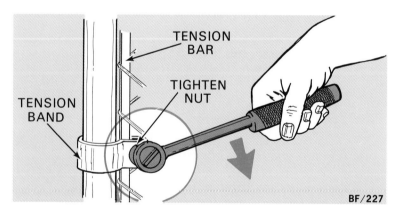

4. *Thread a stretcher bar in the fabric about two feet from the terminal post at the opposite end of the fence line.*

5. *Attach the fabric to the top rail with a loose tie wire between each line post.*

   These tie wires support the fabric while it is being pulled tight.

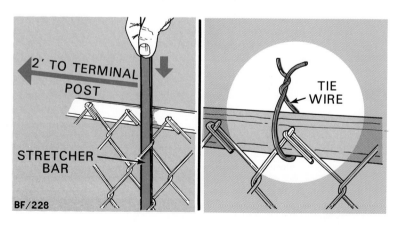

168

6. *Attach the stretcher.*

7. *Apply sufficient tension to pull the wires taught without distorting the diamond shape in the fence weave.*

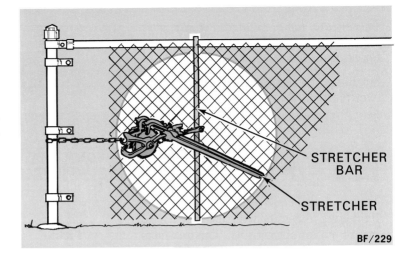

STRETCHER BAR

STRETCHER

BF/229

8. *Cut the fabric to the proper length.*

   This is done by straightening out the end of a wire (called a picket) and unscrewing it.

9. *Thread a tension bar through the end of the fabric and the tension bands previously installed on the terminal posts.*

10. *Tighten bolts on tension bands.*

11. *Release tension on the stretcher.*

12. *Repeat the above process until all sections of the fence are installed.*

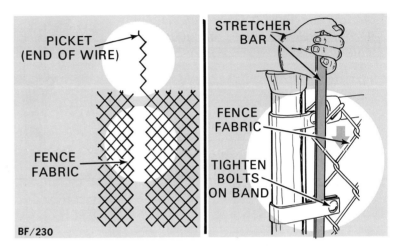

PICKET (END OF WIRE)

FENCE FABRIC

BF/230

STRETCHER BAR

FENCE FABRIC

TIGHTEN BOLTS ON BAND

## HANGING THE GATE

Proceed as follows:

1. *Attach hinges to gate.*

   Hang the top hinge upside down so the gate cannot be lifted off.

   Remove the nut and bolt in each hinge. Insert the hinge over the terminal post. Insert the bolt in the hinge and secure the nut. Be sure to locate the hinges an equal distance from the top and bottom of the gate.

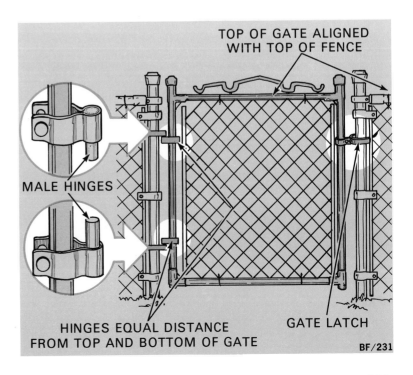

TOP OF GATE ALIGNED WITH TOP OF FENCE

MALE HINGES

HINGES EQUAL DISTANCE FROM TOP AND BOTTOM OF GATE

GATE LATCH

BF/231

2. *Loosen the female hinges on the gate frame and slip them onto the male hinges attached to the terminal post.*

Set hinges to permit full swing of gate over the fenced property. The top of the gate frame should line up with the top rail of the fence.

3. *Tighten all hinges securely with a wrench.*

Tap the bolt head with a hammer while tightening the nuts with the wrench to insure maximum rigidity. This prevents the gate from sagging.

4. *Attach gate latch (unless you have a forked latch) to other gate post with bolt and nut.*

5. *Attach gate latch to gate frame with bolt and nut.*

Double swing gates require special provisions for securing them in the closed position. A favorite method is to use a metal drop rod attached to the unhinged end of one of the gates.

A simple spring latch is used to connect the two gates. The dropped rod is inserted into a pipe set in a concrete base at the center of the overall gate opening in line with the fence.

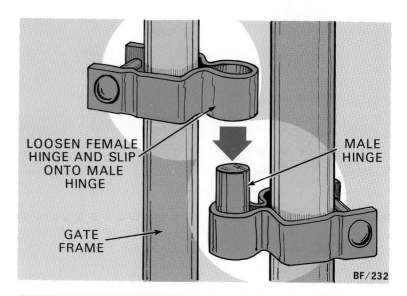

LOOSEN FEMALE HINGE AND SLIP ONTO MALE HINGE

MALE HINGE

GATE FRAME

BF/232

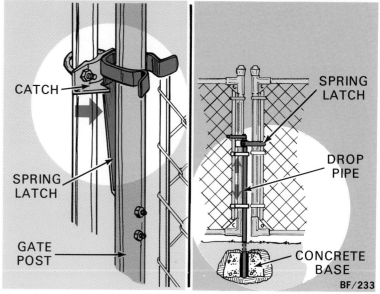

CATCH

SPRING LATCH

GATE POST

SPRING LATCH

DROP PIPE

CONCRETE BASE

BF/233

# Building Gates.

Gates are used mostly where machinery, trucks, cars and livestock use the same passageway. Some cattle guards can be used in this manner but they will not be discussed in this publication.

The materials and designs used for gates vary widely. Many gates are bought ready to hang. These are usually metal gates of aluminum or steel. Both types are durable, but are usually more expensive than those built by the owner. If you build your own gates, the kinds of readily available material may determine the type of gate to be used. The size of the gate to be built will also influence the type of construction and materials used.

In determining the width of the gate it is important to consider what vehicles and equipment will be passing through it. Normally a 10- or 12-foot gate is wide enough for livestock.

Fourteen and 16-foot gates are becoming much more popular as farmers and ranchers increase their use of combine harvesters, hay balers, cotton pickers and other large equipment that require a wide gateway. Most equipment will pass through a 12-foot opening. However, some equipment is built that requires a 14-foot width and the probability is that more will be built in the future. A 16-foot gate is needed if a turn must be made while moving large equipment through a gate such as when passing from a field into a lane. Most gates are 52 to 54 inches high.

Building gates is discussed under the following headings:

A. Building Metal Gates.

B. Building Wood Gates.

C. Building Temporary Gates.

# A. Building Metal Gates

There are several types of metal gates you can build. Procedures are given here for building one from ¾-inch pipe and woven wire.

Upon completion of your study of this section, you will be able to do the following: **build the frame for a metal gate, attach and stretch the woven wire** and **hang the gate.**

Building metal gates is discussed under the following headings:

1. Tools and Materials Needed.

2. Building the Frame.

3. Attaching and Stretching the Woven Wire.

4. Hanging the Gate.

## TOOLS AND MATERIALS NEEDED

Electric drill, ⅜″ drill bit   Hammer
Brace and ⅝″ bit              Vise
⅝″ die and threader          Grinder
Welder and rods              Framing square
Adjustable wrench            Hacksaw
Pliers                       Chalk or soapstone

For gate, 12′ wide x 52″ high:

2 pcs. ¾″ pipe 12′ length
3 pcs. ¾″ pipe 4′ length
1 pc. ¾″ pipe 3′-10″ length
2 pc. ¾″ pipe 3″ length
1 pc. 1″ pipe 4′ length
1 pc. ¼″ x 1″ flat steel 9′ length
13′ of 47″ stock and field fence (or type wire used on fence)
2 pcs. ⅝″ steel rod 15″ length
2 ⅝″ flat washers
2 ⅜″ x 5″ bolts with washers and nuts
Chain and harness snap

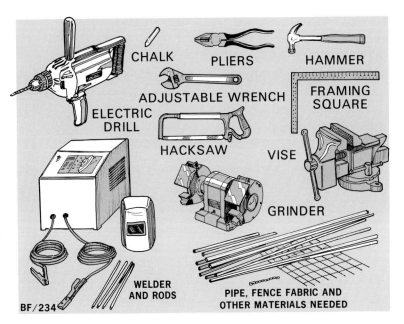

CHALK   PLIERS   HAMMER
ADJUSTABLE WRENCH   FRAMING SQUARE
ELECTRIC DRILL   HACKSAW   VISE
GRINDER
BF/234
WELDER AND RODS   PIPE, FENCE FABRIC AND OTHER MATERIALS NEEDED

## BUILDING THE FRAME

To build the metal frame for the gate, proceed as follows:

1. *Lay out and weld frame.*

   Use the 1″ pipe on the hinge end of the frame only. Make sure the frame is square. The outside edge of the 4′ pipe must be square with the ends of the 12′ pipe.

2. *Weld hinges to frame.*

   Use the ¾″ x 3″ pipe. Measure 6″ from the top and bottom of the frame and weld to the 1″ pipe.

3. *Weld ⅜″ bolts to frame.*

   Measure 12″ from the top and bottom and weld to the 1″ pipe.

4. *Weld the brace.*

   Use the ¼″ x 1″ x 9′ length of flat steel. Weld the brace on a diagonal. Weld the upper end to the frame at the hinge end. Weld the lower end to the bottom of the frame.

5. *Mount the wire-stretcher pipe.*

   Use the ¾″ x 3′-8″ length. Drill ⅜″ holes to match the size and location of the welded bolts. Fit the pipe over the bolts. Place the washers and nuts on the bolts and turn about 2 revolutions.

## ATTACHING AND STRETCHING THE WOVEN WIRE

To attach and stretch the woven wire, proceed as follows:

1. *Attach one end of the wire to the latch end of the frame.*

   Wire the ends around the frame evenly.

2. *Attach other end of wire to the stretcher pipe on the hinge end of the frame.*

   Wire the ends around the pipe evenly. Pull ends snug but not tight.

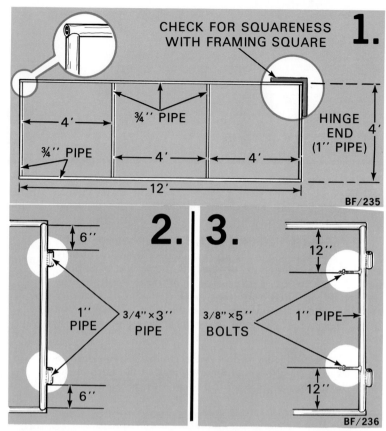

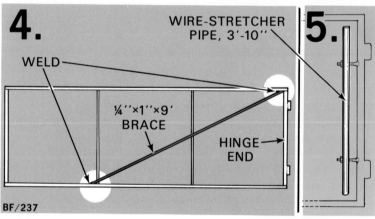

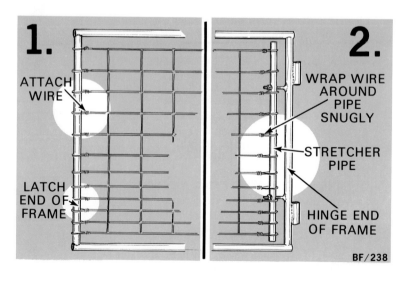

3. *Stretch the wire.*

Tighten the nuts alternately until proper tension is applied.

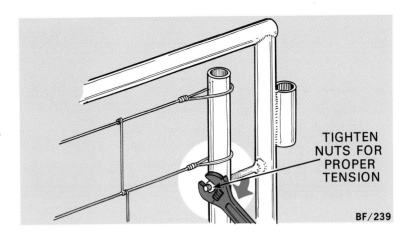

TIGHTEN NUTS FOR PROPER TENSION

BF/239

## HANGING THE GATE

To hang the gate, proceed as follows:

1. *Prepare the stationary (male) hinge.*

Shape the ⅝″ by 15″ rod by bending to "L" shape. The short end must be 3″ and long end 12″. Weld a ⅝″ washer on the long end 1″ from the short end. Thread 3″ of the long end.

2. *Drill holes for hinges.*

Measure the distance between pipe hinges on the gate. If you wish to reverse the top hinge to prevent the gate being lifted off the hinges, measure the distance from the upper edge of the top hinge and the lower edge of the bottom hinge. Otherwise, measure from the bottom edge of both hinges. Drill ⅝″ holes in the gate post so the top of the gate will be even with the top of the fence.

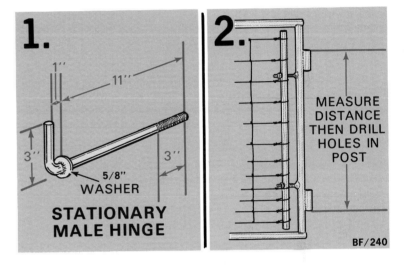

1.  1″  11″  3″  3″
5/8″ WASHER
**STATIONARY MALE HINGE**

2.  MEASURE DISTANCE THEN DRILL HOLES IN POST

BF/240

3. *Engage hinges.*

Stand gate in position and engage hinges. Insert lower male hinge at bottom of female hinge. To reverse the top hinge, insert the male hinge from the top down. Otherwise, insert both hinges from the bottom.

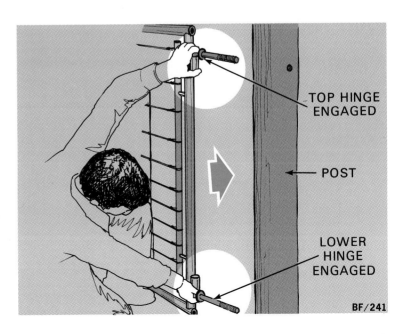

TOP HINGE ENGAGED

POST

LOWER HINGE ENGAGED

BF/241

4. *Mount the gate.*

Lift the gate and insert hinge bolts through holes in the gate post. Place washers and nuts on bolts while supporting the gate. Tighten nuts securely.

5. *Install chain latch.*

Staple one link to latch post at desired height. Loop around the post and over the gate frame. Fasten with harness snap.

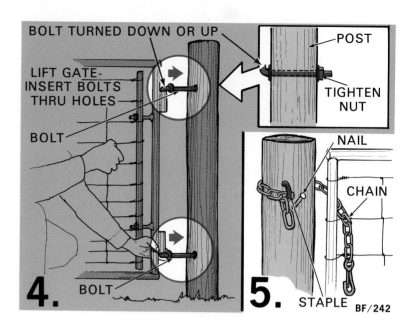

# B. Building Wood Gates

Wood gates are often built of 1″ lumber. Where heavier or longer gates are required, 2″ lumber may be used. Treated lumber is often used for a more durable gate. Procedures are given here for building a 12′ gate using 1″ x 6″ lumber. The gate post used with this gate must extend $8\frac{1}{2}′$ above ground to accommodate the cable brace.

Upon completion of your study of this section you will be able to do the following: **lay out and build the frame for a wood gate, install the braces,** and **hang the gate.**

Building wood gates is discussed under the following headings:

1. Tools and Materials Needed.

2. Building the Frame.

3. Hanging the Gate.

## TOOLS AND MATERIALS NEEDED

Electric drill
Drill bits 3/8″ and 5/8″
Adjustable wrenches
Handsaw or electric saw
Rule
Pencil
Claw hammer
Framing square

Cable for brace 1 3/8″ x 15′
Horizontal boards 3 1″ x 6″ x 12′
Upright boards 6 1″ x 6″ x 4′
Braces 4 1″ x 6″ x 7′
Clevis 1/4″ x 2″ (or turnbuckle)
Eyebolts 2 5/8″ x 12″
Latch 1 1″ x 3″ x 18″
Hinge support blocks 4 1″ x 6″ x 30″
Carriage bolts 22 3/8″ x 2 3/4″
Carriage bolts 8 3/8″ x 3 1/2″
Latch brace 1 1″ x 6″ x 27″
Machine bolt 1 5/8″ x 3 1/2″
Hinge straps 1/4″ x 2″
Male hinge bolts 2 5/8″ x 15″
Nails, 3 lbs, 10d common

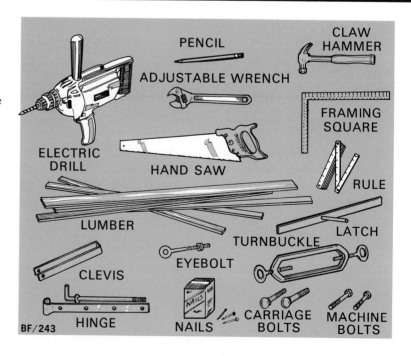

## BUILDING THE FRAME

To build the frame for the wood gate, proceed as follows:

1. *Lay out the gate frame.*

    (1) *Lay out the 1" x 6" boards to be used for framing the gate.*

    Upright boards are used in pairs —on both sides of horizontal boards.

    Square the corners with the framing square.

    (2) *Nail the 4' upright end boards to the 12' top and bottom boards.*

    Two nails at each joint will hold the frame in position for drilling holes and installing bolts.

    (3) *Center and nail the middle 12' board to the frame.*

    (4) *Center the middle 4' upright boards and nail in place.*

2. *Install the diagonal braces.*

    Place the 7' diagonal brace boards in position. Mark the angles and saw each end as marked. Nail the four brace boards in position.

3. *Install the hinge support blocks.*

    Lay each board in position. Mark the angle. Saw blocks as marked.

    Nail the four hinge support blocks in place.

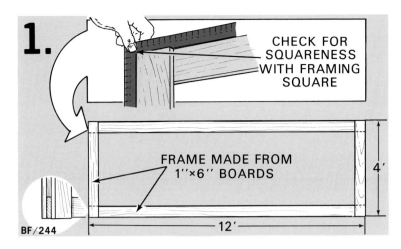

**1.** CHECK FOR SQUARENESS WITH FRAMING SQUARE

FRAME MADE FROM 1"×6" BOARDS

4'

12'

BF/244

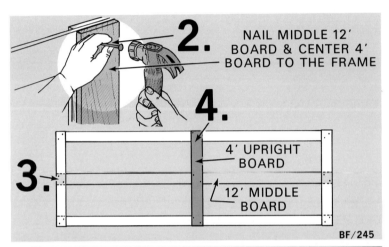

**2.** NAIL MIDDLE 12' BOARD & CENTER 4' BOARD TO THE FRAME

**4.**

**3.**

4' UPRIGHT BOARD

12' MIDDLE BOARD

BF/245

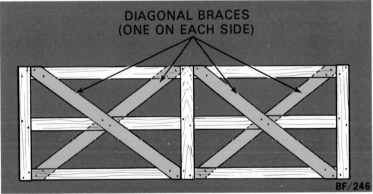

DIAGONAL BRACES (ONE ON EACH SIDE)

BF/246

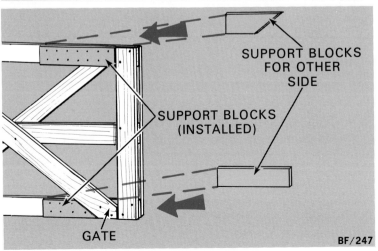

SUPPORT BLOCKS FOR OTHER SIDE

SUPPORT BLOCKS (INSTALLED)

GATE

BF/247

4. *Install the latch and latch brace.*

Slide the 1″ x 3″ x 18″ latch between the end upright boards.

Nail the 1″ x 6″ x 27″ latch brace in place.

5. *Install the latch handle.*

Insert $\frac{3}{8}$″ x 5″ bolt through the latch.

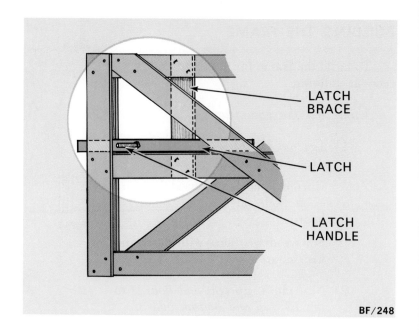

LATCH BRACE

LATCH

LATCH HANDLE

BF/248

6. *Install bolts.*

Drill holes as indicated. Install all bolts except those for clevis and hinges. Tighten nuts with wrench.

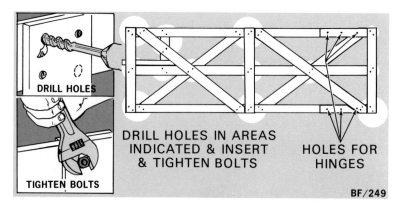

DRILL HOLES

TIGHTEN BOLTS

DRILL HOLES IN AREAS INDICATED & INSERT & TIGHTEN BOLTS

HOLES FOR HINGES

BF/249

## HANGING THE GATE

Hinges can be purchased or they can be fabricated.

To hang the gate with purchased hinges proceed as follows:

1. *Install female hinges on gate as indicated.*

2. *Drill holes in gate post for male hinges.*

Measure the distance between hinges on the gate. If you wish to reverse the top hinge to prevent the gate being lifted off the hinges, measure the distance from the upper edge of the top hinge and the lower edge of the bottom hinge. Otherwise, measure from the bottom edge of both hinges. Locate and drill holes in the gate post so the top of the gate will be even with the top of the fence.

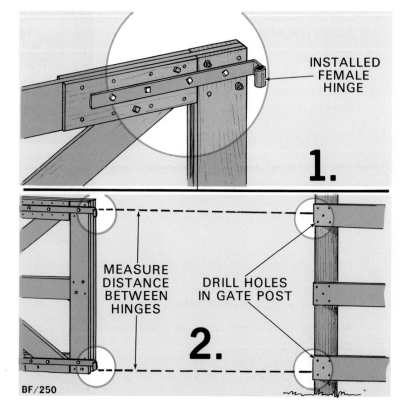

INSTALLED FEMALE HINGE

1.

MEASURE DISTANCE BETWEEN HINGES

DRILL HOLES IN GATE POST

2.

BF/250

176

## 3. *Engage hinges.*

Stand gate in position and engage hinges. Insert lower male hinge at bottom of female hinge. To reverse the top hinge, insert the male hinge from the top down as shown. Otherwise, insert both hinges from the bottom.

## 4. *Mount the gate.*

Lift the gate and insert hinge bolts through holes in the gate post. Place washers and nuts on bolts while supporting the gate. Tighten nuts securely.

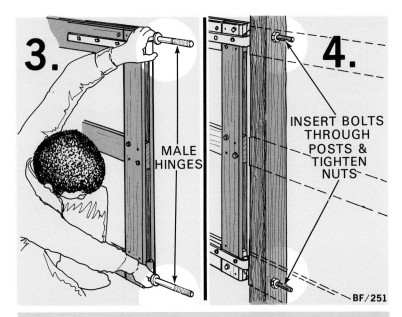

## 5. *Install cable brace.*

Assemble cable brace. Drill 5/8″ hole in gate post 8′ from ground level. Insert the eyebolt with cable attached and fasten washer and nut. Attach clevis to gate and tighten nut.

## 6. *Adjust tension on the brace cable (use clevis or turnbuckle) to level the gate.*

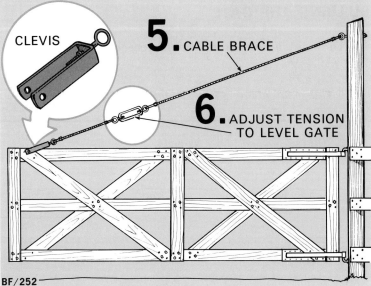

# C. Building Temporary Gates

For some fences, it may be necessary to build a temporary gate.

From your study of this section you will be able to **build a temporary gate.**

Building temporary gates is discussed under the following headings:

1. Tools and Materials Needed.

2. Building the Gate.

## TOOLS AND MATERIALS NEEDED

Claw hammer
Pliers (wire cutting)
Axe
Pole 2″ diameter, 6′ long
Wire (barbed or woven)
Staples (for wood posts)
Wire clamps (for steel posts)

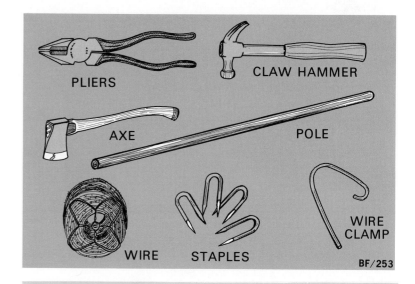

## BUILDING THE GATE

To build a temporary gate, proceed as follows:

1. *Cut pole about same height as fence post.*

2. *Attach barbed (or woven) wires to pole.*

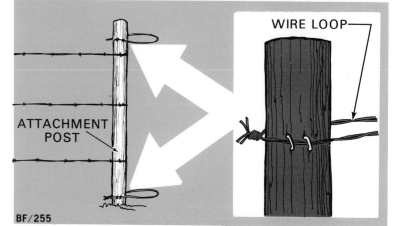

3. *Make upper and lower wire loop on attachment post.*

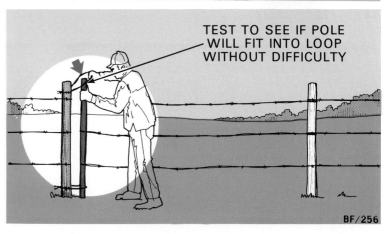

4. *Test assembly to see if pole can be fitted into wire loops without difficulty.*

# Index

# Index

# NOTES

# NOTES

# NOTES

# NOTES

# NOTES

# Other Bestsellers From TAB

☐ **BASIC ROOF FRAMING—Barnow**

Leading off with an in-depth look at various different types of roof styles, Barnow carefully identifies and describes the framing members of each one. You'll find an invaluable introduction to the tools used in roof framing, including a complete explanation of the steel framing square—the most important tool of the framing carpenter! And you'll also get a look at professional techniques for choosing and buying needed materials with plenty of practical advice on proper material estimating. 192 pp., 250 illus. 7" × 10".

**Paper   $11.95**                                        **Hard   $19.95**
**Book No. 2677**

☐ **111 YARD AND GARDEN PROJECTS**
**—from boxes and bins to tables and tools—Blandford**

Expert woodworker and metalcrafter Percy Blandford gives you step-by-step building guidance that's based on years of experience as a teacher and author of bestselling project guides. Plus, he provides a wealth of basic know-how on how to choose and work with wood and metal. He gives invaluable tips on constructing tool handles. And he shows how to custom design exactly the outdoor tools, accessories, and gardening aids that are right for your own particular needs! 416 pp., 301 illus. 7" × 10".

**Paper   $16.95**                                        **Hard   $25.95**
**Book No. 2644**

☐ **HOW TO CAST SMALL METAL**
**AND RUBBER PARTS—2nd Edition—Cannon**

Using this excellent sourcebook as a guide, you can easily make high quality, defect-free castings for almost any purpose and at an amazingly low cost! Just some of the countless uses you'll find for this potentially profitable skill . . . making obsolete or vintage car parts, hood ornaments, garden and fireplace tools, kitchen utensils, automotive parts, replacing broken antique parts, reproducing sculpture, plaques and other art . . . all kinds of decorative and useful objects for your own use or to sell! 176 pp., 143 illus.

**Paper   $9.95**                                        **Hard   $15.95**
**Book No. 2614**

☐ **TILE FLOORS—INSTALLING,**
**MAINTAINING  AND  REPAIRING—Ramsey**

Now you can easily install resilient or traditional hard tiles on both walls and floors. Find out how to buy quality resilient floor products at reasonable cost . . . and discover the types and sizes of hard tiles available. Get step-by-step instructions for laying out the floor, selecting needed tools and adhesives, cutting tiles, applying adhesives, and more. 192 pp., 200 illus. 4 pages in full color. 7" × 10".

**Paper   $12.95**                                        **Book No. 1998**

☐ **BUILDING OUTDOOR PLAYTHINGS FOR KIDS,**
**with Project Plans—Barnes**

Imagine the delight of your youngsters—children or grandchildren—when you build them their own special backyard play area complete with swings, climbing bars, sandboxes, even an A-frame playhouse their own size or a treehouse where they can indulge in their own imaginary adventures. Best of all, discover how you can make exciting, custom-designed play equipment at a fraction of the cost of ordinary, ready-made swing sets or sandbox units! It's all here in this practical, step-by-step guide to planning and building safe, sturdy outdoor play equipment. 240 pp., 213 illus., 7" × 10".

**Paper   $12.95**                                        **Hard   $21.95**
**Book No. 1971**

☐ **ROOFING THE RIGHT WAY**
**—A Step-by-Step Guide for the Homeowner—Bolt**

If you're faced with having to replace your roof because of hidden leaks, torn or missing shingles, or simply worn roofing that makes your whole house look shabby and run down . . . don't assume that you'll have to take out another mortgage to pay for the project. The fact is, *almost anyone can install a new or replacement roof easily and at amazingly low cost compared with professional contractor prices!* All the professional techniques and step-by-step guidance you'll need is here in this complete new roofing manual written by an experienced roofing contractor. 192 pp., 217 illus. 7" × 10".

**Paper   $11.95**                                        **Hard   $19.95**
**Book No. 2667**

☐ **66 FAMILY HANDYMAN® WOOD PROJECTS**

Here are 66 practical, imaginative, and decorative projects . . . literally something for every home and every woodworking skill level from novice to advanced cabinetmaker: room dividers, a free-standing corner bench, china/book cabinet, coffee table, desk and storage units, a built-in sewing center, even your own Shaker furniture reproductions! 210 pp., 306 illus. 7" × 10".

**Paper   $14.95**                                        **Hard   $21.95**
**Book No. 2632**

☐ **UPHOLSTERY TECHNIQUES ILLUSTRATED—Gheen**

Here's an easy-to-follow, step-by-step guide to modern upholstery techniques that covers everything from stripping off old covers and padding to restoring and installing new foundations, stuffing, cushions, and covers. All the most up-to-date pro techniques are included along with lots of time- and money-saving ''tricks-of-the-trade'' not usually shared by professional upholsterers. 352 pp., 549 illus. 7" × 10".

**Paper   $16.95**                                        **Hard   $27.95**
**Book No. 2602**

☐ **CABINETS AND VANITIES**
**—A BUILDER'S HANDBOOK— Godley**

Here in easy-to-follow, step-by-step detail is everything you need to know to design, build, and install your own customized kitchen cabinets and bathroom vanities and cabinets for a fraction of the price charged by professional cabinetmakers or kitchen remodelers . . . and for less than a third of what you'd spend for the most cheaply made ready-made cabinets and vanities! 142 pp., 126 illus. 7" × 10".

**Paper   $12.95**                                        **Hard   $19.95**
**Book No. 1982**

☐ **HOW TO TROUBLESHOOT AND**
**REPAIR ANY SMALL GAS ENGINE—Dempsey**

Here's a time-, money-, and aggravation-saving sourcebook that covers the full range of two- and four-cycle gas engines from just about every major American manufacturer—from Briggs & Stratton, to West Bend, and others! With the expert advice and step-by-step instructions provided by master mechanic Dempsey, you'll be amazed at how easily you can solve almost any engine problem. 272 pp., 228 illus.

**Paper   $10.95**                                        **Hard   $18.95**
**Book No. 1967**

# Other Bestsellers From TAB

☐ **THE COMPUTER FURNITURE PLAN AND PROJECT BOOK—Wiley**

Now, with the help of this first-of-its-kind handbook, even a novice can build good looking, functional, and low-cost computer furniture that's custom-designed for your own special needs—tables, stands, desks, modular or built-in units, even a posture supporting kneeling chair! Computer hobbyist and craftsman Jack Wiley provides all the step-by-step guidance, detailed project plans, show-how illustrations, and practical customizing advice . . . even basic information on tools, materials, and construction techniques. 288 pp., 385 illus., 7″ × 10″.

**Paper  $15.95**                    **Hard  $23.95**
**Book No. 1949**

☐ **DO-IT-YOURSELF DESIGNER WINDOWS**

If the cost of custom-made draperies puts you in a state of shock . . . if you've had trouble finding window coverings of any kind for cathedral or other problem windows . . . or if you're unsure of what type of window decor would look right in your home . . . here's all the advice and information you've been searching for. It's a complete, hands-on guide to selecting, measuring, making, and installing just about any type of window treatment imaginable. You'll even get an expert's insight into selection and installation of decorative storm windows and thermal windows, stained glass windows, woven or wooden blinds, and workable treatments for problem areas. 272 pp., 414 illus. 7″ × 10″.

**Paper  $14.95**                    **Hard  $21.95**
**Book No. 1922**

☐ **MOPED MAINTENANCE AND REPAIR**

Guaranteed to save you time, money, and inconvenience, it is packed with practical troubleshooting and repair information, preventative maintenance tips, safety advice, even important facts on state moped regulations and operating guidelines. Generously illustrated, it provides solutions to these routine problems that plague every moped rider—flat tires, fouled spark plugs, broken or worn cables and chains, and more. 256 pp., 229 illus.

**Paper  $14.95**                    **Book No. 1847**

☐ **DO YOUR OWN DRYWALL —AN ILLUSTRATED GUIDE— Kozloski**

Professional expertise for the amateur builder and remodeler! Proper installation of interior plasterboard or drywall is a must-have skill for successful home building or remodeling. Now, there's a new time- and money-saving alternative: this excellent step-by-step guide to achieving professional-quality drywalling results, the first time and every time! Even joint finishing, the drywalling step most dreaded by do-it-yourselfers, is a snap when you know what you're doing. And this is a guide that leaves absolutely nothing to chance and that leaves no question unanswered. 160 pp., 161 illus.

**Paper  $10.95**                    **Hard  $17.95**
**Book No. 1838**

☐ **PRACTICAL LANDSCAPING AND LAWN CARE—Webb**

Make your lawn the envy of the entire neighborhood . . . *without* spending a fortune or putting in never-ending hours of maintenance time! Here's absolutely everything you need to successfully plan, plant, and maintain lawn grasses and groundcovers, vines, and flowering ornamentals . . . annual, biennial, and perennial flowers . . . shade trees, lawn trees . . . even decorative (and delicious) fruits and berries. It doesn't matter whether your climate is cold and damp or hot and dry . . . whether your soil is sandy, rocky, or gummy clay . . . *everything* you need is here! 240 pp., 84 illus., 7″ × 10″.

**Paper  $13.95**                    **Hard  $21.95**
**Book No. 1818**

☐ **HARDWOOD FLOORS —INSTALLING, MAINTAINING AND REPAIRING—Ramsey**

Do-it-yourself expert Dan Ramsey gives you all the guidance you need to install, restore, maintain, or repair all types of hardwood flooring at costs far below those charged by professional builders and maintenance services. From details on how to select the type of wood floors best suited to your home, to time- and money-saving ways to keep your floors in tip-top condition . . . nothing has been left out. 160 pp., 230 illus. 4 pages in full color. 7″ × 10″.

**Paper  $10.95**                    **Hard  $18.95**
**Book No. 1928**

☐ **PANELING WITH SOLID LUMBER, including projects— Ramsey**

Home remodeling expert Dan Ramsey shows you how to use solid wood paneling to give almost any room in your home a new look that's comfortable, convenient, economical, and practically maintenance-free plus gives you an exciting selection of projects. Included are step-by-step directions for building a cedar closet . . . storm doors and shutters . . . a bathroom partition . . . a sauna decor for your bath . . . storage walls . . . a home bar . . . an attic study . . . book cabinets . . . a fireplace mantel . . . a kitchen corner cabinet . . . and more! 192 pp., 288 illus. 7″ × 10″.

**Paper  $12.95**                    **Hard  $18.95**
**Book No. 1868**

☐ **58 HOME SHELVING AND STORAGE PROJECTS—Blandford**

From a two-shelf book rack or table-top organizer to a paneled chest, basic room divider, or hall locker . . . from shelves or a spoon rack to a period reproduction of a Shaker cabinet or a Welsh dresser, you'll be amazed at the variety of projects included. And, each one includes easy-to-follow, step-by-step directions, plenty of show-how drawings, and complete materials list. 288 pp., 227 illus. 7″ × 10″.

**Paper  $14.95**                    **Book No. 1844**

☐ **BUILD YOUR OWN FITNESS CENTER**

This sourcebook gives you expert guidance on everything from planning your facility to constructing it, step-by-step. It shows you how to choose and install all the needed equipment, and in many cases gives you direction for building your own equipment and accessories for a fraction of the commercial cost! Plus, there's practical advice on the proper use of your equipment once it's installed. 224 pp., 301 illus. 7″ × 10″.

**Paper  $12.95**                    **Hard  $18.95**
**Book No. 1828**

☐ **CASTING BRASS—Ammen**

A highly respected metalcasting professional shares his secrets for casting almost any type of object—from art works to mechanical fittings in copper, brass, bronze, or other copper alloy—in this easy-to-follow sourcebook! Whether you're a first-time metalcaster, an experienced amateur, or a metalworking professional, you'll find this book packed with practical information and expert advice that's simply not available in any other metalcasting guide! Plus, the author has included an invaluable section on how to set up and run a successful small brass foundry business! No matter what your interest in brass casting, this is an invaluable sourcebook! 252 pp., 200 illus.

**Paper  $11.95**                    **Hard  $18.95**
**Book No. 1810**

# Other Bestsellers From TAB

☐ **HOUSE CRAFTSMANSHIP:**
**A GUIDE TO RESTYLING AND REFURBISHING**

An information-packed sourcebook for every homeowner and do-it-yourselfer! Here are all the practical tips and step-by-step procedures you need to accomplish your restyling and refurbishing projects quickly and easily. Like having a skilled craftsman at your side. This illustrated guide shows you how to do just about every interior and exterior job imaginable, easily and inexpensively. 288 pp., 291 illus. 7″ × 10″.

**Paper $14.95**                                    **Hard $22.95**
**Book No. 1809**

☐ **GLUE IT!—Giles**

Here, in one easy-to-use reference is everything anyone needs to know about glues, adhesives, epoxies, caulkings, sealants, plus practical how-to's on when and how to use them! If you need to glue or seal anything—from plumbing to glassware or from toys and airplane models to a cabin cruiser, this is where you'll find the needed information! 112 pp., 32 illus. 7″ × 10″.

**Paper $8.95**                                    **Hard $14.95**
**Book No. 1801**

☐ **WHAT'S IT WORTH?**
**A Home Inspection and Appraisal Manual—Scaduto**

Here's a guide that can save home buyers and home owners thousands of dollars in unexpected maintenance and repair costs! You'll find out what types of structural problems occur in older and in new homes, even condominiums . . . cover everything from foundations and crawl spaces to attics and roofs . . . learn simple "tricks of the trade" for spotting problems and discover how professional appraisal techniques can be applied to any home! 256 pp., 281 illus. 7″ × 10″.

**Paper $12.95**                                    **Hard $21.95**
**Book No. 1761**

☐ **ATTRACTING, FEEDING AND**
**HOUSING WILD BIRDS . . . with Project Plans—Moorman**

Here is a thorough, up-to-date look at how you can provide a total environment that will attract the most birds—both common and rare varieties. It's also a rich source of project plans for practical and easy-to-construct bird feeders and birdhouses that can be inexpensively built from space age materials. Includes a year-round bird feeding schedule, recipes for custom seed mixtures, and detailed plans for birdhouses and bird feeders. Plus landscaping ideas for making your yard more attractive to birds! 154 pp., 33 illus.

**Paper $8.95**                                    **Hard $15.95**
**Book No. 1755**

☐ **EFFECTIVE LIGHTING FOR HOME AND BUSINESS—Ramsey**

Now this completely up-to-date sourcebook provides all the information you need to update the lighting in your home or business . . . indoors *and* outdoors! Find all the most modern lighting theories, wiring and fixture information, and installation techniques given in easy-to-follow, step-by-step format. Plus there are 16 complete lighting plans! 224 pp., 380 illus. 7″ × 10″.

**Paper $13.50**                                    **Hard $18.95**
**Book No. 1658**

☐ **TROUBLE-FREE SWIMMING POOLS**

Here is the ideal sourcebook for anyone thinking of installing a swimming pool—inground or above ground from wading pool size to large indoor public pool. It shows how to plan, excavate, construct, and safely maintain all types and sizes of pools. You'll find out how to have your own pool for as little as $1,000 . . . or how to get more pool for the money no matter how much you're able to spend! 176 pp. 306 illus. 7″ × 10″.

**Paper $11.95**                                    **Hard $18.95**
**Book No. 1808**

☐ **HOW TO BE YOUR OWN ARCHITECT—**
**2nd Edition— Goddard and Wolverton**

The completely revised version of a long-time bestseller gives you all the expert assistance needed to design your own dream house like a professional. You'll save the money that most custom-home builders put out in architects' fees—an estimated 12% to 15% of the total construction costs—to pay for more of those "extras" you'd like your new home to include! 288 pp., 369 illus. 7″ × 10″.

**Paper $14.95**                                    **Hard $22.95**
**Book No. 1790**

☐ **PROFESSIONAL PLUMBING TECHNIQUES—**
**ILLUSTRATED AND SIMPLIFIED—Smith**

This plumber's companion includes literally everything about plumbing you'll ever need! From changing a washer to installing new fixtures, it covers installing water heaters, water softeners, dishwashers, gas stoves, gas dryers, grease traps, clean outs, and more. Includes piping diagrams, tables, charts, and arranged alphabetically. 294 pp., 222 illus.

**Hard $16.95**                                    **Book No. 1763**

☐ **FASTEN IT!—Self**

Here in easy-to-use format is all the information you need to find exactly the right fastening method or almost every job imaginable. Plus, you'll get complete guidance on the tools you need for each type of fastener—from claw hammers to specialty chisels, from welding rods to drill presses, and more. You'll learn how to join any two objects together permanently, temporarily, flexibly, or rigidly. It's an indispensable sourcebook that no hobbyist, craftsman, or home handyman should be without! 304 pp., 364 illus. 7″ × 10″.

**Paper $14.95**                                    **Hard $23.95**
**Book No. 1744**

☐ **CONSTRUCTING AND MAINTAINING**
**YOUR WELL AND SEPTIC SYSTEM—Alth**

A practical, money-saving guide for do-it-yourself homebuilders, homesteaders, and non-urban homeowners! Here, in step-by-step format, is all the information you need to plan and construct and maintain efficient water and septic units that will stand up to your needs for many years to come. Even if you're not interested in doing all or part of the work yourself, this guide can still prove an important money-saver by showing you what should be done and how it should be done, so you can deal more effectively with professional well drillers and septic contractors. 240 pp., 206 illus. 7″ × 10″.

**Paper $12.95**                                    **Hard $19.95**
**Book No. 1654**

# Other Bestsellers From TAB

☐ **WOODCARVING, WITH PROJECTS—Wiley**

Whether you're a woodcarver who's looking for some pro tips on carving techniques, woods, or tools . . . a novice who's looking for a practical introduction to the basic how-to's of woodcarving . . . or a craftsman who wants to add an extra dimension to your woodworking skills . . . this is the ideal guide! Here's where you'll find expert advice on all kinds of woodcarving possibilities, how to select the right woods for the project you have in mind, how to choose tools and set up your work area, about basic grips and cuts with knives, chisels, and more (even power tools), and all about patterns, designs, wood finishing, and more! 360 pp., 319 illus.

**Paper $11.50**  **Book No. 1639**

☐ **BUILDING WITH SALVAGED LUMBER—Williams**

Build an $80,000 home for as little as $15,000 . . . have new paneling, decks, furniture, and more *for next to nothing*! This first-of-its-kind guide lets you in on a surprising, money-saving secret—how to find top-quality wood virtually FREE in old buildings, begin salvage operations, transport and store lumber, then use it on your own amazingly, inexpensive do-it-yourself building projects! Here are all the work-in-progress photos and step-by-step directions you need to turn painted lumber studded with rusty nails into beautiful, polished wood! 272 pp., 122 illus. 7″ × 10″.

**Paper $10.25**  **Book No. 1597**

☐ **THE ILLUSTRATED HANDBOOK OF WOODWORKING JOINTS—Blandford**

How-to-do-it techniques on all the ways to join two or more pieces of wood together: the hundreds of methods, the specific uses for each type of joint, the tools and hardware needed, and step-by-step instructions for making a perfect woodworking joint every time! Covers over 1,000 joints, all conveniently arranged for quick and easy reference! 352 pp., 352 illus. 7″ × 10″.

**Paper $15.95**  **Book No. 1574**

☐ **Th COMPLETE BOOK OF LOCKS AND LOCKSMITHING—2nd Edition**

If you've every spent hours trying to locate a locksmith because you locked yourself out of your home or car, here's a book that can show you how you can do all your own locksmithing chores, easily and inexpensively—even if you're an inexperienced do-it-yourselfer! If you're looking for a profitable full- or part-time business that's virtually recession proof, this book also has all the information you'll need—from locksmithing techniques to laws that apply to the trade, from the types of key blanks and machines you'll need to know-how to lay out your shop and advertise your services! 352 pp., 637 illus. 7″ × 10″.

**Paper $15.95**  **Book No. 1530**

☐ **THE TAB HANDBOOK OF HAND AND POWER TOOLS**

Just think how much easier every home, hobby, gardening, and shop task would be if you had expert, easy-to-follow advice on tool selection, use, maintenance, and storage plus pro tips on safety precautions and special tool characteristics and applications! Well now you can have it ALL because here's a comprehensive, easy-to-use sourcebook that provides all the information you need on just about every hand and power tool imaginable! Logically organized, this generously illustrated guide is packed with authoritative, up-to-date know-how that just isn't available anywhere else. 512 pp., 553 illus. 7″ × 10″.

**Paper $17.95**  **Hard $26.95**
**Book No. 1638**

☐ **MASTERING HOUSEHOLD ELECTRICAL WIRING—Kittle**

Now you can add ultra-modern conveniences to your home, such as a handy electric garage door opener, extra outdoor outlets, a brand *new* door-chime, and more—without paying the high cost of an electrical contractor. Step-by-step instructions, photos and diagrams of work-in-progress show you how to handle large and small electrical jobs with no prior experience. 304 pp., 326 illus. 7″ × 10″.

**Paper $13.95**  **Book No. 1587**

☐ **BE YOUR OWN CONTRACTOR: THE AFFORDABLE WAY TO HOME OWNERSHIP—Alth**

If you've put your dreams of home ownership on "hold" because of today's sky-high building costs, this single guidebook can change all that! It shows you can save thousands of dollars on the cost of a new home by becoming your own contractor. It shows how to build an attractive, secure, comfortable home at minimum cost. 256 pp., 207 illus. 7″ × 10″.

**Paper $12.95**  **Book No. 1554**

☐ **HOME REMODELING—A HOW-TO, MONEY-SAVING HANDBOOK—Wahlfeldt**

Join the ranks of in-the-know home owners who've discovered that today's best and most affordable home buy is an *older* house. This is a sourcebook that outlines the key things to look for when buying an older home (which faults are easily fixable and which ones can mean major renovation work). You'll find information on everything from finances to location and utilities. 400 pp., 505 illus. 7″ × 10″.

**Paper $16.95**  **Book No. 1515**

*Prices subject to change without notice.

---

**Look for these and other TAB books at your local bookstore.**

---

**TAB BOOKS Inc.**
**P.O. Box 40**
**Blue Ridge Summit, PA 17214**

---

**Send for FREE TAB catalog describing over 1200 current titles in print.**